D1274028

religious psychology

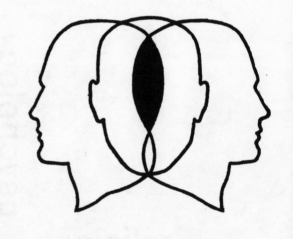

mental
health
series

5

VINCENT V. HERR, S.J.

religious psychology

alba house
A DIVISION OF ST. PAUL PUBLICATIONS
STATEN ISLAND, NEW YORK

First edition, April, 1965
Second edition, February, 1966

Nihil Obstat:
John B. Amberg, S. J., Censor deputatus
March 25, 1964

Imprimi Potest:
John A. McGrail, S. J.
Provincial of the Detroit Province
October 22, 1963

Imprimatur:
Most Rev. Cletus F. O'Donnell, J.C.D.
Vicar General, Archdiocese of Chicago
March 26, 1964

2019
H564

The Nihil Obstat and Imprimatur are official declarations that a book or pamphlet is free of doctrinal or moral error. No implication is contained therein that those who have granted the nihil obstat and imprimatur agree with the contents, opinions or statements expressed.

Library of Congress Catalog Card Number 64-20109

Copyright 1965 by Society of St. Paul, Staten Island, New York. (10314)

Designed, printed and bound in the U.S.A. by the Pauline Fathers and Brothers as part of their communications apostolate.

contents

preface and acknowledgements

THE content of this volume was taken from lectures given by Rev. Vincent V. Herr, S.J., Director of the Loyola Mental Health Project. They were given in similar form over a period of several years, and have been extensively revised by the author in collaboration with many graduate students from different religious orders and seminaries. It is intended for students who have had at least two rather thorough courses in modern psychology. It therefore presupposes they are capable of reading the current literature that deals with the analysis and interpretation of empirical findings in psychology.

Critical comments were made by Rev. William J. Devlin, S.J., M.D., the co-Director of the Project, and by Frank J. Kobler, Ph.D., consultant to the Project. Numerous other persons aided by their suggestions, and as experimental subjects. We take this opportunity to thank them all most cordially.

A special debt of gratitude is due the officials of the National Institute of Mental Health who helped plan and who approved the Project; the late Dr. Seymour Vestermark, Dr. Robert H. Felix, and Dr. Raymond Feldman. Special thanks are also due to Rev. George C. Anderson, Director and Founder of the Academy of Religion and Mental Health. He it was who made the initial suggestions to the President of Loyola for the Project, and who has continued to aid the Project workers by his advice and encouragement.

Typing and bibliographic assistance were given by the psychology staff, by Miss Lucrezia LaRusso, Project secretary, and Miss Laura Logsdon, research assistant. Research assistance was also given by Mr. Abraham Rittenhouse and Miss Mary Kay Egan, graduate assistants at Loyola University.

The continued guidance and support of the Project's advisory board have been invaluable, and certain new members were added from time to time. Of particular importance has been the wholehearted support of His Eminence, the late Samuel Cardinal Stritch, and of his successor Albert Cardinal Meyer. As of 1961 the board members were: The Very Reverend James Maguire, S.J., President of Loyola University, *ex officio;* Rev. Paul F. D'Arcy; Msgr. Edward M. Burke; Rev. John Connery; Rev. Charles A. Curran; Rev. William J. Devlin; Rev. Charles I. Doyle; Msgr. John Egan; Rev. Joseph M. Egan; Rev. Walter A. Farrell; Msgr. Malachy Foley; Rev. Vincent V. Herr; Dr. Frank J. Kobler; John J. Madden, M.D.; Rev. John A. McGrail; Rev. Bernard McMahon; Rev. William Schmidt; Rev. Sylvester Sieber; Rev. Leo D. Sullivan.

Vincent V. Herr, S.J.

1 psychology of religion

IN a recent issue of one of our national magazines there is an interesting account of a young Japanese student's experiences during World War II. He was in his second year at Tokyo University when war broke out and "swept along on the surging wave of patriotism, (he) enlisted in the Submarine Corps of the Japanese Imperial Navy." The long months of war that followed eventually brought production shortages for Japan and the shortages in turn forced thinking on ways and means to get the most out of the limited supply of munitions still available. "One of the more unorthodox plans was the creation of the Human Torpedo Squadron."

"At this time," the young man writes, "I believed with all my heart in the divinity of the Emporer. To die for him was the supreme glory of the Japanese fighting man. To sacrifice one's life in the Imperial service was undoubted assurance of an eternal reward. It was quite natural for me to volunteer for the manned torpedoes." Days of training and practice followed. These were days of anticipation each marked with the recurrent, indescribable thrill of hearing the names of comrades read who had died gloriously for the Emperor. And finally there came the morning when practice ended and there was a summons to man a live torpedo. He climbed into the cockpit; he even splashed cold water on his face "to insure complete consciousness in what

* The introduction was prepared by Rev. Walter Farrell, S.J.

I thought would be my last moments on earth;" he waited. The signal to move out never came; instead, he was recalled to dockside only to learn that on this August 15, 1945, Japan had unconditionally surrendered. The terrible blow of this announcement crushed many and drove others to take their own lives. But more was to come.

> A short time after we stood and listened to the Emperor declare over the radio in his own voice that he was not divine. This denial of his heavenly origin and attributes was almost more than I could bear. Lost in my thoughts, I wandered through the debris. My most frightening nightmares were nothing compared with the crushing loneliness and fear that I felt in my heart.
>
> I don't know how long I wandered aimlessly through the streets. My first moment of awareness came when I heard the laughter of a group of children who were leaving the remains of a bombed-out building. The knowledge that anyone could laugh happily in such circumstances piqued my curiosity. After much hesitation, I approached the ruined building and entered.
>
> The first words I heard were, "Jesus Christ, true God and true man, loved us before we came to be, and died for each one of us that we may save our souls."
>
> At the sight of Christ on the cross, my empty heart was filled and I was overwhelmed by what I now know to be the power of grace. In that moment of discovery, I felt the reality of Christ and His love.

That this conviction of conversion was permanent is attested to by subsequent events, since the quondam student and Navy man is now a priest ministering to his fellow countrymen in Imperial Japan.

Thus run the details of a rare individual experience; thus, in exceptionally brief compass, we are afforded a privileged case of religious experience cut from actual living. This is not to say, however, that what is recounted here belongs uniquely to the psychologist of religion, for many another scientist also could profitably ponder this autobiographical selection. It may be of service at the outset, then, to try to distinguish the interests of other scientists in this story from that of the psychologist of religion and thus to come to some understanding of the distinctions between these various sciences. No attempt, of course, will

be made here to give a complete account of the work of such
scientists as theologians, philosophers, and sociologists, and only
broad lines will be drawn to separate these scientists from the
psychologist. Similarly, no attempt will be made to indicate the
total process which each of these scientists would employ. Rather,
within the confines of the story just recounted (for the sake of
clarity, while admitting that no scientist stays with just one case),
the various facets that are of interest to these scientists will be
indicated. In a word, using the autobiographical account as an
example, we will attempt to distinguish those areas in it that
interest the theologian, philosopher, and sociologist from those
that are of interest to the psychologist, and thus to underscore the
proper objects of the sciences in question and their distinctive
functions.

The context within which we will be working is that of the
conversion story just outlined. More specifically, the context is
that of a young Japanese with now one, now another religious
orientation. In both instances the religious commitment is lived
out against a background, in a setting, which is Japanese. In the
first case, belief is in the Emperor, dedication is to his person,
and reward is hoped for from him; in the second case, faith,
hope, and charity are directed through Christ and in Christ to
the God of Catholicism. What should be emphasized, however,
is the paradox of this religous context: it is at once open to endless
variety and yet it is invariant. The believer, for example, can be
(1) oriented by nature or grace to (2) an absolute that may be
an ideal, an emperor, or God and this is (3) a setting that is
Japanese or occidental, in times past or present. In short, the
content of the picture admits of kaleidoscopic changes, while
the structure remains unchanged. For there is always a believer;
he is always oriented to an absolute; the whole is always in a
setting.

It is the elements in this picture of paradox that give the
clue to the areas of interest for the theologian, philosopher,
sociologist and psychologist; while it is the divergent interests
of these scientists in turn that alert us to the proper objects of
investigation and hence, ultimately, to the distinctive ways
travelled by each.

That a theologian would be interested in the events here described goes without saying since there is evidence of two religious systems in the life of this young man. The first was from the Emperor; the second, from God. The first took its origins in the nation and in the line of Japanese Emperors, who, as the young man indicated, not only announced their divine origins but also asserted their divine attributes and prerogatives. It is about the origin and content of this imperial religion (creed) that the theologian would concern himself, while at the same time wanting to know what response, in terms of acknowledgement and service (code) as well as reverence and praise (cult), would be expected of the individual believer in this imperial religion.

Although we keep referring to the data of the theologian in terms of the autobiographical account provided by a young Japanese, still it is obvious that this example is a mere sample and this account but a token of the data with which the theologian actually concerns himself. In fact, the theological scientist would not only make a wider sampling than this individual instance but he would transcend any mere description, historical or otherwise, of religious data. He would push on to a search for some intelligible pattern that would characterize as well as systematize the data discovered.

Our theologian, to return to our example, would also be interested in the picture presented by the young Japanese after conversion. Here again origins and response, i.e., descriptions of God and His attributes, as well as the appropriate response expected of the creature to such a God, would be considered. Here too the interest would transcend phenomenological detailing of the findings in this individual case or other cases and the effort would be for understanding and the discovery of the intelligible scheme that would characterize this religion as Christian, as Roman Catholic.

Lastly, by way of concluding this presentation of the theologian's work, it should be added that beyond mere description and/or experience, beyond discovery of patterns in either or both systems, the theologian would be constantly checking his systematization and thus verifying its validity with the data at his disposal, with the teaching, practice, and worship of both religions.

Within the context of our conversion story, then, we can locate the interest of the theologian at the point of religious orientation. He is interested in contacting and penetrating the an adequate, verifiable scheme. Such however is not the concern data of both religious systems so as to specify their content in of the psychologist of religion.[1]

If one were to turn to the philosopher of religion, then, would his perspective differ from those of the theologian and psychologist? To be concrete, would he be interested in a distinctive element in the autobiographical experiences outlined earlier? To indicate the direction of development in subsequent paragraphs, let an immediate affirmative answer be given both of these questions.

It is true that, like the theologian, the philosopher of religion would want to go far beyond the individual case cited here. He too would want to transcend all individual instances in order to concern himself with what he finds in any of the individual cases. Further, rising above mere description or detailing of

1 The wording of the last sentence should be remarked. What is spoken of here is the religious psychologist as psychologist; the statement refers to this scientist as scientist. It does not refer to nor intend to open the question of the religious psychologist *as a man*, i.e., as one who must assess in his own conscience and according to his own lights the religious systems known to him. As a person the religious psychologist, just as any other person, must investigate the questions of origin, destiny, and the like; as a person the religious psychologist must make his commitment. Yet just as a commitment *as a person* to one religion does. not preclude the theologian *as a scientist or theologian* from studying the content and character of another religion, so the *personal* commitment of the psychologist does not prevent him from a scientific investigation of religious behavior in any religious context.

Hence, it follows that the personal commitment of the authors to the Roman Catholic faith does not exclude them as scientists from investigating the religious behavior of their fellow men regardless of the similarity or diversity of confession.

phenomena, the philosopher of religion would with the theologian also be looking for a structural pattern and hence he too would note with interest that this young Japanese was first related to the Emperor as his god and later ordered and orientated to the Triune God of the Christians. Yet all these similarities should not lead us to confuse the search of the philosopher with that of the theologian. For where the latter was concerned with the content of two religious schemes, the former is intent on the structure of the relationship in either and in both schemes. In other words, the philosopher of religion has an interest that is methodological, the way of being related to an absolute. The proper object of his investigation is structure, the structure of a person's orientation to the absolute. He is concerned with this invariant structure and with the characteristics of this structure, namely, what relation is implied in the two terms of this structure; what sort of dependence is here involved; and what sort of expression of dependence is implied in being thus related.

Where the theologian, then, would turn to the case in hand and to similar cases only to transcend any individual cases, the philosopher would turn to the data of experience (as presented in this or some other case) only to move from there to a higher viewpoint. But where the theologian would seek intelligible patterns in the dogmatic content of the religious data (whether revealed or otherwise), the philosopher would rather seek out the structural relationship (of a being to the absolute) embedded in any content whether revealed or not. And thus where the concern of the theologian would be the stuff of religion and revelation, the concern of the philosopher is rather the common relational structure of dependence on an absolute and all that this implies, whether the absolute be the God of Israel, the Emperor, or the God of the Christians.

Within the context of our story, the structural element, the aspect of invariant orientation, is the point at which we would locate the interest of the philosopher of religion. And yet, although it is true that the psychologist of religion is working within the framework that is the proper object of the philosopher's investigation, still this framework or structure as such is not the concern of the psychologist as such.[2]

If the theologian takes a terminal viewpoint seeking characteristic patterns within the data of religious belief and practice, and the philosopher takes a methodological viewpoint seeking transcendent structure, and if neither of these viewpoints is that of the psychologist of religion, what aspect of our initial story-context is proper to him and his investigations? The answer to this question seems to call for a reanalysis of our sample data.

In an earlier page we listed the first element in our context as the believer or individual faithful, the one oriented or committed. Now in one sense one could think of everything else in the context as opposed to him. (Opposed not in the sense that everything is at odds with the believer but rather in the sense that everything else is and can be distinguished from him.) He could be thought of as the subject and all else as non-subject. Hence, where seemingly one element remained in our story-context there are actually two. Again, it should be remembered that while the subject as such was considered an invariant element in the structure of religion, still in the existential order the subject *as such* does not exist *as such*. It most certainly exists but as *this* subject, our young Japanese for example, or as this other subject and so on. Similarly, all that is non-subject does not exist as such either, but is rather concretized, for example, as the Emperor, as this setting of time and place which can be denominated the Japanese culture of the 20th century, and so on. Now it takes little imagination to see that all that we have grouped under the rubric *non-subject* (provided we subtract the elements of structure and dogmatic content assigned to the philosopher and theologian) is what we have earlier called back-

2 Here again it should be noted that the psychologist *as man* may well have to make the question of the philosopher his concern of conscience. But this does not change his perspective as scientist. As scientist he is neither theologian nor philosopher and hence not concerned with either the content or the structure of religion or religious schemes. This is the affirmation of an important distinction; it is not a statement of religious indifference nor absolution from personal responsibility.

ground and setting. These are the circumstances, surroundings, conditions, and atmosphere which shape and qualify the variable content of diverse theologies as well as influence and modify the multiplicity of response that is made to the absolute in the various religions. For if one can say in general that time and place or, more specifically, historical periods, cultures, and social milieu have an influence in shaping a man's behavior, then surely it can be said that these same environmental factors have an influence not only on the human expression of religion and worship but even on the contentual pattern of various religions themselves.

This area of investigation, then, is properly the province of the sociologist of religion. It is he who is concerned, to return to our example, with the social implications of an imperial religion and with the cultural grounds out of which such a religion and its complementary religious expression would grow and prosper. He too would be interested in a social phenomenon like Catholicism which, at first sight, would seem to be an import in Japan; he would question and study the social implications of the coming of Catholicism for Japan and for this individual, its adaptability to the oriental mind and manner and to this particular person.

When we come to locate the interest of the sociologist, then, in the context of our conversion story, we would point to that whole area which is neither dogmatic content nor invariant structure and yet is other than the subject. This location at once points up the difficulty of distinguishing between the sociologist and psychologist at the same time that it puts the distinction between them in focus. For the setting, the environmental factors of time and place, are the domain of the sociologist; the subject, the context as viewed through the eyes or in the behavior of the subject, is the domain of the psychologist. The domains are distinct; one is subject, the other non-subject; but the domains overlap since what is subject as well as what is non-subject is influenced by background and setting.

If we translate these statements and distinctions in terms of our conversion story, what does the area of interest for the psychologist of religion come to be? His area is the Japanese youth himself, the subject, with all his thoughts and desires, feelings and emotions, actions and reactions; it is this youth and the amplitude of his behavior viewed in the religious framework of our discussion.

The psychologist of religion, then, not only has a different name than the other scientists (theologian, philosopher, sociologist, *et al.*) but he has:

(1) a different viewpoint, namely, that of *the subject;*
(2) a different area of investigation, namely, the *subject's behavior,* which he considers
(a) in its fullness,
(b) though only in as much as it is found *within the invariant structure* of religion,
(c) by an appropriate *scientific* methodology.

This view of the psychologist's work, it can be noted, answers difficulties and meets developments that appear in the history of religious psychology over the past eight or ten decades. For a psychologist with such a distinctive viewpoint and subject-matter is not one who is easily embroiled in Freud's problem of religion as mass-delusion. As a psychologist, of course, the man we have described will concern himself with delusional behavior, even on a mass scale. As a psychologist he will do more, too, than just record the phenomenon of delusion; he will take note as best he can of its origins and growth, its pattern of development and recurrent manifestations. But such concern for the study of mass delusional behavior is quite different from the pronouncement that religion is a mass delusion. The former is proper to the psychologist; the latter (or similar pronouncements on religious systems) is a structural statement (or a matter of dogmatic content) which it is the right of the philosopher (or the theologian) to make and validate.[3]

3 A psychologist having the outlook assumed here would have an entirely different problem when dealing with Freud's theory on the relationship of sex and religion (a position inconsistent, it would seem, with the philosophical assertion of mass delusion). For here, even if one disagrees (1) specifically, with the genetic explanation of this relationship in terms of the Oedipus complex or (2) generically, with the development of a total theory from abnormal cases, still the discussion is about behavior and about behavior within the framework of the psychologist.

Again, a psychologist whose area of investigation extends to the religious subject's behavior in all its amplitude is one who prevents a recurrence of an earlier trend in the history of religious psychology such as the *Varieties of Religious Experience* by William James would represent. The work of James is still a classic of its kind; it also contains fruitful insights. (Seeing religion as a source of composure after upsets and crises whence examination of motivational systems derived, would be an example.) And yet the *Varieties* does not live up to its name; there are whole areas of religious psychology that it does not even mention. In effect it comes to be a treatment of the varieties of extraordinary religious experience.[4]

Lastly, a psychologist who approaches his work as a scientist will be one who profits by the developments in his field: he does more than imitate the court chronicler or reporter since he editorializes about events. He would note, for example, that most writing in religious psychology prior to 1920 spoke of religious experience in only one way: a special emotional arousal, a feeling of "intense union" with God and a sense of "being saved," all of which is described after the manner of the mystics. And yet

4 Some readers who think in terms of religious action as grace-produced may wonder at this point how a religious psychology can expect to handle religious behavior *in all its amplitude*. It may be objected: psychology can never explain acts produced by grace. An answer to this objection can be developed from either of two principles held by the objectors: (1) to distinguish is not to deny; (2) grace builds on nature.

Certainly, grace-produced acts are also human acts and hence part of human behavior. As such, under this behavioral aspect, they are, then, the proper object of study for the psychologist. This distinction neither denies the supernatural or grace nor disproves the worth of religious psychology; it merely keeps things in intelligent order.

Again, if grace builds on nature then the appropriate contribution that religious psychology can make is to prepare, promote, and sustain psychologically sound religious living as a basis for the work of grace. This is not to deny that grace is a gift. Grace is gratuitously given but it is also true that, other things being equal, when grace is given a man who is psychologically adjusted will profit more from it than one who is maladjusted. That seed which is the gift of grace grows better when planted in soil properly tilled and cultivated.

he would know that this psychology profited by the work of Kulpe and the Würzburg school, adapted its research methods to the religious field, and hence broadened our notions of religious experience considerably. He would be conversant too with the expanding research going on at present.

As we have hinted, the scientist envisioned here would not be satisfied with mere descriptions and the cataloguing of religious events. He would be looking for the initiation and development of behavior, for recurrence of manifestation and cycles of growth. More concretely and in terms of our opening story, the psychologist would notice that the pivotal phenomenon expressed in the autobiographical account was the discarding of the imperial religion and the movement toward Christianity. Conversion, then, becomes the central treatise (Chapter VI) in the study that follows. However, conversion is not, as we shall see, a kind of particular action that might be likened to *running,* but rather it would better be thought of·as a complex activity such as we might designate by the phrase *playing a game.* There is a core phenomenon of commitment; there is the individual's existential sense both of helplessness and security as he stands between a commitment already made and its fulfillment yet to come. Further, it is in this context that the love of altruism and union become meaningful. In a word, faith, hope, and charity (Chapter V) are behavioral elements involved in the story of conversion.

Adult behavior such as we have just described does not occur *ex abrupto.* It has its antecedents. True, the Japanese we heard from earlier had but a brief introduction to Catholicism in our story (although more came later) but the beginnings and growth in the imperial religion were a lengthy process which extended back through adolescence and childhood to infancy. A full behavioral study in the religious framework, then, would consider these stages along with their problems and influences, especially the influence of other persons (Chapters III and IV). Adult religious behavior also has its atmosphere or, better, the conditions it requires for the maintenance of religious health in a psychological way. Prayer and worship are certainly implied in our conversion story and these along with many other types of action (penance and contrition, petition and thanksgiving, sacraments and vows, *et al.*) are matter for detailed study by the psychologist of religion (Chapters VII and VIII). The extraordinary character of our conversion stories reminds us of William James and earlier psychologists of religion, and indicates to us that (even without taking up abnormal and pathological cases) there is place for an examination of behavior and experience that goes beyond the ordinary types of action listed above.

Lastly, like other scientists, the religious psychologist becomes reflective as his science achieves a more adult stature. With this reflection comes an assessment of the instruments and tools at his disposal, an appraisal of his methods. Hence after all else there are two appendix-like sections (Chapters X and XI) in the first of which methods are shown concretely in empirical studies and in the second, a more theoretical essay on methodology is developed.

An outline of the study to follow is easily sketched from the foregoing paragraphs:

The study opens with an introduction	Chapter I
Then comes some background material	Chapter II
There follow, logically, the development stages in	*Infancy and Childhood*, Chapter III *Adolescence*, Chapter IV
Whence we arrive at the various religious aspects manifested in the adult which are	*Religious aspects of the mature man: faith, hope, charity*, Chapter V
And thus we are in a position to consider the central theme of	*Conversion*, Chapter VI
Thereupon means are taken up: the ordinary first in	*Ordinary Means of Growth*, Chapters VII & VIII
Followed by the extraordinary in	*Ascetical Phenomena*, Chapter IX
Two sections, like appendices, are at the end, the first of which is	*Empirical Studies*, Chapter X
And the last is	*Tools and Methods*, Chapter XI

2 historical foundations and background

THE bases or foundations for a psychology of religion, so far as its materials and methods are concerned, are the same, at least in part, as those for any field of psychology. This is because the various fields of psychology all treat of the same subject matter, namely, the mind of man and his behavior. Just as there can be an abnormal psychology, if the investigator wishes to study the deviant forms of behavior and thought especially; and there can be a psychology of childhood, or child psychology, if the investigator wishes to study this level of development mainly; so there can be a psychology of religion, if the investigator wishes to study those aspects of human life and action which have a very close relationship to religion.

Of course there are many different definitions of psychology, as there are of religion. The term "psychology" will here be taken to embrace any and all of the activities which characterize the psychophysical composite called man. It must be taken to include all levels of man's development, and so it will be extended to the study of the mental processes of children, youths, mature persons, and the aging and aged. In regard to the definition of religion there is more debate than with regard to the meaning of psychology. But by adhering to the root meaning of the word "religion," namely, the binding back of man to God, much difficulty will be avoided. Of course, man will here be treated as one who owes his beginning and continuation in existence to an outside power which is God, one who owes some homage and service to the God to Whom he owes existence, one who will be called back to God one day to give an account of the service which he has rendered. It can be said then with the theologians that religion is the sum total, or embraces every instance, of actions of man which show his particular relationship to the supernatural, to the divinity, to God. Among these activities there will be some which are external and observable to other people, and some which are inner and secret, known only to the person himself. And among both kinds of activities will be some which have moral worth, some which bear a peculiar relationship to God, that is. What is important here is the fact that some of man's acts are such that they will bring him closer to God, and others will not do this, and may even remove him far from God. All these truths and considerations have to be taken for granted in any generalized account of the relationship between psychology and religion. The reality of the Divinity and His creative act will not be demonstrated or called in question, nor the reality of man's destiny and the means necessary for him to fulfill it. The phenomena which arise in the world of man and his fellows will be studied because of the fact that men are as a matter of fact religious. A religious psychology might just as well be spoken of as a psychology of religion. In this case, however, the adjective "religious" would be used as a modifier of the experience of man, rather than as a separate relationship between man and his creator. It probably comes to the same thing; in some instances one expression might be clearer, in others the opposite might be the case.

To summarize thus far, religion means the sum total, or each instance, of acts which man performs which have a specific relationship to the "other world," the supernatural, the divine. It will then be taken to include a belief or creed, a set of norms or a code, and a ceremonial or ritual. Very much will be said about the ceremonial aspects of religion, so they must be kept in mind right from the very beginning of the study. The threefold aspect of religion has been neglected by many writers, and they thus give a one-sided view of the totality of religious psychology, stressing either the belief aspect to the neglect of the other two, or again the normative aspects. The threefold aspect becomes a necessity when it is considered that man is a being who thinks and judges about his destiny (holds a creed); who acts somehow in accordance with his creed (has a code); and who distinguishes, among his various actions, those which bear directly upon his final destiny, by reason of the purpose or intention of the acts themselves, from those which by themselves do not, but which could be made to serve this purpose by an inner act of choice and intention. The observable aspects of man's behavior, so commonly studied by psychological investigators, may or may not be the subject matter of this psychology. But these behavioral aspects certainly do become incorporated into such a psychology, if and when man uses a ritual or ceremonial to indicate in a clear and observable manner the purpose of his actions. Thus, three rather clearly delineated phases of our study can be distinguished, which will be introduced into every chapter, namely, the ritualistic or ceremonial of religion; the body of truths accepted, or the dogmas, the creed; and finally the ways in which these two modify the behavior of men on many occasions, the moral or ethical side of religion. For those writers who wish to prescind from the reality of the existence of God, or otherwise wish not to become involved in discussions of the fundamentals of all religions, natural as well as revealed, this last phase becomes synonymous with the study of man's conventional or culturally determined behavior. To avoid confusing moral behavior with convention, the presuppositions have been laid down with which this study of the bases for a psychology of religion will begin.

It is not the intention to speculate at the outset about the apparent great issues of religion, like the problem of evil, or of predestination. These topics may easily get the reader so involved in controversy that he cannot launch a successful inquiry into the psychology of religion. There are some readily admitted, easily observed, simple foundations or bases which would justify a special branch of learning known as the psychology of religion. For instance, one might bring in the efficacy and use of prayer. Again, there are some tendencies which one meets quite frequently in dealing with persons who are emotionally disturbed, such as exaggerated ritualism, or magical practices, or guilt feelings. These topics ought to be handled particularly in a psychopathology of religious life, but they do give a foundation for the study of the normal kind of behavior which is found to lead to such deviant forms; that is, the very existence of a necessary ritual, or of an act of sorrow following conversion, or an adolescent doubt leading to scruples—all these show how intimately interwoven must be the study of psychology of the normal, of the abnormal, and of the religious experiences of man.

It might be asked at this point why there has to be a psychology rather than a sociology or biology of religion. Why are the phenomena mentioned above proper topics for the study of psychology rather than of sociology? It would seem that there should and could also be a sociology of religion, insofar as the institutions of a given era have brought to bear upon the course of religious experiences and development. So there is no doubt that there is a real place in libraries for a course designated the sociology of religion. But insofar as such a discipline would be forced to rely upon the actual experiences of the individual persons who constituted the groups, it would overlap with the study now being undertaken.

As for the biology of religion, it is obvious that none of the infra-human species have ever been seriously thought to have possessed a religious life. Since, then, the proper objects of biological studies, exclusive of those which treat of human beings, are plants and animals, there need be no further discussion of the religious biology of man. But in just so far as the biology of man, or the sociology of man, includes elements which are common to men and animals, so far does our study extend out into and borrow from the study of both. An instance in point might be the study of the mystical phenomena characteristic of the saints, in which biological laws seem to have been held in abeyance. But more of these in their proper place.

There is a final reason or foundation for taking up the psychology of religion seriously at this time. Introspection is one of the methods proper to psychology, and philosophers of all times have been given to reflection. By means of reflection, the great minds of all time have been brought to bear upon the great problems, such as the origin and destiny of man, his relation to the universe, his power over nature and over himself. Thus, were it not for the fact that man is a thinking, or better, re-thinking, reflective creature, one could never hope to fathom the depths of his being, or attempt to probe his subtler, but nonetheless real, deep and solemn religious experiences. Thus, the method which has been so useful in the traditional psychology of human nature, namely introspection and inference, gives sure grounds for the pursuit of a thoroughgoing and serious study of the psychology of religion. Self-analysis and curiosity about man's destiny, plus considerations of the means needed for working out this destiny, have been phenomena of the world from the earliest days of recorded history. And even prehistoric remains show evidences of man's universal interest in the "other world" and his relation thereto. Lastly, the recent revival of interest in the relation of religion to man's well-being, and of extra-sensory phenomena to those of normal sensory response, make it timely to rewrite a psychology of religion that incorporates the more recent findings of modern investigators. For there is no doubt about it, in the minds of those who do reflect upon their experiences, that religious experience is a unique relationship found expressed in various ways by men of various ages and in places far distant from one another. Men are spontaneously moved to further considerations of the special kind of relationship which exists between the experience they have of a material world, and that which they say they have of an "other world" not of the senses. This special kind of experience is of an even deeper, and sometimes more vitally significant, kind of reality than is man's experience of the material world of sense.

LOGICAL AND HISTORICAL GROUNDS

One might expect that a Catholic writer on the subject of the psychology of religion would be challenged by certain historical events which would give him an argument for writing a predominantly defensive treatise. Several non-Catholic writers have recently been so challenged by recent events of history and science now commonly known and discussed by psychologists and religionists alike. Reference here is made to the writings by Sigmund Freud on *Totem and Taboo*, *Moses and Monotheism*, and *The Future of an Illusion*. It is common knowledge that Freud relied heavily in these works upon the *Golden Bough* by Frazer, and that much of the data from this account of primitive peoples have been called into question since Freud wrote his treatise. Nevertheless, the opinion seems to have persisted among scientists that the Father of Psychoanalysis has finally and effectively disposed of the myth of religion by his researches and publications. In the opinion of sincere thinkers and earnest researchers of all religious denominations, Freud was working outside his proper sphere of competence when he chose to write on the subject of religious experience. It is not to enter upon a controversy regarding these documents that they are mentioned here. It is merely to show that there have been certain events in our recent times which have pinpointed the main ideas that had been traditionally discussed in the psychology of religion.

Nor is the present treatise being written because William James did an inadequate job of writing on the subject forty years ago when he wrote his *Varieties of Religious Experience*. This work still remains a classic even though it does not touch whole areas of thought which are elementary materials for persons not professing the same religion that James did.

The writings of George Stanley Hall on adolescent doubts have also been acclaimed as classics, and some psychologists still quote these pages as if the last word had been said about this period in the development of religion in human beings. Again, the present findings will not be based upon any of the arm-chair philosophizing of these three men; it will be admitted, however, that all of them have done a service to psychology in that they have stimulated thinking on three important areas. They are the area of religious motivation, that of the value to the individual of his religious experience, and that of the significance in the life of each individual of passing through a period of doubt. There is a grain of truth that is contained in Freud's "escape" theory of religion—perhaps some men do use this roundabout way of shirking responsibilities, namely, to go to church and pray. Such people are not therefore to be taken as representative samples of the whole human race. Others may, as James surmises, use religion in order to regain their balance and composure after upsets and crises. This also gives objective grounds for investigating such motivation systems in man, but in *Varieties* one has not the whole truth. Stanley Hall did a service to psychologists also by reminding them that the phenomenon of "doubt" is as objective a fact as that of "choice," but he spoiled the effect of his writing by over-generalizing this experience of doubt.

These three classic sources for a psychology of religion will not be relied upon in this treatise as giving the real historical foundation to the study. There is another historical fact which does give such a foundation. In all the great religions of the world, from as far back as 6000 years before Christ, there has been a recognition of a force drawing man outside himself, toward the divinity. There has been a corresponding realization and admission of the fact that certain essential relations exist between man and the "outside" or "supermundane" being, and that these relations are expressed in a form of worship or at least a respect for the deity, and a belief in his power to reward or punish, to measure out his sanctions in accordance with human goodness, human deserts. So the real foundation or real basis for a psychology of religion is the fact of the essential body-and-soul, that is, the essentially dependent constitution of man, attested to by thinkers of all times and places. This demands a serious consideration of how man carries out the activities connected with the special kind of relation he has to the divinity; this relation has a very noticeable effect upon his creed, his code and his ceremonials.

Thus the chief bases for a psychology of religion are: the fact that man universally recognizes that he is in the position of a small, dependent and subservient being when he compares himself to the divinity; that the natural expression of such an attitude of dependence is a feeling of wonder and of awe, joined to sentiments of respect, homage and worship. Men are known to have arrived at this attitude even apart from any special revelation, simply by considering, for example, the grandeurs of nature, the marvels of the visible world, or the great wonder of the world evidenced by the fact of human goodness and philanthropy. Allied to the sentiments here mentioned are those excited by the unending revelations of more and more wonders in outer space, the macrocosm; more and more power in the electron, the microcosm.

When man recognizes his weakness and nothingness, he spontaneously seeks to rise from this condition. He strives to be rid of total dependence, by pursuing a course which, it is his hope, will lead to some measure of independence; his very weakness is a stimulus to becoming stronger. This is part of the normal maturing, or development from within, of human nature. Thus, being weak and close to nothing, he strives to become something, to reach a goal, to do something to satisfy his inner craving and need for self-actualization. Following from the deep inner striving and need for fulfillment is a need for security, for freedom from disturbing threats to his existence and well-being; included in his striving for total well-being is a state of mind that we call the wish or craving for peace and contentment, for happiness which is the natural destiny of human beings.

Since the very constitution of man results in these states, namely that of dependence on an outside cause, and the feeling of inadequacy joined to striving for fulfillment, psychological manifestations or expressions most often associated with such feelings are acts of worship and adoration; statements of a friendly relationship between man and God his father; feelings of awe, wonder and longing. Associated with the strivings and craving for security are expressions of man's need for outside help, his petitions and supplications, his desire and hope that he may someday, somehow, be relieved from too terrible a suffering, secure from threats too awesome to meet. All this gives the natural foundation for a psychology that helps one to understand and interpret these strivings, this feeling of being too small to mean much of anything in such a large or nearly endless universe.

But to stop here would be to have but a very small portion of the reality which is the true foundation of man's religious needs and strivings. Though helpless, and while seeking to lift himself from the total abyss of nothingness which seems to encompass him, man comes to realize that there is really something of value in himself and in other selves when viewed against a larger scheme of things. His insignificance is continually being counteracted by the reality that each man knows he possesses. It is his not by accident nor by choice, but by the actual accomplishments which accrue to him whenever he actualizes any of his potentialities. He knows he is not a "nobody" when he sees the effect of a single good deed on the life and happiness of another human being. This new awareness of being of value somehow to another, and to oneself, gives the motivation, or even courage, to strive to become more fully the self for which one is equipped by native endowments. Let it be noted here that the need and tendency to go out of the self in the service of another is so closely tied in with the basic tendency toward self-actualization that it is hard to discriminate between them in a mature person. Thus the group need, or the conviction that "not I but we" have value, is satisfied by bringing out one's talents to their fullest capacities, and is as essential to human nature as are the individual needs. Religion and religious group-striving sustain human efforts, give direction and meaning to human striving, confirm the weakling worn out with fruitless or misguided efforts or opposed by unexpected and immense frustrations.

Through the addition of props or supports, then, by means of the courage and hope which religion engenders, men are supported so that they can really become of value to themselves and to others, and so that the value they see in themselves is not merely a fiction or an illusion. What would be the value, one might reason, inherent in a human being, apart from the atoms of which he is compounded, were it not for the extra-mundane destiny of which man is capable and desirous of attaining. The realization that life is meaningful for a helpless striving creature like man is furthered by giving expression to the feelings it engenders, it is disseminated to those around one by participation in group acts of religion, and it is perfected on the attainment of unity with the corporate body of all humanity. So by means of religious acts, to be discussed in detail later, man acknowledges his dependence. He asserts his rights with humility. When possible he shares his benefits with his neighbors, and he activates with zeal his tendency and capacity to direct, control and develop the weak self. He also tries to express, enhance and perfect the active, real self. The destiny of many such selves in a final unending infinitely just but happy Utopia, cannot but be a source of attraction to thinking men.

ONTOLOGICAL GROUNDS FOR A PSYCHOLOGY OF RELIGION

Since consideration has been made of some of the bases for a psychology of religion which are derived from the nature of man and from history, it might be fitting to look briefly at some more fundamental facts that have a bearing on the issue. These facts are so straightforward and uncomplicated that it is a wonder that they have not been given full treatment in discussions of personality, or of character, or of the relationship that religion has to both of these.

The constitution of man has been described as involving a very humble beginning, an existence which is totally dependent upon parents, tutors, and outside help generally. His existence reaches outward and upward, in the direction of an independence of the self, or self-actualization, of goal-striving for an absolute and unconditional state of happiness and rest from conflict. There is in the very nature of man, if his beginning and his end upon earth be considered, the foundation for both an active life of deeds and accomplishments, and for decay and deterioration in old age terminating in the biological passivity of death. Thus the grounds are laid in early days of childhood for an unending conflict within each man, because of the fact that from birth he is continually but surely tending toward death. This notion is reached without making any postulates such as life-death instincts. As soon as man is able to reflect upon things, and to make even the most elementary speculations about the meaning of life, he is faced with the problem of the meaning of this in terms of a possible non-life. Observation attests to the fact that the life of man is not permanent nor gratifying in every aspect. This ontological fact that faces generation after generation of human beings might properly be thought of as the fundamental reason for the minds of men turning so universally toward the beyond, the permanent, the eternal. Life is not unmixed with an element of death and decay, not simply because of the ravages of the time and old age, but also because of the physical dangers that threaten happiness and health on every side. Thus, the basic ontological fact which leads logically to a study of the psychology of man's relation to God is the reality of death.

This is obviously a far cry from saying, as do some authors, that there is in man a life and a death instinct; or that there is an innate faculty for religion and morality. The difference lies in the fact that such authors see in man's physical nature only the foundation for conflicts, the opposing forces. On the other hand, instead of regarding the life-death conflict as instinctual, it can be seen as an indication of the precarious nature of human existence, and the consequent total dependence on a power which can preserve man in life after death. The result of recognizing this dependence, then, is acceptance of religion and cultivation of morality. It is our position that man, with the right use of his powers of judgment and reason, grounded upon the fundamental reality of an intact and unimpaired human nature, comes spontaneously to a realization of religious reality as defined above. Even the most confirmed materialist, provided he thinks at all seriously about the meaning of life and the destiny of man, will set up a kind of philosophy of man, a *Weltanschauung*, that guides his thinking and behavior generally. This for him will be the code and the creed, even though he claims that he will have no dealings with the religionists. It will obviously at times also lead him to the establishment of certain rituals which will enable him to get what he most desires from material objects, since he looks upon these as the ultimate for human happiness.

It is profitable at this point to speculate about the meaning of this natural opposition or conflict that is built up in every thinking human being, lest it be confused with the views of Freud on this subject. It is a conflict or opposition between the desire to be, and the knowledge that earthly being is not permanent and satisfying, or the conflict between the urge to live and the need to die. The more a person concentrates upon the benefits of existence, of remaining sane and happy, of perfecting his natural powers by exercising them in a healthy and purposive manner, the more he will be likely to be active rather than passive.

For in the joy of doing things there is little room for quiescence or repose. On the contrary, the more a person dwells upon the certainty of death that ends all the psycho-physical functions and operations so laboriously perfected during the life span, the more he might tend to cease from the daily struggle and let well enough alone. Thus there are bases in human nature for both a life of activity and of passivity; the two aspects of religious life and asceticism which correspond to these bases are the active and contemplative lives respectively. The latter, however, involving effortful activity, is passive only in the sense that it is primarily directed toward disposing the individual to perfect reception of the goodness of God. All that is known from revealed religion about the happiness of the blessed will come in to help solve the riddle of activity-passivity; the problem of evaluating the active-contemplative lives. That is theology, however, and the pleasure of entering upon this very exciting field of inquiry will be foregone here.

A third consideration may be mentioned, one which touches everyone at some time in life, connected with the death-life realization. It is the question of whether religion is to be a positive value that attracts one to itself for the benefit which can be received from it, and for enhancing the value that religion has in and of itself—the positive pull aspect of religion; or whether notions of the divinity are built up as something so mighty and awesome that it repels one, especially with its reminders of the certainty of death, and the necessity of suffering and of self-denial. If this latter happens to be the state of affairs at some time in life, it might be expected then that one would be morbid and morose, inactive to the point of being driven away from the ordinary pursuits of everyday existence, in a family or in a community. The two possibilities are always present, and there is scarcely a person designated as religious, by his own opinion or by the verdict of those around him, who has not felt at times the opposition between these two forces.

Finally it can be mentioned that there are those who use religion as an escape from the world. They withdraw from their responsibilities and seek solace in the quiet of religion or in endless retreats. They have become disgruntled by events, perhaps only for the moment, and keep asking themselves, "What can religion do for me?" "What has it done except to take me out of contact with reality?" In connection with such an idea it not infrequently happens that an overconscientiuos and somewhat misguided person may blame religion for his morbidity and isolationism. What he ought to ask himself is rather, "What have I done, or what ought I to do to fulfill my religious obligations?" This double aspect of life and of religion, the activity-passivity, or the simultaneous positive and negative outlook, can and often does lead to morbidity and withdrawal; but a good psychologist of religion will be able to help such morbid and withdrawn persons to realize that their behavior under the conditions which led to these disturbances was not the inevitable outcome, either of the use of their native endowments, or of the adjuncts of religion and religious activities. Such persons can often be helped by the same means which may have been instrumental in injuring them psychologically, but the question of cure belongs properly to the psychopathology of religion.

AN ANALYSIS OF THE FORMAL MEANING ATTACHING TO A PSYCHOLOGY OF RELIGION

If one were to ask just what is the object of psychology of religion, the answer would be, it is the natural psychological aspect of mental religious habits and traits. The first part of the definition to come under discussion is the idea of a mental religious habit. Every being which is relative is by that token ordered to an absolute one; and every created spirit is ordered toward worshipping and possessing God, by means of a natural relationship, which may even be subconscious. As has been seen, man's nature is absolutely subordinated to and totally dependent upon God.

To this quasi-religious aspect of the essence of created things there corresponds, in rational beings, that attitude in which one consciously thinks, not only theoretically about divine reality, but is also borne onward in the practical realm toward finding and adoring God, as he conceives Him to be, and is united to Him in heart and mind.

There are many and even variant forms which these religious attitudes may take. Some might be mentioned, such as reverence for the divine being, and devout love, adoration and petition; self-dedication with faith and hope; contrition, conversion, etc. At times a person experiences this religious dynamism as a certain active attempt at approaching God, and at other times rather as a passive experience of being drawn to God. For some the religious experience is locked up in the silent secrecy of the mind; for others it makes itself known in the outer world in the form of expressive symbols. Often it is a purely personal experience, yet again it may be a collective one and one that is closely bound up with the social life of man. All over the world instances of religious experience are found, and these are extremely dependent upon the unique character of individuals, upon social groups and cultures, and upon geographic and cosmic conditions. In all cases, however, this habit or attitude implies a conscious relation—one of worshipping God. Currently the relation is more often expressed as one of a mental reconsideration of divine things, i.e., attentively weighing and relishing them.

Besides this positive habit of religion there is what might be called a negative habit, which belongs indirectly to the object of religious psychology. It consists in an aversion for divine things, and a cool religious indifferentism.

By the term "psychological aspect" psychology is distinguished from other parts of the science of religion. Psychology does not proceed in the way that philosophy of religion does, by inquiring into the essence and metaphysical grounds of religion as such; nor in the way natural theology puts forth the truths about the nature of God. The fundamental question in religious psychology is the psychic structure of religious experience: the conscious and unconscious psychic processes which together constitute religious experience; its rational and irrational, personal and social characteristics; and the manner in which this experience emanates from the total psychic entity and culminates in the total psychic life.

There are questions in the psychology of religion dealing with the relationship between the type of personality of an individual and the type of religious activity he prefers. These questions are concerned with the relation which seems to exist between religious experience and the unique character of a person or group. Also, there is a psychology of religious evolution, which deals with the mutual relation between psychic evolution in general, and religious life. Finally there is psychopathology of religion, dealing with relations existing between a deformed or sick psychic structure and a healthy or an unhealthy religious disposition.

Are any characteristics of religious habits natural? Actually any religious act that is perfect is not something which is merely natural. By means of elevating grace it is raised to the supernatural order; through illuminating grace it is changed and directed. Nevertheless the religious act remains an act of the soul, and as such it is subject to the laws of psychic life. Only in this respect is it the object of religious psychology. This point needs greater emphasis, and will be explained in greater detail below.

Let it be noted at the start that there are limits and difficulties inherent in a psychology of religion, and that these arise from the supernatural character of a religious act. Since religious psychology is concerned only with the natural quality of a religious act, and yet a perfect religious act is not purely natural, nor explainable solely by means of psychic laws, this study appears to be dealing with an object that does not exist as such. Therefore psychology of religion seems to be a pseudo-science.

Our answer is simply this: to abstract is not to deny. A person does not deny nor necessarily neglect the action of grace, just because he abstracts from it within the limits of a certain method. Of course the psychologist should state that he never attains the full reality of a perfect religious act by using psychological methods exclusively. In a similar way thinkers in philosophy and speculative theology are careful to report that they never exhaust nor fully express the fullness of the divine reality by means of their analogous concepts. However, from the very fact that the total reality of an object is not encompassed, it does not follow that not even a good part of it is perceived.

Again it may be asked: Is religious psychology able by its methods to show, at least in some instances, that a certain psychic event cannot be explained without the intervention of divine grace? First let it be noted that the entitative supernaturality of a religious act is never attained by psychological methods, because such an act simply transcends the capacity of positive scientific investigation. Yet the effects of illuminating and comforting graces can sometimes be reliably established, as for example when a person says he got an inspiration to visit a church, and while so doing received sensible consolation. Again, a distinction must often be made between cases of ordinary graces and those of favored persons. As a psychologist one studies the structure of psychic acts, trying to distinguish the purely natural aspects of mental life from those aspects which are known only through revealed religion. It is a fact of revealed religion that intervening graces exist. There seems to be no good reason why a believing psychologist should not accept the fact of grace and then attempt to describe its natural concomitants. Statements about these natural concomitants can be as reliable as those one would make about any psychological process whatever.

If, however, it is asked whether limits can be set for certain, by psychological methods only, beyond which a specific psychic event must be designated as one which is inexplicable on the basis of natural psychic law, the answer would seem to be that in ordinary cases the grace of God so well adapts itself to nature that any certain designation of such limits by means of psychological methods alone is scarcely ever if at all possible. In an exceptional case, however, the view which denies the possibility of a natural explanation is more easily tenable. Yet men highly skilled in very exceptional phenomena of religious life invariably caution especially to proceed with care here. So long as there is question of a physical event, it can easily be shown that this event, for example, a healing, or a raising from the dead, is beyond a natural explanation. But the psychic unconscious is so complex and at the same time so capable of influencing the conscious life that it would be most difficult, by psychological methods alone, to prove with certainty that the natural psychological explanation of a certain conscious experience is impossible. Neither is it proved that the natural explanation is in itself impossible simply from the fact that a satisfactory explanation has not yet been forthcoming. The Church therefore proceeds most cautiously in judging the supernatural character of any religious experience, no matter how sublime or pious it may be.

Certain objections arise against an "exact" religious psychology. It would seem that the exact scientific observation of a religious experience would entail so much reflection that this would be injurious to the genuine religious life. The reason is that religious experience delves into the secrets of hearts, and flees from the public gaze, especially that of scientists. There seems then at least to be a profanation of a holy experience connected with scientific observation of the religious life. Moreover, here too there seems to lie a danger of psychologism; a relativism weakening the vigor of religion and the objectivity of religious doctrine.

It is answered: Whether such a danger will be present or not depends on the manner in which the study is undertaken. It is surely possible to treat holy things in a profane and irreverent manner. So too, for example, it is possible to treat the life of the Blessed Trinity in a rationalistic manner. Should all speculative theology on this account refrain from discussing this most profound mystery? Many psychologists, it is true, have approached the study of religious life with relativistic bias. But it does not follow that for that reason the study should be dropped; rather it follows that religious men are obliged to devote their efforts to the study of religious experience in a reverent manner. Thus, they can show the beauty of religious life and serve the cause of truth.

SOME EARLY HISTORICAL ANTECEDENTS TO THE PSYCHOLOGY OF RELIGION

In this part of the investigation some highlights of history will be sketched briefly, which will enable the reader to grasp the significance of modern trends. There will be a larger historical summary at the end of the work, with ample annotated bibliographies.

The reader of books and articles on the psychology of religion prior to 1921 will be struck by one thing. There was only one acceptable view with regard to the nature of religious experience. It was a special emotional arousal, a feeling of "intense union" with God and of "being saved" much after the manner in which the mystics have described their highest religious experiences. It was definitely not in any way in the nature of an intellectual experience and therefore was not rational or logical.

It was mostly because of the researches and writings of Girgensohn and his followers in Germany that this state of affairs came to be changed. The workers of this school had been able to take advantage of the new methodologies that became acceptable in scientific psychology. These were perfected largely in the Würzburg school of Oswald Külpe. The Würzburgers instituted the method whereby moments of psychological experience could be fractionated. Then upon reflection the person trying to analyze mental experience into its components could more easily refer to each part of the train of thoughts. For instance there would be the fore-period, the middle period, or time of actual insight, and the after-period in a problem-solving situation. In the fore-period one described his feelings of anticipation, fears, desires; in the main period he more often concentrated upon the real relationship of ideas; and in the after-period again there were significantly large numbers of feelings and emotions, as for example those of satisfaction and release.

Altogether apart from the immense value which the discovery of this new method had for science, it became a new tool in the hands of the psychologists of religion. Girgensohn, then, utilized these methods and was able to give a more complete account of the deeper aspects of religious experience than had ever been given before his time. He and his workers now claimed that the religious experience when analyzed more thoroughly could be found to be made up of parts or phases which were not purely emotional. They partook more properly of the character of intellectual or rational features. For example there was reported a real intellectual representation of the divine being, during religious experience; there was a reaction of man's whole being to the divine reality, and a recognition that this was the divine to which man reacted. This was like a functional relation of the total ego of man towards the apprehended aspects of the divinity.

Of course religious experience contains emotional elements, and these might predominate over the rational. But they were by no means the sole characteristic of the experience *qua* religious. For instance there would be feelings of fear, desire, grief and blame—typical human negative emotions; and there would be joy, elation, devotion, reverence, dedication, peace, love and confidence on the positive side. The investigators found that these emotions, while they were secondary to the basic religious characteristics, still could arouse or activate spiritual powers. That they could even sustain these powers under stress was a real discovery among religionists. More specifically, the investigators distinguished clearly in the religious experience the intellectually-represented object of the same, from the ego-reaction. In this reaction the person was found to make more intimately his own the pious and devout thoughts which came into his life, and then to assimilate them; so that he now opened his soul to the divine light in a new way, and vowed allegiance and service to the Master, to the fullest extent possible for man, being so dedicated that he "lost all to find All."

Under these circumstances a man also evaluates his religious fantasies in a new way. They are now no longer mere symbols only, nor are they of prime importance in the reaction; they are certainly not to be equated with mundane objects which become symbols of further and deeper, perhaps magical and mystical meaning. The experiencer also discovers in his repertoire of mental content some volitions and strivings which come into reality spontaneously in the course of the religious experience, but are not actually part and parcel of the experience itself. The peculiarity of these strivings, as compared to ordinary non-religious strivings, is that they seem like certain dispositions of the mind or of the whole self, which dispositions came into being without awareness of freedom or of self-determination of the process.

This new point of view, which has been very sketchily presented, met with much opposition among traditional religionists, and particularly with the psychoanalysts. In 1924 a Catholic student of Girgensohn, W. Gruehn, refined and elaborated upon the doctrine of his master and produced a monumental work known as *The Experience of Worth* (Das Werterlebnis). Some 20 years later Gruehn collected and published the results of many scientific and empirical researches on religious experience, in a volume entitled: *Die Frommigkeit der Gegenwart*, (Munster, Asschendorf, 1955). Besides the work done in Germany there have been similar studies in Switzerland done by the Eranos Group; in Brussels by the Lumen Vitae group, and in Canada by the eminent Dominicans, Father Mailloux and Father Salman. All this renewed activity followed in the wake of the encouraging remarks of Pope Pius XII in his now famous 1953 address on Psychotherapy and Religion (See *Acta Apostolicae Sedis*, 1953, 45, 278).

All in all, the amount of real positive scientific contribution in this field was disappointingly small up to 1930, but lately it is increasing rapidly. More and more research is being done on mystical and religious phenomena, especially by Catholics. Leagues of mental hygiene are being formed among groups sponsored by religious persons. Finally, real basic research is being done by many groups in the field of religious development of the psychic life of the pre-school child. This is a healthy sign, indicating that Catholics are coming to realize that they have nothing to fear from science, while they may have something to gain. These trends also indicate to the present writer that Catholic thinkers may but recently have gotten over their feelings of relaxed security, engendered by the possession of the true doctrine of Christ. They have not felt the need to study deeply the almost infinite ramifications of this doctrine in the lives of everyday Christians, on the purely natural level of their existence. It is one thing to sit back and calmly enjoy the truth without trying to apply it to everyday life; it is quite another to go out and work among Christ's chosen ones, bringing to them the savory elements of the truth which alone can save men's minds from stress and illness; and which also require continual re-application to the changing needs of the times, if they are to reap the elegant fruits the Master expects of them.

3 the psychology of religious development: a

Part I. The Period of Total Dependence—Infancy

1. *Infancy*

PARENTS CANNOT BE INDIFFERENT

DURING the period of infancy the activity of the human consists mainly in the two life processes of taking in food and elimination. Even in carrying out these activities, the infant is in need of the ministrations of others, if life and health are to be maintained. Purely passive or indifferent care on the part of the elders will not satisfy the need, for it extends beyond that for mere existence—the infant has a real need for healthy existence, that is, for that kind of treatment which will make it possible for him to grow into a healthy and happy member of society. Hence he has above all a need for affection or loving attention. To satisfy this need, the infant demands that he be given love along with his food, with his mother's milk, as the saying goes. As far as the infant is concerned, this love is all of a receiving kind; love is for an infant a taking-in process. It will have to be changed into something else as the child grows older, but at the beginning it must be at least a process in which the child's need for others is satisfied by others, or else his development will suffer.

GOD AND PARENTS PRODUCE

Now Christian parents and nurses will easily realize that in the Christian era, reasoning adults cannot claim absolute power and dominion over their offspring. Since the child is both a child of God and of human parents, both God and parents have an interest, and parents must feel their responsibility to supply what the new-born babe demands for a healthy and happy existence. This ability to supply love and affection, along with sustenance, is well within the scope of any healthy parent. Not all parents realize the importance of the act of pouring out affection upon their children, in conjunction with the act whereby God Himself loves and sustains the infant. The more the parent is imbued with the notion that he and God work together in this process of giving, the more will the deep inner needs of the child be satisfied—not for a moment or two in the morning, nor for an hour or two a day, but for 24 hours a day, for seven days a week. Any failure on the part of parents to impart to the fast-growing infant this feeling of being loved by others will surely place a mark upon the child that will remain for the rest of his life. If the scar is, perhaps, somewhat obliterated later on in life, it will still be healed over only at the expense of some portion of the tender affective life that the child will need in order to maintain his balance in a hostile and difficult world. The need for affection on the part of the infant is absolute, because the dependence is total and absolute; the infant is weak, and could not even withstand the inroads of disease and privations, were it not for the gift to him of kind and loving care. The psychology of religion must specially emphasize this role of the parent in taking the place of the Divine Creator, not only in placing the conditions necessary for God to implant the soul in the child He loves, but also in prolonging the loving act of God and parent throughout the life of the new and beloved individual.

GOD AND PARENTS SUSTAIN

There is more than merely love that parents owe their off-spring, even in the physical order. There is a support or sustaining act, that differs but slightly from love but can be distinguished as the years go on. It is one thing to nourish the child with generous portions of food and love; it is another to carry him around when he cries, to relieve him from tension due to clothing, prolonged remaining in one position, etc. These acts of loving ministration may be classed under the heading of cooperative or concurrent acts of parents with their loved one. Again, whatever these hour-by-hour ministrations are called, their purpose seems to be mainly to preserve the infant from harm, while he is being fed and sustained by the love and care that he needs throughout infancy. There is no more consoling part of the doctrine of Divine creation, conservation, and concursus with the acts of man which are not sinful or malicious. Even as the Divine has stooped to make men out of nothing, to sustain them by allowing nature to supply their bodily needs, and to act along with them in their very movements, as in breathing, for instance; so must the parent reflect upon his own role in regard to the child: the parent, too, must stoop to sustain the child in being, to support him in his actions, and to direct his actions toward what the older and wiser person knows will redound to the greater good of the child of God. All these considerations linking the role of parent to the care and providence of God, could be high-lighted and doubly emphasized, if parents remembered the redemptive acts of God. The goal and *raison d'etre* of these acts is precisely to build up and re-vivify the child of God, who may have failed to keep to his covenant with God, or fallen from His loving friendship.

GOD AND PARENTS PROTECT

Lastly there is the third aspect of the child-parent relationship, reminiscent of another one of God's interests and concerns with the well-being of humanity. When this point has been considered, it will be seen how much truth there is to the saying that even when the parent is nearing the end of his own span of life, he will do well to bear in mind the fact that adults are always children when it comes to their real, essential relations with the Deity. The need referred to at this point is the need for shielding or protecting. It is literally true that every human being is beginning to die the moment he is born. There are disease germs waiting to attack him on every side, even within the very confines of the organism. He must perforce grow to meet the demands made by environment, and by his very existence, upon his endurance; thus he must be strengthened by some outside force, be it that of "nature" or the loving parent. In the act of protection is seen the acme of loving care. What more consoling religious belief is there than the one which pictures the Divine Person as our Father, ever ready to mete out His gifts, His care, and His protection, in ways that suit His infinitely wise plan and eternally loving purpose in bringing us out of nothingness into the realm of His own creation. All that religion means to the parent can be translated into a better understanding of the latter's responsibility toward the child; namely, the parent must sustain, protect, and lovingly accept the child, not merely this or that quality of the child, but his totality. This entire but diminutive person, though seemingly small and of little worth, is gradually going to be set in the direction of becoming a thing of limitless value, eminently worthwhile to himself and to others, a being worthy of God's infinite love and protection.

THE CHILD LEARNS BY IMITATION

In the stress placed upon the relations of parent to child, the growing and changing needs of the child during infancy have been deliberately overlooked. He is never static for an instant, and the needs that are satisfied have a way of generating new needs; and it is the continuous and adequate satisfaction of these needs that alone can result in the favorable outcome called the "well-adjusted and happy child."

On his part, the child will have utilized his natural capacities to give expression to his needs, and to react to the ministrations of the elder, blindly and without appreciation perhaps at first, but in ways that can be catalogued under heads that are classical in the study of child psychology. The child will be dynamically reacting to every act performed in his regard, whether by loving parents or less careful adults and peers; he will be driven by his own inner strivings to attain ends proper to his particular level of existence according to means also proper to his age and development level; he will learn by a process of imitation as much as possible within his limited range of ability. Thus he smiles at being smiled upon, he waves his hand and coos as others engage in these activities. He manifests great dependence here upon his environment for the kind of acts he will be learning to perform. The realization of what this means must startle a thinking parent; but it should not paralyze or render anxious the parent who loves and really cares, for such a parent will know that at some time later this now totally imitative creature will speak and think for himself.

THE CHILD LEARNS CASUALLY, UNREFLECTINGLY

Another kind of response present in child behavior is the conditioning of his native reflexes to different classes of stimuli; thus at first a food response will be evoked by the sight of a bottle, then by the nipple, then by any other similar object— without any amount of reflection on the part of the child. Again, if child learning is thus mechanized and unreflective, how much a loving parent will try to make the kinds of responses generated by the environment the ones best suited to the well-being and happiness of his child.

THE CHILD LEARNS BY SUBMISSION

Lastly, the child learns by both the above means to obey and respond in a desired manner to small signs expressive of the mind and desire of the elder. He learns the power and directive influence of authority, without, of course, considering where such submission to rule will lead him. He becomes routinized, much at the discretion and whim of the parent, in ways that may later be either a hindrance or a benefit for him, depending on how far the habits acquired really serve the needs of the total person. If parents, then, or other responsible persons are aware of the extent of their responsibilities as the vice-regent, the "other self" of God Himself, loving, supporting, protecting, and

directing the child even without the child's volition and consent,
truly the God-like role of parent will appall some of them, but
it cannot fail to engender more real desire and striving on their
part to carry out their expected role to the best of their ability.

2. Religion Aids in the Infant's Striving to Express Himself in Action: Producing Things, Attaining Goals

THE CHILD HAS JOY OF ACCOMPLISHMENT: HE SETS HIS OWN GOALS

When one remembers that every living being is both an active
and a goal-striving creature, he gets another light upon the process of child development and its relation to religion. The child
from birth onward will actually add to his stature, not only
physically, but especially mentally; he will develop his powers
through use, and he will thus become a more efficient, a more
capable individual, by reason of his very striving. But his
squirming, wriggling, and striving, though it seems without
direction and simply a massive and diffuse form of energy-
release, very soon becomes channeled into localized or specialized
habits of reaching for bright objects, for example. These strivings
involve effort—effort which is not merely concerned with that
which is thrust upon the child. At times he feels dissatisfaction
with what is present, and efforts are then directed to obtaining
things he may not or cannot obtain. This frustration of his
striving generates tension, in that he both realizes the goals of
some of his strivings, and derives contentment, and at the same
time he fails to get some of the things he strives for, and experiences displeasure, discontent, or even anger and hostility.

God forbid that one should try to reduce all of his reactions
to those of either anger or hostility or both, when he is frustrated,
but there is not the slightest doubt that he does experience both
pleasure at attaining goals and displeasure at failure to obtain
the desired objects, or at the forced acquisition of unwanted
benefits. In both cases there is need of a wise and cautious tutor,
parent, or guardian to see to it that at some time in the life of
the child both kinds of reaction are experienced. There is need
for a happy outcome to at least some of the infant's strivings.

The reason this is so necessary is that the child cannot remain all his life dependent, but must one day assert his independence; he cannot do this if he has never realized—in a very rudimentary way in infancy—that there is satisfaction in attaining goals set by himself for himself. This means that he must (and will somehow or other) actually obtain certain satisfactions that are eminently his own, and then learn to repeat these as if they were so much his own that they could not possibly belong to anyone else, so that he begins to feel the joy and satisfaction of accomplishing things on his own; this is the joy of achievement, which is the basis for developing a sense of personal worth. This cannot be stressed too much nor at too early a period of child development. When the ego of the child is even partially developed, there is already the possibility of attributing to himself certain outcomes, certain results of his striving, which build up his ego and prepare him for the struggles that lie ahead.

RELIGION SUPPLEMENTS MEANS AND SUBSTITUTES GOALS

The devout religious person cannot fail to see how his religion helps place the proper goal for the child's striving, and helps the parent place the suitable environmental conditions, so that health, happiness and spiritual strength will be the outcome of the infant's strivings. Then the higher satisfactions that come from altruistic enterprises can have some place in the life of an otherwise apparently totally dependent, but selfish, individual child. There will be much more to say later about the meaning and value of religion in the home. Suffice it to say here that there seems to be even more joy of accomplishment experienced by the child in completing a task of a religious nature, such as even imperfectly making the Sign of the Cross, than there would be in his learning to tie his shoes or button up his coat. Since the attitudes of parents toward learning the Sign of the Cross, however, will presumably be different from learning to button a coat, the child cannot help imbibing something of this changed attitude. His growing religion gives new and gratifying outlets for creative and imitative actions.

So the importance of religious considerations is largely indirect via the parents, helping them to achieve deeper realization and fuller execution of their role as parents. This means they will help the child develop his capacities as fully as possible. By restraining the child's sensory and pleasure-seeking inclinations, parents help the child redirect them toward higher goals. In this manner they help the child develop a full, meaningful relationship with God. The ultimate aim of this child-rearing is, of course, to enable the child to perform acts which will aid himself, and those about him, to return to God in accordance with God's will throughout the whole course of childhood development. Parents produce, sustain and protect the child as instruments of God; this involves a dynamic process of cooperating with the strivings and growth processes in the child, in order to enable him to actuate his potentialities to the fullest.

The child is totally dependent on the parent for physical care and nourishment, love and stimulation of his early learning capacities; this dependence on parents is a sign of, and runs parallel to, the real but less obvious dependence of a child upon God its Creator and Redeemer.

Part II. Religion Aids in the Period of Early Childhood Training

The period of early childhood, lasting from one to three or four years, is sometimes compared to that of an impulse-ridden individual, who, if he is to survive and be content, must begin to learn to control his impulses. There are various clearly defined needs which the child has at this time, and these needs and the means for satisfying them will be sketched, insofar as religion is of value in the process. It should be borne in mind throughout that earlier patterns of behavior in the child will remain, but new ones will be added. This scheme is particularly true of the mode or manner of learning. It is also true, though not always recognized as such, that older goals of satisfaction remain in some form, but newer modes or means of satisfying the old needs, of going beyond the old goals, will be found to put in their appearance. Lastly there will be a brief picture of the manner in which childhood emotions will have differentiated into patterns which resemble more and more the patterns which are recognized as those of the healthy adult personality.

Just as in the infancy period the child's chief need was for affection, and this implied the need for support and protection, now a more clearly specified need develops—the need for security. To be secure implies that one lives harmoniously, even peacefully. One tends to think that security implies a negation, an absence of something disturbing. If one speaks about financial security, he means freedom from anxiety about one's future finances. Emotional security has been described as the freedom from hampering fears of disasters, of misfortunes, or of anything that would impair or disturb the peace and harmony among the feelings and desires of a person. Hence when it is said that the child needs security at this age level, it is meant that he wishes to be freed mainly from such disturbances as would be apt to arise during the period of early childhood, not that he desires or needs to be financially or otherwise secure on the adult level. Religion, in so far as it aims at producing and maintaining peace of mind and heart, peace with oneself and with his fellow man, and especially with God, ought to be an important factor in making the parents feel secure, and thus in making the child feel the same.

A. Religion at this Age Already Sets Goals Suitable for Health and Happiness of the Child

It is well to recognize, as did the psychologist Piaget, that during childhood the morality or "goodness" of the child can be somewhat properly characterized as being a morality of constraint. Gradually, however, thinks Piaget, the child comes to realize that there is something more to this process of becoming and remaining good, of doing things which please others around us. There is to be a morality of conscience, whose faint beginnings may be hit upon in some instances during the period of from one to four years. The difference between morality of constraint and that of conscience is that in the former the motive seems to be nothing more than immediate satisfaction. The avoidance of pain might be one of such immediate rewards; another might be to obtain praise, money, sweets, etc., right at the time, or even some additional show of love, attention, and affection. All these motivational factors are expected to occur and to be observable by adults who rear children. These adults should be reminded, however, that there will come a time when the child is not fully pleased or quiescent in the pursuit of such motives as these. He wants to know more of the "why"; for what reason he should be constrained to do so-and-so rather than its opposite. The fully developed conscience will not appear suddenly, nor is it likely to be there before five or six years; adumbrations of its appearance might be seen in some of the questions asked by the child in this period of early childhood, e.g., "Why is it wrong to lie?" (the implication being that he sees his mother's behavior as inconsistent with her teaching). Other stock questions have to do with the goodness or badness of various touches, words, etc.; and in every case the child's questioning should be definitely answered, in so far as the child is capable of understanding, lest there be a break in the smooth and harmonious affective relation between parent and child. Religion can be a tremendous motivating factor, making the parent more keenly aware of the part he must play in this delicate give-and-take which is the forerunner of the child's actual use of the power of reason, to give him the answers which he so easily obtains now by relying on authority and power. The need for submission on the part of the child will go on throughout the process of seeking to know the why and wherefore of various so-called good and bad actions.

The goal, therefore, of development is now the beginning of a control of impulses, that is, not simply a physical binding and enslavement of the individual; he must be somewhat independent, not that emancipation from authority and from obedience is expected, but that while following rules and orders, the young individual guides his own behavior, getting experience in selection of a course of action. He tries his hand sometimes at least at deciding a point on his own, e.g., is it right for Johnny to eat meat on Friday? Authority says no, if one is old enough to be responsible for his acts; Johnny says he thinks he is old enough, so he decides to do as the elders do, which also makes him feel more adult and grown-up.

B. Religion Supplies New Means for Attaining the New Goals

It is seen that with the new goals of development which are set by nature and religion for the youngster, there are additional means which are more suitable than others for carrying the child through this period. It is not a trifling accomplishment to remodel the manner of behavior of the lively youngster, so that he is now not just an impulse-ridden individual. He becomes more sedate and calm, more inclined to deny that he wants to be like a baby all the time, and to assert his feeling of amounting to something—"being like Daddy." Indispensable means for this attainment are a feeling of security arising from the accomplishment of tasks which the child chooses for himself. Nothing enhances the feeling of self-worth so much in a child as to let him show off an accomplishment, even though it be a mere house of blocks; if it cost him effort and planning and decision, he will be proud of it and feel that he is worthwhile. The feeling of self-worth is necessarily enhanced by the accomplishments in the physical or material order. Johnny makes a dog-house, or Jane furnishes a doll-house. Even greater self-worth and value are experienced if and when Johnny, secretly and all on his own, decides to befriend little Jane or some other needy person, when the chips are down. Little Jane can likewise feel a new sense of personal worth if she can cooperate with John to the extent of showing her appreciation by somehow reciprocating—and both will grow in independence if their little plot can be kept as a top-classified secret between them. The principle involved, it would seem, is that human beings, endowed with power of free choice, must have some opportunity of exercising the power in early life, or else it will not become actively or effectively directive of the person's behavior later on.

C. Religious Institutions Help by Sustaining, Encouraging, and Protecting the Child, Even by Means of Restrictions

While the impositions placed by organized churches upon the behavior of small children are very few, still it is well for the ministers of religion to remember that even the restrictions placed upon adults have repercussions in the lives of children. Take the law of abstinence, or that of church attendance, for example. In addition, family devotions also include small children. Thus all these help to keep the child in a world of close contact with his elders and the institutions to which they belong. The moral support received by some parents from their church organizations, like P.T.A. and the Altar and Rosary Society, can never be fully appreciated by those who do not participate in such activities.

D. The Child Acquires New Ways of Learning and Acting

The ways in which the child learns are the same as those for the previous period of infancy, but in addition there is the effect of suggestion, and the crude beginnings of insight. By suggestion is meant an action brought about in another without his having fully chosen it or thought much about whether it should be performed or not. It is traditional that children are very suggestible, with the result that the elders will be doing most of the thinking for them, but not all of it. It is well known that when there is a break in the emotional bond between two persons, then there will be lessening of the effects of suggestion. It can hardly be imagined that the child will have the proper affective relationship with his parents to make absolutely all of their suggestions effective of action on his part. This means that in place of mere uncritical and parrot-like response on the part of the child there will be some reflection. He must and will experience his own new insights in relationships, those between his acts and their consequences, and those between his own and the acts of other persons, peers as well as superiors.

Thus the poor, helpless, totally-dependent infant tends by his very nature to become independent, thinking, choosing, and responsible for his actions. Morality can be taught in principle, but moral behavior and choice can be learned only by doing. How must a zealous minister interpret his own responsibility here? He is delegated by the parents, but both must shoulder the responsibility of initiating the processes whereby our infants and those in early childhood will become mature.

E. The Child Now Learns to Act Not Merely for Fun, Not Just to Release an Impulse

Probably the difficult task known as impulse-control will not assume so repelling an air if one looks to the natural processes involved in its attainment. "Release" of impulse energy can be spoken of as a motivating factor, and the mechanist will understand this model. But by thinking about the strivings of the child as something more than energies directed by means of physical energies and vector quantities, one can visualize an individual who has learned that delayed satisfactions are fruitful and desirable, and that they are not just another way of getting more thrill out of the release when it does take place. There is a motive called fun-playing with things that serve no other purpose than enjoyment; and there is a different kind of activity known to adults, and coming to be understood by the young child; it consists in using things for the goals to be obtained by means of them. These goals are not always and only just the satisfaction of ourselves or those around us. The goals are very distant and very much isolated from concrete reality at times; thus the child who works for the reward of money works for a distant advantage, the candy to be purchased next birthday or holiday; or the child who does the same chores in order that his sister may be better able to have a nice rosary for her First Communion; these children must have grasped something of the abstract nature of "doing good to others." In either case, however, our children are learning to react not just for fun any more and to pass the time all day; they practice working for values that extend beyond the child's present needs and desires; they strive for goals, reaching out for the good that is contained in the benefit to others, the benefit of goodness, the goodness of kindness and of unselfishness. These new goals, means, and satisfactions in using means toward the ends make up the pattern of early childhood training in so far as it reaches out beyond the activities of an impulse-ridden individual human being.

F. Emotions Progress and Develop from Early Childhood

Most observers of infant behavior agree that the rudiments of all the various emotional responses put in their appearance very early. And one can see a progressive differentiation from a basic emotionality pattern or matrix. For instance, before the age of one-half year the child's responses could all be classed as approaching and withdrawing: the positive emotion of attraction and negative one of repulsion. Out of each of those we can see several patterns emerging. For instance, from attraction comes joy, love, confidence or trust, and devotion. From the negative comes fear, anger, hate, and sadness. With these common-sense categories in mind, one can learn to detect the main emotional storms of pre-school children.

Part III. Religion Aids in Late Childhood, From Three to Six Years; Period of Sharing, i.e., Taking in Less and Less, and Comfortably Giving out More, or at Least the Same Amount

A. New Goals

The need for new experiences has been called a primary need by W. I. Thomas. Other experts speak of an exploratory tendency as basic to small children as well as animals. Their helplessness makes them fearful of small threats and obstacles, and causes them to wish for shelter, protection, and affection. The more of this affection and protection they receive, the more secure and masterful they feel in difficult situations. This added security makes them feel capable of accomplishment, mainly in combatting dangers, and eager to be successful in doing ever harder and harder things. They are growing in feelings of self-worth and of being good-for-something instead of good-for-nothing.

Children learn first impulsively, and later calmly, to evaluate their own worth, and to estimate the value of things they have and use. They learn to appreciate even the value to themselves of some restraint of their impulses. They get an occasional sample experience or packet of experiences which they themselves feel as good rather than the opposite. They see good even in delays of response, or denial of immediate pleasure. This transition from doing what-I-want-to, to doing what-I-ought-to, is contemporaneous with learning to enjoy activities which are not just play; with a new experience of being comfortable in giving as well as in taking. This means that the child is ready, after he has had several of these new experiences, to lean on other human beings and respect them not merely for what they shower upon him, but also for what they mean to him and he to them.

In this newest of all experiences our child recognizes that he is a member of a group, and that group-needs and satisfactions are often equal to or greater than individual ones. In a word, he has or will soon learn a kind of rule for regulating his behavior which is not just avoidance of pain or displeasure, not just designed to regulate himself, but especially well-suited toward group or corporate experiences of various kinds. To summarize, the child who was once a mere bundle of impulses, striving sometimes vainly and even madly for self-expression and self-benefit, now yearns for and appreciates some of the benefits of self-restraint and group benefits. He is endowed with a new energizing or triggering device for action. He is said to be maturing more along the lines of morality of conscience or because of group values, and of following a code, instead of simply a morality of constraint, or the feeling of being pressured into group patterns and of being guided only by the cultural norms and conventions. The child is truly about ready to accept and incorporate into his own system of thought and desire a code which really guides to actions without effecting them, a sanction which stimulates and orients to proper actions without compelling them, and a satisfaction which builds and strengthens his ego without inflating it.

The child is satisfying his needs for new experiences by the new and gratifying discovery that there may be a joy in sharing, a comfort in giving, a solace in belittling oneself provided others can be permitted to grow in stature and worthwhileness. The exploratory tendency now serves to enable the child to experiment with more and more ways in which his own "ego" can be enlarged while no one else's ego is deflated; even for ways in which one's own self can be deflated and still enlarged with awareness of benefits shared, without his wishing to be known as the benefactor. This is the change in goals, and there are corresponding changes in modes of striving expected of late childhood. Religion obviously sets a high value on these experiences and goals; it never ceases to inculcate group goals and group benefits, incessantly and even artlessly at times urging youth to cultivate a habit of sharing, an attitude of respect for group striving, and an appreciation of the real value of group participation.

B. New Means

To share that which one values is not of itself an easy task for any man. For animals it is either a brute necessity, as in the case of the social insects, or it does not occur—witness the turtle, the most unsocial animal known. Means can be supplied by psychology and education to aid in cultivating a habit of sharing, or to strengethen the habit when already present. The basic tool of such training known to positive science is an attitude of respect for other persons, not using them as a means for one's own gratifications. This respect includes a special kind of fraternal relation between intimates and peers, and a paternal or hierarchical homage and respect shown parents and superiors.

With religious sentiments welling up in the heart of old and young alike, respect and honor and even worship of a superior and a benefactor should be easier. Thus the cultivation of real religious feelings and their expression in song and ritual can and should help children channel their respect and devotional sentiments into desired areas. The ritual always tends to be a group response, and it fits nicely into the classical picture of a circular or self-reinforcing response. That is, when one person expresses himself audibly and visibly, he becomes a stimulus to excite others to similar patterns of behavior. Incidents of a kind of chain-reaction in devotional activities are not unknown to history and anthropology. Sometimes authority may have to be appealed to in order to mitigate the intensity of these circular responses. A deep-seated, warm I-Thou relation between creature and

Creator fosters the healthy and normal reaction of group worship. The Father-son, man-God, creature-Christ-God concept prevalent in Christianity solidifies the devotional relationship and makes it effectual in building a personal ego strong enough to withstand the ravages of time and tension-causing transitional states in human development. With science and religion joining hands to fashion the foundations of a healthy human personality development, what personal benefits for all in the way of happy adjustment may not be expected.

C. Development of Powers and Added Motives

In this period the child continues, but at a very rapid rate, to develop his powers. Verbal and manual skills are learned, with a positive acceleration which often astounds investigators. No new powers are apparent during this period, but owing to the fact that children talk so incessantly and move about so energetically, they seem to have a whole set of new talents and abilities. The child's vocabulary actually increases by geometric proportion during the first six years. His most notable accomplishment seems to be in the use of his power of moral judgments. This new-found self-actuation becomes of vital importance when there is question of learning to share without demanding, to give out some of the good things he has learned to claim as his own. His moral sensitivity will of course continue to grow, and his appreciation of persons with whom he shares becomes his guide to healthy and happy social adjustments.

In setting himself new goals the child opens new opportunities for himself as he participates in new experiences which offer new challenges for his exploratory urge every moment. He finds new tools and accessories to aid him in the armamentarium of native endowments and cultural tradition, and especially in the codes and creeds of religions. Christ's example and the virtues of Jesus as Man become a stimulating source of energy for the child. This presupposes that the picture which our pre-school child receives of Jesus is an adequate and appropriate one. It will be inadequate if it stresses only the divine in Him. It will be less than appropriate if it makes the child Jesus an adult with fully matured ways of thinking and acting. The finding in the temple incident cannot be put forth as the only narrative about the Child Jesus or else youth may become repelled by His Omnipotence rather than attracted to His Goodness.

Presenting Jesus as a perfectly normal but absolutely faultless youth never fails to captivate children. The fact that He was so much united to His Father, God, that all good things were shared with His Father, makes the modern family also want to share its benefits. Then finally the fact that everyone, old and young alike, is made by God our Father in a likeness to Him and His Divine Son, gives a prop in one's weakness, a protection in one's fears and a loving parent in one's littleness and insignificance. Yet the fact that He would make man at all, let alone send His Son, born of Mary, to heal and repair him when damaged through his own neglect, is man's newest and best experience of reality from another world, because it gives him a new courage, solace, and Friend Divine, Who not only bolsters his ego but guides him away from danger that threatens him, and finally goads him on to efforts of untold magnitude for his greater self-actuation and expression.

4 the psychology of religious development: b

I. The Pre-School and Early-School Child and His Religious Growth

MEANING OF RELIGIOUS DEVELOPMENT

WE will accept the excellent explanation given by Dr. A. Schneiders[1] for the term *moral development* as a starting point. He says it really means the intellectual development: that is, gaining intellectual insight into moral values, principles and ideals. And it involves the actual use of the volitional capacity for self-determination. All this also implies a certain level of emotional and social maturation. It also seems obvious that morality and moral conduct require essentially the exercise of the capacity to seek the good not *through compulsion* but *for itself;* to conceive ideals and to strive for their realization; to understand some meaning and value in life apart from immediate satisfaction of needs.

Religious needs seem to be basic to human nature, in all times and places. Since religious beliefs and practices are common to all cultures and societies, it seems healthy adjustment will require appropriate religious adjustment. Bearing this in mind it will be clear that the growth of religious consciousness in children proceeds both from their inner natures and from extrinsic factors, such as education.

Thus the development of the child's moral concepts will go along in parallel with all his concepts, including those about

1 See Schneiders, A. A. *Personality Development and Adjustment in Adolescence,* Bruce, Milwaukee, 1960. pp. 309-331.

God and religion. This means that, during childhood experiences, there is built up a system of values, or principles and judgments about the worthwhileness and goodness of different things; of attitudes or propensities to act according to these judgments; and of sentiments with feelings of adequacy, sufficiency and their opposites. All these processes pass through lower stages, intermediate and higher stages, until the adult level of behavioral machinery is fully elaborated and ready to function. It is a slow and continuous process not easily delineated, yet a few of the outstanding stations or anchoring points will be indicated, especially for the period of early childhood up to age 10 or 11. Although moral knowledge will be necessary before morally responsible behavior can occur, nevertheless, we must accept the fact that knowledge by itself is no determiner of action. Knowledge must first become a motive before it can guarantee action. Yet many of the studies reported in the literature trace nothing more than the development of moral knowledge in children. If this distinction between knowledge and motive power were kept in mind, the problem regarding the existence or non-existence of a positive correlation between moral knowledge and moral conduct would be solved. If concepts of right and wrong are necessary but not sufficient for moral behavior, we might expect to find some relationship between them. This is actually the case.[2]

One of the most painstaking studies done on the evolution of moral concepts and moral behavior in children was done at Loyola University (Chicago), by a Sister (whose family name is Eleanor Doyle). Her study, unfortunately for our purpose, begins with the fourth graders, and extends through 5, 6, and 8. Her main purpose makes the work pertinent for a psychology of religion and particularly for the developmental stages. She designed her experiment to study the effects of a course in character education, by the use of stories about the boy Jesus in the classrooms for the experimental groups, and without using these stories in the control groups.[3]

2 See Schneiders op. cit., p. 318-19.
3 Doyle, Eleanor M. The Use of the Concrete Ideal in Character Education

She did show very notable changes which took place after the course in all the grades except the sixth grade. She is to be considered one of the pioneers in the field of religious education, and besides showing the effectiveness of teaching good behavior by means of the model, Jesus, she was able to cross-validate the findings of Hartshorne, May and Mallers with regard to some fundamental character traits in children. She studied particularly the habits of self-sacrifice, cooperation, and persistence. She also was able to describe changes in the sentiments, motives and conduct of these upper-grade elementary school children.

Another study of grade school children had to do with truthfulness. Miss Marcella Twomey performed this study as part of the requirement for her degree at Loyola University. According to her study the word "truthful" has a definite meaning for children as low as the second grade, but here the concept is limited to the understanding that a *truthful person* is either one who does not tell a lie, or one who tells the truth. Two years later the child recognizes the possibility of deceiving by keeping silent, or withholding the truth. After two more years the concept is expanded to include avoidance of any kind of deceit or exaggeration.

The children's attitude is one of disapproval of untruthfulness. This is true from the very lowest grades on upward, but a certain set-back seems to appear in the sixth and eighth grades. There lying may be justified for about one third of the children, if the reason is serious enough. However, Twomey and others found that sometimes the child is quite inconsistent in that it approves lying in practical concrete cases, yet it disapproves all lying in the abstract. She goes on to elaborate upon the manner in which these concepts and attitudes have been built up through home, school, and other environmental forces. She says the most influential factors are fear, love, sympathy, shame, intelligence and desire for social approval. Factors of less importance are disgust, remorse, admiration of others and self-respect.

with Special Reference to the Consistent Presentation of the Boy Jesus as a Model throughout the School Life. (*Unpublished Doctoral Dissertation,* Loyola University. 1936)

The findings of Miss Twomey are particularly meaningful, since she is a trained child psychologist, and since she gathered her data by the questionnaire method, using 168 randomly chosen children in grade schools as her subjects. She makes a very pertinent observation when she notes that grade-school children differ from adults in their ways of thinking about truthfulness. Their chief arguments for veracity are based upon authority, whereas adults base their arguments more upon rational and social grounds. Children are aware of only a few devices for making "truthfulness without offensiveness" easy to practice. They are inferior to adults in the ability to distinguish the relative evil of various types of lies, such as jokes and mental reservations broadly so-called. This last difference arises largely, no doubt, because of the paucity of the child's social experience and its otherwise general lack of sophistication.

The study[4] does show that *one* of the most important of social virtues, namely truthfulness, develops only gradually in the life of the child. One could hardly expect the other notions of the child about virtue and sin, good and evil, God and Satan, to be different in their origin.

Another example of a slowly developing concept is that of obedience. Here we will rely heavily upon the research of Sister Arnoldina Mertens.

This researcher set as the goal for her study the finding of the answer to the question: What does obedience mean to the child? She was especially interested in the first grade, the intermediate grades, and the ninth. We shall be mostly concerned with the first and intermediate grades. Sister very aptly makes her comparisons with respect to the child's concept, its attitudes, and its motives for obedience. We call attention to one of her conclusions particularly. It is that the children in the primary grades (first and second) know what they are expected to do in simple situations, but not in more complex ones. They think obedience consists in external compliance with commands and they are unable to interpret a command in any but a literal sense.

4 Twomey, Marcella. Children's Truthfulness. Unpublished M. A. Thesis, Loyola University, Chicago, 1931.

Primary children attribute authority to any one who is in any way superior to them, whereas only later will they grasp the meaning of delegated authority. Primary children give only authority as a basis for obedience, whereas those in the fourth grade already add the notion of social fitness, convention, prevision of consequence, and so forth, as bases for compliance.

Sister used 426 children in her study.[5] The subjects were at 9 different grade levels, and equal numbers of them were boys and girls. She used the very direct approach of interviewing parents as well as children. Her tests contained "behavior samples" both in narrative and in pictorial style. It would thus seem that her findings are reliable. She tried to obtain answers to such questions as whether age changes were due to the change in the child's concept of knowing what-to-do, or rather in the concept of the ought-to-do. Her conclusions fall very nicely in line with the present author's description of the developing God-man relation in the child contained in the previous part. Another way of stating our view might be to say that the religious and moral concepts of children develop out of a diffuse matrix of compulsive pleasure-seeking activities which at first serve to give only an immediate satisfaction to the child. Later on the actions will be placed for the purpose of obtaining delayed satisfaction, and they will be more deliberate than impulsive and spontaneous.

II. The Age of Psychic Expansion: Eleven to Thirteen or Fourteen

The following is a tentative account of the religious evolution of a boy and a girl, ages eleven to thirteen. The authors are indebted to many persons for assistance in collecting the data for this chapter. They borrowed very heavily from Fr. Gruber's excellent chapter.[6]

5 Mertens, Sr. Arnoldina. A Study of the Concept of Obedience of Children. Unpublished Doctoral Dissertation, Loyola University, Chicago, 1930.
6 Gruber, J. The Religious Evolution of the Child. Lumen Vitae, Vol. XII, No. 2.

They are also deeply indebted to the members of the class in the psychology of religion of 1960 for critical comments on the descriptions found here. This class was made up of graduate students, equal numbers of both sexes. Lively discussions took place regarding many of the sex differences mentioned below.

The whole chapter is, of course, partly the result of "reflective recall" on the part of adults, and partly built up out of letters, diaries and conversations of growing boys and girls. The study made by Fr. Gruber gives this overall model for the chapter. He, in turn, claims to have gleaned many of his ideas from actual interviews as well as from letters and diaries.

Speaking of both sexes, one may say that they show a turn in the direction of greater inner reflectivity and serious thoughtfulness. The world is no longer just a place for fun and light-heartedness. Things take on a more serious aspect, more so than they really deserve. But running along with the seriousness, one finds a certain intermittent frivolity, an unpredictable series of mood swings which sometimes alarm the adult. Now there begins the first arousal of sexual feelings and images, and the Catholic boy or girl knows that the previously-noticed differences between the sexes have a deeper meaning. They do not as yet fully realize the significance of this, but may feel somehow that they have been deceived in the way in which adults have treated them. Older persons and even parents are accused of keeping great secrets from their children; the boy and the girl feel they have as much right to know all the "secrets" of life as the older persons. Yet their own immature stage of development makes them incapable of grasping the full meaning of sex and sex experience.

Some boys and girls have been known to give expression, at this age, to the most outlandish views about the conception and birth of children. They have very varied notions, if they allow themselves to think at all about sex, about when and how children are conceived, about the meaning and frequency of sexual intercourse between parents, about the difference between the virgin birth of Our Lord and the Immaculate Conception of Our Lady.

Yet with all the strangeness of the experiences at this level of development there is, for most boys and girls, a real solace and support in the practice of religion. Confession and Communion take on new meanings. Because life is not so simple as it used to be, the boy and girl need to study it attentively. This they do by prayer, and even by more serious reading of the lives of the saints. The youthful saints are of course the favored ones, but some turn spontaneously to the lives of the saints who were parents, like St. Louis and St. Elizabeth.

Now is the period of uncertainty rather than doubt. The two sexes both react to this by feelings of insecurity and of loneliness if not rebelliousness. When an older person is available in whom they have the fullest confidence they will pour out their thoughts very readily to him. These ideas and problems will usually be ones which have to do with the mystery of life, of life after death and of giving solid meaning and grounds to the doctrine of the Church concerning marriage, the sacraments, especially of Matrimony and Holy Orders. The child will already have felt some security in his newly garnered strength gotten from the Sacrament of Confirmation. This added fortification may, however, only serve to remind him of his weakness. Boy and girl alike turn easily to God and Our Lady to help them solve their problems and obtain new security and hope. Each one does this in a slightly different way.

The boy tends to be more theoretical than the girl. This is in line with his more abstract kind of intelligence. It probably also reflects his tendency to assume leadership in matters connected with business, planning for the future, becoming the bread-winner. The boy is more concerned about problems in the area of natural mysteries, such as the origin of life on the earth, the details about the creation of Adam and Eve, the real meaning of sin looked on as the death of the soul. The boy also wants to know, in theory at least, how it can happen that God will answer prayers, when people ask for contradictory things, as when one parish prays for rain while another wants nice weather for a picnic. In general, then, it seems that the boy's problems all have a turn in the direction of armchair philosophizing; he knows he can use his power of abstract thinking, and he wants to make it give to him the explanation about the most difficult of mysteries. Not succeeding in this, he feels helpless. Unless he has a confidant to whom to turn, he may become a doubter.

His own apparently unlimited ability makes him uncertain as to the true answers, because when one mystery is solved another two arise to take its place. Again he may turn to the hero and warrior saints for help. The ideal of power appeals to him especially if the able person happens also to be holy. We are reminded here also of the investigation of Mother Loyola on the efficacy of character training in imitation of the Boy Jesus.

Turning to the girl, we may say that her concerns and questioning have a much more practical bent. She is not much concerned about the philosophy of causality or the manner of creation. Rather she feels a growing sense of her own importance; this is because she herself now begins to develop physically in the direction of motherhood. She simply accepts the fact of her possible role as parent; also she ostensibly prefers to think of actualities rather than theories. Hers is already the practical down-to-earth realism which admits the facts of life, even though they seem at times unintelligible. Such wholesome admission of the practical value of life's processes, rather than quarrelling about subtle distinctions regarding the ultimate nature of life, makes the inner awareness of the girl vastly more expansive and realistic in outlook than that of the boy. Nevertheless she does have some unanswered questions about sex and parenthood. Yet these stay more or less peripheral so that her peace and calm are not much disturbed. Her hopes and firm grasp of reality make her trust God's power and rely on His goodness to carry her through the uncertainties of life and over the obstacles to her progress.

Taking both sexes together again, it seems that, whereas mysteries would seem to preoccupy their minds more than ever before, still the newness of the problems attracts and holds their attention like a vivid but threatening object. They are moved to ponder more deeply; but at the same time they are frightened at the possible outcomes of their speculations. They love the danger of doubts yet fear the problematical outcome. The painful feeling of having caused their own doubts may at this period easily turn into a *vague* feeling of guilt, vague because they do not know of any specific cause for it. Maybe the very uneasiness they experience in thinking about God, strikes them as sinful;

maybe also they are slightly confused in regard to the real meaning of a deliberate mortal sin which would offend God. Thus intermingled in their emotional lives are the contradictory feeling of joy in religious activity and fear of religious truth, love and attraction to God and the saints with uncertainty and uneasiness in the presence of God and holy things. Now is the time for the devoted parent and guardian and priest to stand by, patiently awaiting the approaches of the child. Adults know very well what the youth is encountering if they will only take the time to reflect upon their own experiences. Their son and daughter are precious pearls entrusted to their loving care. They can help tide the youngsters over this difficult period by realizing that each child has a real need to be dependent upon adults. This need must be balanced by feelings of security and self-worth, so that each can achieve independence and self-control.

III. The 14-18 Year Period of Religious Conflict

Before the onset of puberty, youth develops expansively and at a rapid rate, but at puberty their psyche is creative, vibrant with new vitality. At or around the first experiences of mature sexual activity, such as the monthly periods for the girl and intermittent nocturnal emissions for the boy, youth of both sexes see the whole world with new eyes. They feel somewhat like they imagine our first parents felt, when after the fall their eyes were opened and they knew the meaning of good and evil. Now, instead of an avalanche of uncertainty the youths experience deluges of doubts; and their growth in power and their realization of newly found creative power lead them easily and treacherously into an era of conflict. Their first and often spontaneous solution to the conflicts is to deny all value to the past; staunchly to criticize adults and society at large; steadfastly to reject the present troublesome situations, to create their own world of unreality, and to fight unceasingly, so as to bring about a new order which would be more tolerable and less threatening to their security.

Let us trace this rebellious meandering of the boy and girl in and out of the world of make-believe, fantasy and wishful-thinking. The boy begins to build up tensions, and these are of an entirely different type from those of the girl. They differ too from those he will experience later. Their first point of origin is in his *new* power and creativity. He feels he must accomplish great things, so he must engage in more and more difficult tasks. Then when unlimited success does not meet his efforts at every turn he becomes disgruntled. He needs to prove himself and win and keep the attention and respect of peers and superiors alike. He does not always receive these rewards and so he turns to religion. Now, however, he seems more prone to deny his earlier reactions to God and the saints. He senses his own increased vitality as a proof that he has less need for God and the divine realities that had appealed to him so much a few short years ago. During these few years of conflict he allows his religious sense to become somewhat dulled and this state of affairs worries him.

Again, being virile and an ardent lover of manliness, he must assert himself more, lest he be unable to prove his worth. The more self-assertive and demanding he becomes, the more often he comes in conflict with superiors and teachers generally. All too often the outcome of the battle against authority is an unbridgeable chasm between youth and superiors. This is the ideal situation, then, for the development of delinquents. The predominant feelings accompanying youth's war against authority are, we must remember, those of fear, doubt, and insecurity. The boy, as a sort of compensation, now comes to rely more and more upon his own sagacity since he cannot *trust* his elders. He now thinks he can solve all problems better than his elders; no mystery is too deep for him. Hence he builds up his own private philosophy of life; removes the veil from the deepest mysteries of religion by creating a totally new world. No traditional religious view will satisfy him. He is an innovator and he prides himself in his new role of universal interpreter and world philosopher, to such an extent that the old order must change to suit his extravagant tastes and desires. This, then, is the picture of a Catholic boy, troubled severely, and in need of the kind counsel and prudent guidance of his elders.

A third consideration throws light on the boy's revolt. His

sexual impulses are strong and demanding; he still thinks he can control them within tolerable limits if he gets his mind settled in regard to his theoretical problems. He tries and persists in trying to reason away his sex difficulties, only to find that instincts rule him eventually. Thus, were it not for his wise and frequent use of Confession, he would find himself alone in the conflict. Should he already have come to distrust the benefits to be derived from sacraments, then he is truly headed for trouble. When he finally comes to think that his craving for sexual gratification cannot but collide with his religious conviction, then he may actually deny God and say to himself—"How could God do this to me, if He is what I thought He was?"

As for the girl, fortunately, no such serious disturbances seem to occur. At least they are not reported in diaries if they do. The girl, less often than the boy, goes into an open rebellion against God and religion. She does experience similar theoretical difficulties centering around the mother-child relationship. Yet she rather expects that a girl's speculative ability is of such a quality that she does not have the same need to solve her problems intellectually. However, changes do occur at this time in her religious life. She admits certain conflicts between childhood fancies and the cold realities and now turns from her previous attitudes of recollection and prayer. She seeks now not so much the inner sentiments of piety and devotion as external show and fanfare. The dramatic side of religion appeals to her more at this time than ever before. The ritual of the Mass entrances her, perhaps in part because of the colorful vestments and altar decorations. Beautiful and artistically designed costumes are the order of the day. Not so much does she doubt her religion. Rather she acts out a part chosen by herself for herself, and seems to derive subtle sorts of satisfaction from playing the role of a romantic even heroic follower of Christ. We see how the spontaneous tendencies of the adolescent girl towards a life of "dedication" can fairly blossom into a more mature vocation to the religous life.

Our treatment highlights the differences between boys and girls especially at this point. Whereas boys are troubled about sex, girls are more troubled concerning parenthood. The boy believes his intellect can solve all his problems but the girl relies more upon her good practical commonsense. She will experience some changes in her moral outlook on the world. Some difficulties are created, as seems natural, by the awakening sex urges, but they usually arise more in connection with experiences that were initiated by others, chiefly by those of the opposite sex. Her sensitive and often high-strung nature will be upset by certain tensions. These soon form a pattern of behavior indicative of how she reacts to her periods. Thus at stated intervals she is forced to expect a tension-building and tension-releasing series of events. Her preparedness for these periods and subsequent reaction to the same will be delicate indicators of the quality of her emotional development and maturation. Her deep and firm faith in the Fatherhood of God seems to carry her past a period of doubts. Her realization of the power of motherhood gives her stability and often makes her turn more wholeheartedly to religion than ever before.

A neat summary of a few pivotal points in the development of pre-adolescent concepts may be had from an analysis of the data collected by Kuhlen and Arnold in 1944.[7]

Five hundred and forty-seven children of various faiths and of both sexes were asked to check their reactions to a series of 60 propositions concerning God, heaven, hell and the like. They could check one of three answers, namely "Believe," "Not Believe" or "Wonder About." Let us pay attention only to those statements which showed the greatest differences due to age, since all of them seem to have something to do with notions of good conduct and reward rather than with ideas about God and immortality. To say this in another way, there were virtually no age differences in response to the proposition: I know there is a God - in which 80 - 94% believed, nor to the statement: Only our soul lives after death - in which 60 - 70% believed, nor to the statement: Heaven is here on earth in which 50% - 70% disbelieved.

But in response to the statement: God is someone who

7 Kuhlen, R. G., and Arnold, Martha, Age Differences in Religious Beliefs and Problems During Adolescence, J. Genet. Psychol., 1944, 65, 293.

watches to see that you behave yourself and who punishes you if you are not good, 70% believed at age 12, 49% at age 15 and 33% at age 18. The rest either disbelieved or wondered, and the differences between age 12 and age 18 are all highly significant.

And to the statement: Only good people go to heaven, Age 12, 72%, Age 15, 45%, Age 18, 33%. The rest either disbelieved or doubted.

And to the statement: People who go to church are better than those who don't, Age 12, 46%, Age 15, 26%, Age 18, 15%. The rest either disbelieved or doubted.

And to the statement: Prayers are to make up for something that you have done that is wrong, Age 12, 47%, Age 15, 24%, Age 18, 21%. The rest either disbelieved or doubted.

Since the sample of respondents was fairly large and representative of the youth of our country, the findings seem to illustrate the progressive nature of some of children's and youth's concepts. There appears also an inclination for the respondents to "believe" in theory only, and to question or deny the practical implication of religious doctrines. It would be illustrative to follow the religious development of these same youths and adolescents onward through their days of college and adult life. The authors say that an analysis of the items about which the subjects wondered did not substantiate the hypothesis that adolescence is a period of generally increased religious doubts and problems. They also noted that Catholics had fewer subjects who wondered about the doctrines than did non-Catholics. All in all it is the present writer's opinion that there was a different kind of age progression shown in the youths' responses to dogmas, as compared to their responses to partially true items such as "People who go to church are better than those who don't." This differential change accompanying age changes serves to emphasize the fact that these adolescents are learning to live their doctrines and not just to mumble them by rote memory.

When 18 or 19 years have been completed both the boy and the girl seem more calm and more at peace with themselves and the world. They are engaged, no doubt, in some sort of gainful occupation, and soon will be able to choose their respective vocations for life. What more desirable outlet is there for the limitless energies and capacities of the boy than the career of a missionary priest or religious; and what more suitable channel is there for the practical mother-oriented impluses and the decorative dramatic urges of the girl than the career of a devoted nun or nurse.

5 religious aspects of the mature man

INTRODUCTION

MANY pages have been written on the stages through which various religions develop. One can hardly deny that there is change, and for some man-made religions there is steady but sure change in a given direction. For divinely-instituted religions, on the other hand, the changes are more of the nature of incidental variations in techniques of worship, rather than in fundamental beliefs.

Our course began with the notion that religion involved a code of action, a creed or belief, and a ritual or ceremonial. It stands to reason that wherever the code is of divine origin, its principles will not be found to change radically. And if code and creed are both in reference to a personal deity, then the ceremonial will also bear some marks of such beliefs. The rituals may be fully enriched with symbols, and the manner in which the symbols are understood and interpreted becomes stabilized also by reason of codes and beliefs; nevertheless this is not the whole story.

For instance, altars serve as places of sacrifice and of worship, and worship is the most respectful act a person can perform toward any other being. Any religion which professes belief in the supremacy of the deity may so worship Him upon an altar. Sacrifice of precious gifts upon the altar causes those who participate in the worship to feel at one with each other and with the deity. Thus a second end or goal is achieved by means of this altar, a social end, namely the group's participation. Many kinds of altars exist, and the styles change from time to time; yet the significance is always there for one who is duly instructed; the essential meaning remains, whereas incidental qualities of altars and places of worship run the gamut of almost all possible variations. There is a development or a variation in the means used for worship, but the essential core or meaning remains the same.

To speak of a maturing personality, of a maturing crop of rye, or of a maturing social organization conveys meanings that are readily grasped. In each case a peak of perfection is being reached, allowing the mature entity to serve its purposes, to achieve its goal in the fullest possible manner. Churches, too, mature; religions rise and fall throughout the course of history. Theistic religions are notoriously resistant to change, due to their intimate connection with an unchanging reality, the divine. However, modes of expressing human dependence upon divine help and support may be as variant as, or more so than, any other cultural element one may care to mention.

Why the psychologist should concern himself with the maturing of a religious organization is not altogether clear. Perhaps it is because he is habitually oriented toward explaining human behavior in terms of the cultural changes which engender it. We for our part prefer to allow the culture historian to trace the subtle influences which have resulted in the gradual evolution of some religions. The proper sphere of this invesigation shall rather be the enumeration of changes internal to the human being in whatever culture he finds himself, particularly those changes in him which bear a real relation to his own and his neighbor's religious beliefs and practices. These changes could probably be spoken of as experiences in the area of religion which help him as an individual to achieve a fuller amount of meaning, value, and accomplishment in his life on earth. Not the coming of age or maturing of religion as such, but rather the ripening and maturation of a man under the influence of religion will be considered here. Another way of stating this would be: We now consider the religious, experiential aspects of a psychologically mature man. Perhaps the level of attainment, the degree of growth, maturing and fulfillment proper to any one human being at a given time will be some sort of index of his participation in the activities proper to religion itself. That is, since religion by its very nature tends to the betterment of humanity, the more a man tries to better himself spiritually, the more he finds the acts of religion suitable, helpful, and gratifying to his own higher aspirations, fulfilling his own basic needs, perfecting his nature, satisfying his desire for happiness.

The elements of religious belief and practice will not be rationalized or defended here, but rather they will be defined in their relationship to the mature and well-adjusted person.

FAITH

Faith is above all a positive attitude, one which gives support and permanence to the believer. This is because faith, psychologically defined, is basically reliance upon another. Notice that it can and often does engender certainty rather than doubt: one firmly believes that his parents generated him, and this is because he trusts them not to have deceived him. Reflect now that faith in God, or faith theologically speaking, adds the authority of Infinite Truth to the compelling force of evidences which move men to assent. When anyone habitually trusts the infinite source of Truth and Goodness, he is endowed with the habit of faith. He is secure from disturbing doubt and dejection, because he is carried along almost against his will, to bring his mind into agreement with the divine ideas and wishes.

Let us consider several aspects of faith too much neglected in an age which demands sensible evidence, and that alone, for most of its beliefs. Thus when person X does come back from the other side of the moon, we will trust his statement because it involves concrete, sensible reality. If he happens to say that he saw God out in the immense reaches of space, we should doubt this statement until we had as much proof of the reliability of his testimony as we have in regard to our parents having generated us. In the fuller analyses of belief there will often have to be considered the possibility that one believes what one wishes to believe, and rejects its opposite; nevertheless, that which directs one's wishes is often enough the compelling nature of evidence, not just the person's preference for sensible evidence.

Faith is traditionally regarded as a gift. Curiously enough, some seem to think that, in order that one might have faith, he must be able to prove positively the truth of the mysteries to which he gives his assent. This is not the case. The man who assents to the truth of a strict mystery also remembers that the · most his natural, unaided reasoning power can achieve for him, is to make him see that he cannot prove that the mystery, e.g., of the Trinity, is impossible. He cannot be able positively to prove, by reason alone, that the Trinity is possible, although he may be able to show the lack of repugnance, namely, that the Trinity is not impossible. Here the human mind is simply dealing with concepts too large for finite human nature. Secure faith results from admitting finiteness, from striving to submit to the infinite. One does not feel very secure psychologically when told that there are no mysteries that are too deep for human comprehension. Rather one would seem to tend toward distrusting anyone who would make such a claim.

VERBALIZATION OF BELIEFS

The believing person cannot remain very long in silence about his faith. If he wishes and strives to cultivate a living and enduring faith in divine things, he will do well to express this frame of mind at least occasionally. The very expression of faith tends to give meaning to the belief. Behaviorists would say, of course, that the belief is nothing more than the words expressing it. The *granum veritatis* here is that words are linked to ideas. Saying the thing often enough helps to bring about assent to its truth.

Faith in the divine is reassuring, let us note, not merely because it moves to assent to the truth itself, but also because it draws one to the source of all Truth and Goodness—the God of Wisdom and the Ages, Who cannot deceive nor be deceived. Deep faith adds solidity to a shaky personality foundation; it engenders consistency and perseverance; it is as far removed from the escapes of the disturbed person as are the loving embraces of a child in his mother's arms removed from such deviant mechanisms.

DIFFERENCE BETWEEN FEELING AND ACCEPTANCE

Not every kind of affirmation of a religious truth is entitled to be called a living and vital faith, a belief which vivifies. When one's mind is set at ease after a logical explanation of a truth, e.g., the law of gravitation in relation to outer space, he is not even then fully at ease. Rather, he seems to want to know more. And yet he knows he cannot know the infinite or even entirely grasp the indefinitely large. What is important here is the fact that although assent to truth about nature may be cold and objective, this is not so in the case of assent to the truths of religion. This is what authors mean when they say that faith, to be effective, must be warm and full of feeling. One gets the impression that what may be implied here is the fact that any kind of cold intellectual activity is not as effective of sustained action as is judgment supported by feeling. And the meaning could be all the more pronounced if one remembers what mob psychologists knew ages ago, namely, that the feelings and emotions erupt quickly and give new energy for emergency reactions; whereas the cool states of mind designated as thinking and reflection keep men steadily directed and also sustain their efforts at self-direction. Faith deeply felt aids particularly in emergencies. Faith fully accepted and relied upon implicitly can guide strivings in every instance. Faith joined to religious zeal and other apostolic virtues can lead to extremes of behavior not yet clearly described in real history or in fiction.

RITUALISTIC BEHAVIOR AND IDEOMOTOR ACTION

It was mentioned earlier that the more or less thoughtless repetition of a formula, or of a statement such as "I am getting better and better every day in every way," has a tendency to focus attention upon the idea. Somehow the added attention seems to bring in its wake an acceptance of the truth contained in the proposition. Then the fact expressed also tends by some unknown process often called autosuggestion to become a reality —one does improve! Similarly by saying over and over to oneself, "God is good," one's judgmental power may begin to acquiesce—he admits the truth, he accepts the fact of God's goodness. This explanation is proposed here as a tentative explanation of the phenomenon whereby "acting out a belief" often results in having the belief.

A phenomenon related to the above is called ideomotor action. In everyday life it would seem that an image of oneself acting, be it a body image or otherwise, always precedes and leads to the action which is intended. Thus if one wishes to execute some fancy step in dancing or movement in skating, he may visualize another person doing it, then put himself in the other's place, and so picture himself to himself, swinging gracefully around doing his school figures, or the latest rock and roll; the self image of an act tends to get him going in regard to that act. The image of an act is the initial stage of the act. This is called the law of ideomotor action, and it is no mere figment of the scientist's imagination. It is a fact which usually can be demonstrated to anyone who wishes to investigate the matter.

The bearing this phenomenon has on a study of faith is the following. Were a person to experience a sudden doubt about the reality of the crucifixion, or of Christ sitting at the Last Supper, he might look toward a cross, or make the sign thereof, or view Leonardo da Vinci's picture of that love feast, and these actions would somehow tend to rivet his mind upon the realities which he has been suggesting to himself. But now action tendencies are added to imaged processes; these spontaneously aroused action-tendencies lead the person to continue in the action and/or to actuate the image of the action. Thus by signing oneself with the sign of the cross when under stress, a person consequently may see new meaning in the symbol under those circumstances. The symbolic carrying out of a meaning, however vaguely realized, does have a way of accentuating the idea in the mind! The act-as-if-you-believed, of the German philosophers, is a case which belongs under this category of behavior. The smiling at oneself in a mirror, following the theory of William James, is another such process. And if the acting-as-if one had a real emotion can initiate such an emotional experience, then at least the emotional side of belief, if not the real acceptance of the truth, can be acquired by applying this law of ideomotor action. To repeat, the mental representation of an act to any human being tends to bring about the act represented. The tendency is, perhaps, even stronger in children than in adults. And it matters little whether this is a physical act like swimming, a psychophysical act like typing, or a predominantly psychic act of accepting a truth upon the authority of another person.

A word of caution is in order here. Prolonged repetition of a ritualistic act long after all meaning has ceased to accompany the act, if there ever was any attention to the meaning of it, gives the phenomenon so common to obsessive-compulsive persons; they wash and wash and cannot help doing it, or feel uncomfortable if they do not wash. The analysis and treatment of such compulsive behavior should more properly be made by fully qualified persons and goes beyond the scope of this work. It differs from the patterns of action involved in religious ritual in at least one significant way: the healthy believer in God who learns to make the sign of the cross early in life, in order to keep clearly before his mind the meaning of the Redemption, is highlighting the meaning and not merely the act itself. This act is only secondarily the object of his attention. With the compulsive person the act is the first object, often the only object of his attention. It is likely that this act becomes mechanized largely through shutting out the real reason for the washing, and riveting the mind on the effective release, the wanton satisfaction gotten out of a self-imposed ritual. Thus mature persons who sign themselves with religious signs, such as signs of the cross, though they very often go about the act quite unreflectively, seem seldom to develop compulsions about it.

Group phenomena are found in which acts of worship become mechanized, and lead to such interesting spectacles as Vitus dances or flagellations. It is these extremes of purely externalized religious performances which often poison the minds of healthy persons who are diligently seeking to understand religion. From the abuses it is difficult to discover the right uses of a thing. "Perfectionistic" ritualism is as far removed from orderly, meaningful, and devout religious ritual as a paralysis or convulsion is from sound neurological functioning.

HOW FAITH KEEPS ALIVE

The question of the vitality of faith has troubled experts in psychology. The fact remains that St. Teresa of Avila gave up all practice of mental prayer, as if her faith had weakened or was lost, only a few years after she had entered upon the new way of life. Many moderns in science scoff at the notion of spiritual or intellectual faculties. They very illogically then proceed to bring into their discussions the concept of human abilities in order to explain performance, or they factor out clusters of traits which seem to point up one kind of ability rather more than another.

We squarely face the fact that man's intellectual power, along with volition, is his crowning glory. If there is to be admitted in every man a real power for sensing the visible changes in his environment, and for directing meaningful movements toward suiting his behavior to these changes; so, too, does he have real rational and volitional powers. By healthy exercise of reasoning power, whether it be directed toward understanding the laws of nature or the nature of God, one strengthens and embellishes the power. No one would hold today that the skilled scientific investigator was able to make his important discoveries by remaining intellectually passive and emotionally indifferent toward the progress of science. Then the expert in religious activities needs the outlet of activities whereby he learns more and more of the divine, and knows how to deal with the truths of religion for his own orientation and security; acts of religion, be they simple prayer, or elaborate rituals of worship, build up the habit of faith. Thus a repeated act of the mind whereby one declares that he knows religious reality not from reason alone, but from acceptance of this same reality because of the divine authority, is the exercise of faith.

EFFECTS OF FAITH

It follows logically that if acts of belief strengthen and vivify the life of faith, faith in turn supports the struggling human being when crises appear in life. When faith is once established, a person seeks to know more and more about the divine; this brings him in close contact with divine things. Thus the circular reaction is begun, something after the fashion of the circularly reinforced muscular twitches mentioned for children: the belief stimulates contact with God and the contact arouses belief, trust, reliance.

Now, obviously, the more one's belief is reinforced with emotion, the more effective it will be. This is the way men are—cold acceptance is productive of passivity and indifference. Full emotional acceptance involves more of the total man, takes more out of him to produce it, and shows itself in whole-hearted enthusiastic devotion of the man to a cause which he sponsors. For the man of purpose, few obstacles are great enough effectively to oppose him. The man of faith joins to his own poor little human designs and purposes the designs of God. He then necessarily grows into a man of hope and love.

Hope: Transition

In practicing the virtue of faith one exercises his cognitive powers mostly, because he searches out the objective grounds for accepting a truth. He never uses only one power in isolation from the others, yet he does concentrate more on finding the truth, so that he may be moved by it to acceptance and assent; to acquiescence in making his own the mind and meaning of another.

In faith God is relied upon, not only because He is so authoritative, powerful and wonderful a Being, but precisely because He is infinite Truth itself. When any part of the divine plan is made known to man, whether it be by means supernatural and religious, or by natural revelation drawn from the purpose and design in the universe, this knowing the truth arouses further questioning. Thus there may seem to arise a difficulty: The more one knows about God, in meditation on His attributes, from reading, from direct experience, the more he must admit His incomprehensibility and mysteriousness. Were he endlessly to go on seeking and striving for more knowledge without a new source of support, doubts and dejection of spirit, even feelings of despair, might spring up in him.

Thus there is another religious aspect of the mature man's experience which has to do with hope. This aspect involves not so much man's intellect to help him know, as it does his will and feeling to help him look forward to a state of being in which he can rest secure from striving. Yet hope does not impel him to a merely passive state of rest. It puts a new stimulus to work on the man; it goads him on to activity by reason of the thought of the future favorable outcome. There is a relation here between hope and the responses called anticipatory by scientists; but in the case of hope the anticipation is always of one thing—the successful outcome with the help of God which will always be there. The outcome will be favorable in our struggle and this is so because He, the infinite Truth, has made man a promise.

Here also we see that the mental states known as confidence, trust, consolation, and self-assurance are tied in with hope. But these states seem to be rather on the passive side, like reliance without activity, or leaning entirely on another. Psychologically hope is the opposite of despair, says St. Thomas. Yet courage is the opposite of fear, and so the more one's fears are allayed, the more courageously he will go out to meet obstacles to his progress; he will not remain paralyzed, as if lacking energy to move in any direction because it all seems hopeless, too hard, or not possible for him. Just as courage involves activity counteracting the inactivity resulting from fear, so hope impels one to act in opposition to the fatalistic repose of despair. It takes hope, and well-grounded hope, in addition to courage, to steer away from the doldrum of despair. When faith in all humanity is lacking in a man, he may indeed be dejected, despondent, depressed; when his God deserts him, he is in desolation; but so long as God can even be approached on bended knee, there ought not to be depression, and there cannot be despair.

HOPE ENLARGES ONE'S LIFE SPHERE

When hopes of the end of a weary journey run high, no road seems too rough, no pathway seems too long, no passage too difficult. How can hope accomplish these changes in us? It seems almost as if anticipation changes one's very perception of reality. When one peers into a dark room expecting to hear a noise, the tiniest rustle becomes audible. When one is not expecting a certain injury, he may be cut and even bleed without sensing the injury. When we say that hope enlarges vision, pushes back horizons, opens up new vistas, we might almost seem to be saying that hope deceives us. This might well be the case in certain instances. However, these illusory perceptions occur mostly in our dealings with other persons. How often have we perhaps been led to expect a sure and true friend to stand by us in our need, only to find that we must stand alone.

In religion hope is founded on other than psychological laws. It is not merely a reliance on and reassurance from a fellow man. Rather man says to his all-wise and provident Father, "I rely upon Your word which is inviolable, Your compact which is sacred, Your credentials which are secure, to see me through this vale of tears, this journey of woes, this task of destiny—unharmed and sure. I place this reliance upon You because You have given me the pledge of honor, Your own word and deeds and example." With such well-founded trust in God, no harm can touch him. He shall come through life fully safe, entirely sound, and totally secure. He so dares to hope because God his Father has told him these things, and therefore they are true. God will never leave him alone in the strife. He will see him through to a happy end of the task, the best and deserved outcome is assured to him—he believes, knows, and so dares to hope.

How can hope continue to direct man onward? The power of hope and confidence is sometimes sought in the nerves which have new sensitivity, or in the glands which secrete new energizers, or in the muscles which draw upon new sources of sugar supply. The real reason, over and above all these, to explain why religious hope gives efficacy, is something quite different.

Hope enables one to tap the divine source of energy, of strength, and of consolation; to become almost person-to-person sharers with the divine in a close and continuing friendly relation. Our lives are bound up in the God of Power. Our strength is in His hands and so the more we distrust self alone, the more we rely on self and Him, the more we surrender self to an outside support. Truly a total self-surrender would be the surest security for a favorable outcome to our lives and all our undertakings, if we could and would but lean on God the way He wants and asks us to. Our support is guaranteed because He will not mislead us or tell us anything untrue.

HOPE ELATES WITHOUT INFLATING

Now, is there anyone who thinks that the person who seems quite sure of himself never has a doubt of his own ability? Some of the most insecure persons put on an air of bravado: the daring stunt flier, the ribald and fearless rabble-rouser. Under influence of fleeting emotions anyone can, for an hour or a day, put up a pretense, but in the long run only those whose basic security is founded upon unlimited power can persist in efforts. Only one whose source of strength and self-confidence arises from his own known ability aided by a divine dynamo—or rather transformer of divine into human energy—only such a one can pass from the state of mild self-confidence or self-assurance into the state of one who is free from earth and the things of earth; unattracted by the passing allurements of sensory and human delights, untouched by the vain desires and petty deceits of worldly men. He has the self-assurance that comes from being one with the divine, which keeps him elated and entranced, if not entirely lost in the immensity of the Divine Being whom to serve is to love. Thus, through the total abandonment of self, one becomes elevated to the divine. This is the elation of hope, with none of the pride or inflation that comes from self-praise. Humble self-submission turns to self-support in the arms of God, as He Himself promised. Hope will not let one down, because of the providence and good promises of our Father, God, to whom we turn, on whom we lean, from whom we expect just deserts, and to whom we totally abandon ourselves and our destinies.

HOPE IN SUFFERING

Just why so many writers, even theologians who should know better, insist upon emphasizing man's problems, the ills and trials which beset his path, as if, almost, there were no possible good reason or grounds for ills and sufferings of man, seems an enigma. There is truly no solution to the problem of evil if there is no recompense in another life; this fact is attested to by millions of persons in East and West, in ancient and modern times. But if the ills one bears, the losses he endures, the pain he accepts—knowing full well he can never really like it—if all these negations of a perfect outcome of some one little life situation have no meaning, then he is truly doomed to be an incurable pessimist. If these ills mean that he should hope for alleviation from suffering because it fits into the Divine scheme of things, then suffering becomes somewhat tolerable, surely not totally unendurable. Hope adds this critical dosage of tolerance, and for many tempted persons it has helped prevent that self-destruction which seemed the only logical sequel to the pent-up feelings of self-deflation and self-depreciation. A self apart from his God, his All, is worthless. In unison with his Father he is not willing to despair or to disappoint his Friend.

THE CONFIRMED OPTIMIST

In a notable chapter on healthy-mindedness one author on the psychology of religion claims that everyone is apt to lean to the one or other pole of life. Either one acts morbidly, feels depressed, and seems to enjoy suffering, or he swings to the opposite pole: he is always cheerful and gay, he is not given to worry or anxiety, and he tolerates suffering with a recklessness that borders on insensibility. The majority of people fit into the one or other category, thinks the author. They are either confirmed optimists, healthy-minded in outlook, not given to worry about sickness and hardship even though they seem to have their share of these; or they are sick-minded, tending to depressed thoughts and attitudes, ready and willing to suffer or even die in suffering.

The present writer doubts very much that such two types of persons exist. Were the two types discernible by any kind of reliable measurement procedures, experts would have published such findings. The fact is that there are two kinds of tendencies existing in everyone. One of them may outdo the other in intensity at times, it is true, but at other times just the reverse is true. Anyone is a bit elated at times without apparent cause. On this account who would think him healthy-minded rather than ill? Again, one is dejected, downcast, or even depressed. The dejected one could be described as falling down, the downcast, as being thrown down, and the depressed, as somehow being held down. One could, if he wished, claim that a person exhibiting one of these conditions is, personality-wise, endowed with an unhealthy mind! Similarly, when elated, one seems easily to enjoy life; when depressed, he seems to thrive on suffering.

Yet the normal, healthy mind of man can and ought to be so much balanced within itself, so well inured to disturbances of this balance that it is able to incorporate all kinds of experience into its program. It tolerates, even if it does not glory in, trials and sufferings when these are meaningful for an end. It also accepts moments of joyful and thrilling experiences, but again not in any haphazard way; it watches, as it were, from the outside, the ebb and flow, the rise and fall of its own emotions, in order to be able, day by day, to stand upright like the rock of ages between these oscillating forces; it is like a pillar of strength, shored up below by the immense foundation of divine hope; it is propped up all around by the all-pervasive presence of the infinity of God's love and power.

Altruism: Transition

Faith, as a divine gift, perfects intelligence to help it know what to accept and gives valid reasons why it does so. It is, of course, built upon the natural knowledge one has of God, but it is also an infused gift.

Hope supports our striving, again even though it is merely the natural perfecting of our volitional or appetitive life. The infused gift of hope builds on the natural desire for a secure source of confidence.

Charity is the third of the great divine virtues. We shall prefer to speak of altruism in psychology; the reason is that charity and love are so complex that even the theologians cannot come to terms with them. Saints and ascetics generally and all but a few mystics were never hampered by these complexities, nor daunted in their pursuit of Divine Love. They almost invariably show their love by way of the second of the great commandments, "Love thy neighbor as thyself"; and this is altruism.

This is not the place to discuss the possibility or impossibility of "pure love"; of total self-elimination in the choice of one's love objects. This way of stating the question involves the whole psychology of the act of free choice. Fruitful outcomes of such discussion should be directed toward understanding how human beings can think less and less of self, while they are trying to go out more and more to the other person.

Altruism, therefore, will be defined here as performance of acts with the explicit intention of having one's neighbor share the benefits of such acts. The other cases in which, for instance, a person forgets to make such an explicit intention to benefit others might be called altruism *per accidens,* provided the benefactor or agent did not deliberately intend to exclude other persons from benefiting by his acts.

Altruism, besides perfecting the higher knowing and striving powers of man, also activates the total being of a man; it involves feeling and emotion; these in turn permeate the innermost layers of the person and actuate potencies which have existed from childhood. The dynamo of love, energizing our strivings from within, propels us onward toward our infinite destiny, which is God. The gyroscope of love and altruism guides and directs these strivings so that the allurements of loved ones will not upset our balance. Dynamo and gyroscope together, regulating the pushes from within and the pulls from without, net a resultant which is man bent on God, leaning on fellow man, with whom he shall fulfill his destiny and return to God.

ALTRUISM UNFOLDS FROM WITHIN

Aristotle called man a social animal. Psychiatrists preach the doctrine of sharing. In their view man cannot keep his balance, mature his faculties, or fulfill his needs as a human being unless he learns to share. Something of their view of the processes was explained in the study of developmental processes in Chapter III. The essence of the view is that during the process of socializing the individual, there must be a growing contentment in the acts whereby others take part in our own benefits. One customarily views sharing as joint ownership, or as several persons each owning part of a totality. Sharing, psychologically, implies so nearly identifying the self with another that it is almost as if one person owns whatever another owns when they share. More practically, perhaps, sharing involves, as stated above, an ability to receive fewer and fewer things from others, and yet to go on giving out, without any notable discomfort or feeling of loss, the same amount as, or even more than, one did before. Speaking purely quantitatively, this state of affairs could not exist without an imbalance. This only shows that the life of affection, the interplay of human emotions, is not a purely quantitative matter. It embodies qualities which may well defy all our crude attempts to measure them.

When parents and tutors are imbued with the spirit of altruism, giving freely of their best gifts and not counting the cost, as religion teaches them, the scene is set for the child's growth in altruism. Shall it be called the uprooting of selfishness? This term rings too much of the negative and the base. Then why not say parents ought not to be egotistical? If by this is meant selfish, then again the term is misleading, because of the ubiquitousness of the self-image and self-satisfaction in all our acts. Let it be said that if parents are thoroughly religious in outlook and feeling, they will, by their very acceptance and cherishing of the child, prepare the home for the development of altruism.

This trait must spring from within the child's innermost being; to try to impose it on a child as a habit, by mere practice according to convention, or to coerce him into being kind and generous to others for the sake of appearance only, will not have the desired effect. It will only cause mental conflict and blocks. To try to use do's and don'ts in a way that will make altruism come to pass without any example and encouragement on the part of parents will only intensify conflicts. Children must learn by means of their own developing power of rational insight and through free, uncoerced judgment, that man is happy when he shares; man practices religion to help him learn to share; man, having shared both the joys and the sufferings with others, shares in the eternal recompense with his Father.

CRUCIAL EXPERIENCES OF PERSONS FAVOR THE GROWTH OF ALTRUISM

No one thinks of all children in the same family as being equally generous, or equally cooperative, or equally truthful. There are easily observable differences among children reared in the same family. The reason for this is not altogether clear, but the fact remains. Some suggestions of an explanation might be given. If we assume that the parents bestow an equal amount of attention upon all their children one can scarcely attribute the differences to the behavior of the parents. Some children become devout parents and very altruistic, others just the opposite, so that one would hardly think that they had been reared in the same home. One theory to account for the differences postulates a different amount of identification of one child with one or the other parent, or even with an outsider with whom he comes in frequent contact. Having stronger ties with this person, he becomes more deeply influenced by this one, so that he takes on the characteristics of this one and no other. The fault in this theory is that it does not seem to work. When a child is more strongly tied to one parent than to the other, he sometimes develops just the opposite qualities. But allowing for these occasional contrary outcomes of the identification process, there does seem to be good evidence that the ideals, goal-satisfactions, and ambitions of an elder somehow get inside the child. They become so internalized that they are part of the child as well as of the parent or elder. We may say, then, that through strong identification between child and parent or parent-figure, there developed strong parent-child resemblances, among which are the qualities of altruism, generosity, etc. This view, let us notice, would also account for the transmission, by reason of identification, of undesirable as well as of desirable characteristics. How great then is the responsibility of parents and teachers generally! During puberty and adolescence, it is true, the child is expected to build up his own standards, and not to follow the parents' ideals in a purely imitative fashion. Nevertheless clear evidence is found that children have strong tendencies to imitate, to take on the traits of some one respected person, and to persist in these during their whole lives. This does not mean that one should underestimate the power of free choice in directing the behavior of the child. He may or may not choose to identify with a particular person, but if he does then these similarities between the older person and the child will put in their appearance quite naturally.

If special personal experiences can shape the destiny of a child, special group identifications can do the same thing. Reasons for this are similar to those just given for the parent-identification. In the annals of great men things like the following have been recorded: "Some particular incident, at church or school, became the turning point in my life—I was never the same afterward." There must have been a strong group feeling, sense of belonging, acceptance and amalgamation with the group, or else these influences would not have been present. The recounting of such incidents, either in diaries or in interviews with adults, leaves much to be desired as far as accuracy and reliability are concerned. Children simply do not know, or seem to have entirely forgotten, who or what it was that influenced their lives in a given direction. They seem to be even less capable after they have reached adulthood of describing how their own particular attitudes arose. Yet many a mature man rejoices in the fact that teacher so-and-so has helped to make him the kind of person that he is, and goes back to thank this older person for many years afterward.

SOME MYSTICAL OR CATASTROPHIC EXPERIENCES AND ALTRUISM

A factor which undoubtedly goes a long way in changing the destiny of youth is surely the inner secret enlightenments or insights obtained in times of prayer or silent thought. There is then a sudden but firm attitude change, a new determination; and it is found to begin, many times, with a rather startling or singularly vivid personal experience never to be forgotten. It resembles the experience of conversion, to be treated later. However, the individual who sees the new light in this suddenly clearer manner, as for instance in receiving the sacraments, or in deciding a vocation, does not by that experience necessarily change himself entirely. People may say that they feel deeply moved and even firmly redirected, but they are not on that account wholly changed, so that no tiny vestige of the former self remains. The new assurance, however, the crisis of the moment in which the self seems to say for sure: "This I know is for me," goes a long way toward building up the ego-strength. And much ego-strength is needed to carry out the ideas contained in the sudden insight, to remain true to the new attitudes, especially when these new attitudes involve changes in the deeper strata of the total person.

PUBLIC AND PRIVATE MISFORTUNES AND ALTRUISM

Such things as plagues and epidemics have been traditionally accepted as causes, or at least as conditions for reforming and perfecting the otherwise selfish natures of human beings. It is likely that these public misfortunes do little more than bring out the already present tendency to altruism; they do not produce it suddenly out of nothing or, if they do, it will not be likely to endure. The idea of service to a leper colony may motivate a few of the more zealous lovers of humanity, but there are other crises and catastrophes which could just as well have attracted them. These others might not have so much glamor attaching to them with the consequent danger of self-aggrandizement or self-seeking motives. Yet humanity generally admires the courage and calm of strong men and women in the face of panic and imminent danger to their own lives. At such times the source of ego-strength will receive its crucial test: either the hero conquers and remains on the spot to save others or he runs out, content only to save himself. Thus in crises we may learn who are the altruists, but it is hardly true to say that the catastrophic fire or earthquake produced the heroic altruists.

Regarding those whose orientation is uncertain, one might say they had been poised between the two alternatives, namely, of becoming total egotists or total altruists. Crises only help them resolve the issue by enabling them to turn in this or that direction: either to excelling in deeds of selfishness, or hiding away in their own cowardice and self-centeredness. There is little in the way of concrete objective evidence to substantiate this view, nor is it clear how long after the crises the newly converted altruists persist in their altruism. For the good of humanity it is hoped that they will persevere in doing good, not fearing the outcome nor weakening in any way.

THE AA'S AND SIMILAR ORGANIZATIONS

This is not the proper place to analyze the techniques of the Alcoholics Anonymous, and yet much can be learned in seeking the causes of altruism from such successful movements as this. One thing these bodies of men all seem to have in common, after the movement has gotten under way, is the feeling that their members are all different from other people—they are all in need of something which the rest of humanity does not need. In the case of AAs, it is that they need special help from God because they are so weak that they cannot do anything alone. This difference, keenly felt and openly expressed among their fellow sufferers, seems to give them solidarity with one another and hope of success in total abstinence. When the history of such organizations for reform has been duly written, it may turn out that a certain religious philosophy runs through their basic structures. Another principle of behavior used by such groups, which we have already mentioned as applicable to child learning, is the principle of "acting as if" we were what we would like to become. This rule acts as a guiding light for the AAs and gives added ego-strengths.

COMMON ELEMENTS IN ALL ALTRUISTIC FACTORS

In the last analysis one must admit that, in moving from a selfish toward an altruistic manner of acting, a human being shifts his emotional center from the intense preoccupation with self-value to that of value-of-others. Put a little differently, it is a movement from undue concern for the immediate benefit of the self to that of the group, from the I to the "I-Thou" relation, with the meaning that the Thou should have a plural rather than singular reference, an all-inclusive you in the sense of all those other than self.

In Sorokin's clever analysis of the great altruists of history he relies very heavily upon a few citations from the writings of the altruists themselves describing how they became so. Rather, one can scarcely be very positive about just how the people turned to their new way of life, whether suddenly or slowly, partially or totally. The author's citations about how they say they came to see the light may very easily be misinterpreted to mean that there came into being a new ego, which seems very unlikely to those who have studied human beings long and earnestly. Of course the power of God could thus bring about the sudden change, but surely, in that case, the changed person would be the last to boast of the event.

What does seem obvious, not only from the writings but also from the deeds of altruists like Assisi, DeSales, Ghandi, and Loyola, is the fact that somehow these people became deeply involved with the cause of others, and let this devotion be the main guide to their conduct, even though it made them seem to others to be queer or even radical. It did not matter much if the number of benefited persons was small or large, or even a whole segment of humanity. The point is that others benefited by the acts and good intentions of the altruists, and the altruists were unaware, or at least unconcerned, that they themselves would thus become acclaimed as great benefactors.

Of course the divine Altruist Himself, Who is the inspiration and Leader in all this search for a model of unselfishness, seems to be the only one who can perfectly seek the honor of saving all men for God and at the same time keep the self-abasement of the lover of the cross each in its proper perspective. This is because He is both God and man, descended from heaven precisely in order to bring this inestimable gift of salvation to all. Besides salvation, He knew that men also needed the example, the ideal and model of a real corporate society in which each would have his own individual role, yet all men would be required to reach the common goal. Jesus Christ was content to be to man the Light showing the way, and giving the means. Man, on his part, should be content to grasp some bit of this humanitarian and all-loving Christ-like spirit, and should nurture the tiny spark of charity so that it blows up into the unlimited glowing fire of heroic altruism. Thus one's well-wishing will include all men, one's kindness will be totally non-discriminating.

6 conversion and its psychological import

1. *Fundamental Notions in Regard to Conversion*

THE topic of conversion is particularly interesting for the psychology of religion because of its close relationship to prayer, worship, penance and finally to altruism as it has been described earlier, as being characteristic of the mature person. There are certain features which distinguish conversion, and which must be present if it is to be said that conversion occurs in a given instant.

To outline the topic briefly: conversion implies a real admission of a fault on the part of a person, and at least a desire to change the situation in some manner; thus self-criticism of some sort is implied in every conversion, although it is not necessarily the most prominent feature of the same. A person will admit that there is something in himself which is not altogether as it ought to be, not quite adequate or suitable; then he will desire, even though he does not put the desire into practice at once, to do something about that which is wrong or inordinate. He will desire to right that which is wrong, to put order in place of the deordination. To repeat: to change or to desire to change the direction of one's life in the interest of bringing order into the whole is the essential feature of conversion.

The desire to change what was formerly the case with regard to oneself, to do something different, means to convert. Such a change or desire to change could hardly be called an escape, at least not in every instance, nor a desire to find release from tension, nor the disease of a disordered brain, as some have claimed with regard to sudden conversions. Such writers say that an individual undergoes conversion just in order to be freed from his inner tensions, and so he goes before the public either in a meeting house or in the open air and publicly admits his faults. He makes a wholesale and sweeping statement about his own wickedness for all to hear, and therefore he feels very deeply what we have called the inner conversion, the inner reform of his life and habits.

Such public conversion and such seeking of release from tension because of conversion has, of course, been known to occur. Again, the seeking of physical relief from tension, or the inner feeling of group solidarity and acceptance which follows from publicly humiliating oneself, are not the essential features of conversion, nor can they rightly be considered the proper motives for conversion.

By way of transition, the attributes of faith, hope, and altruism can be compared with one another and with conversion, in order to relate these processes to each other. Faith involves the believing as true a thing which has been accepted on the authority of another person. If that other person is God, then the faith is divine faith. Faith, then, is in a very real sense an admission of dependence, a submission to the mind of another, because of the attitude which the believing person has toward that other. So faith means yielding to at least one aspect of the Divinity, namely His truthfulness. It also involves another attribute; by submitting to the divine authority, one also assents to the truth which has been transmitted to human beings from that same unerring and authoritative source.

On the other hand, in hope one goes a step further, one reminds oneself that God accepts one, and that God promises to help man in all efforts to reach Him. In this respect faith and hope are the reverse of each other; in faith man accepts God, and God in turn accepts man and promises to do something for him; the acceptance of His help with full assurance of a favorable outcome is the essence of hope.

Finally, in altruism, one accepts his neighbor and puts him on a par with himself, in intending to share his own benefits with other persons. He tends to think those things are of value which he and others agree seem to have real value. He becomes in a true sense a part of the other person, somehow getting outside of himself and moving in the direction of the other person.

In conversion, while admitting mistakes and desiring to improve, one really makes a new and whole-hearted acceptance of himself. In what will be called reform or repentance one takes suitable measures to make effective the changes which he deems desirable in himself, and strives to maintain himself in the changed condition. Self-conquest, contrition, penance, and mortification are means for securing and stabilizing the changes. These activities are studied in the psychology of religion in order to clarify the processes and to enable the psychologist to predict with greater accuracy the final outcome of those efforts at personal change which bear some relationship to the religious activities of the person.

Let it be understood at this point that the self-restraining processes mentioned above are not engaged in by a religious person merely for the purpose of self-torture. Religion never urges mortification and self-denial as ends in themselves. Suffering is not invited or accepted for its own sake, nor for the purpose of making one less susceptible to suffering in the future by a sort of immunization process. Suffering and self-conquest each has a purpose which will be outlined in the proper place.

Love, as will be noted later, is the beginning of all action, for, as St. Thomas aptly puts it, love is an inclination toward an object known to be good or desirable; and thus the love-urge may be said to initiate actions in intellectual beings. Love as an end or goal, however, is the highest state of unity between any two or more persons, because it unites them on the highest plane possible for them, and it thus turns out to be a spiritual-mystical phenomenon. This is especially true when one considers that the bond of love can join a man with God. The love of God as a person elevates the notion of a union with another person to another sphere, namely one in which human concepts and analogies will be at best feeble attempts to relate the intricacies of the love-union process. One thing must be mentioned here at the introductory level of the discussion: Love on its highest plane involves a union between the lovers, a mystical or trans-sensory kind of binding and it is followed necessarily by a new kind of integration within and between the loved persons. It is love that gives human beings the only adequate opportunity to experience group-belongingness, and with group-participation there follows sharing with the Divine, a taking part in the activities which the Divine Person might otherwise claim as His very own, His singular prerogatives.

Love therefore tends to unite the loved ones, and it is for the sake of gaining a better psychological understanding of this process occurring between man and God, between man and fellow-man, that love is studied in the psychology of religion. Here, then, may be envisaged the highest possible kind of union possible for human beings—union between individuals, and between all of them and their Creator. In the total union of human and divine existences, there is a merging of the human and divine natures, and the beginning of the process is always through the spiritual love or spiritual union which ascetical writers so often describe.

After this short digression on the virtues, some of the attributes of conversion will now be described. For this description the author is indebted to Michotte and Pruem of Louvain University, who in turn began many of their investigations and based many of their findings upon the empirical studies made by John Lindworsky, psychologist and author of pioneer works in ascetical theology. Though Fr. John Lindworsky devoted most of his efforts to studies on the will and habit formation, he did this with a view to making clearer certain of the concepts which have been used in the classical writings of German psychologists of religion.

After the attributes of conversion have been discussed, then the motivation in back of conversion, and finally the means for guaranteeing a lasting conversion, including supernatural means, will be taken up. In regard to the attributes, it should be noted that not all those mentioned will be present in every conversion; some persons will show one set, others another set. All of them will follow the usual pattern of motivation which characterizes the lives of rational striving human individuals.

2. The Attributes of Conversion

THE ATTRIBUTE OF SUDDEN INSIGHT

Conversion is often either preceded by or followed by a sudden flash of insight, an insight into a new relationship between the self and God, or between the self and the neighbor. It might be such a sudden insight that it takes on some of the characteristics of a shock experience, so that writers even talk about a conversion "shock" or conversion "crisis." Now conversion always involves the admission of the fact that there is something deviating in one's life, something which is undesirable, imperfect, disordered. Along with this admission of need of change from the former course or direction, the actual change of direction is an essential part of every conversion, while that of suddenness is accidental. It may or may not be present, and still one could experience a genuine conversion.

Now this state of affairs in which a person decides, suddenly or otherwise, to change the direction of the flow of events in his life is a really interesting psychological phenomenon. When the change is very sudden, the person himself is somewhat surprised, and even amazed at the changes which are taking place within himself. And when we say that the change takes place suddenly, in some instances at least, we are not forgetting the fact that deep within the person there may have been some slow process which preceded the sudden change. During the deeper inner process, whether slow or sudden, several things will be found to happen. There will be a desire to change long before this desire is actually expressed, and very long before the emergence of this desire into action. Hence it is obvious that it will be difficult to decide, when one is an observer from the outside and does not share the confidence of the one converted, whether or not the conversion was sudden.

THE IDEA EXISTS BEFORE THE ACTUAL CONVERSION

Another factor which must be considered in all conversions is the fact that the "idea" or "thought" of conversion often exists in the mind of a person long before the time that it goes into action. It may actually exist for a time before it is expressed in words. This statement might startle certain psychologists of the old school for whom it was unthinkable that an idea should exist which was not clearly expressible in the form of words. Yet though the idea of change might be for the person very amenable to expression in words, it does not always follow that such an idea was actually expressed in words, before the actual change occurred. It is noteworthy, however that whenever the thought or beginnings of the thought of conversion were in existence long before the actual change, it is next to impossible to decide whether the conversion was sudden or slow. One reason for this obscurity is the fact that the inner mental movement is first of all not easily observable, not even to the thinker himself; and another is the fact that when the movement is expressed in words, or in some similar form of communication, the inner state might not correspond to the expression.

Here is a case, then, similar to those known to the psychologists of learning, in which the actual improvement might take place when there was no effort, no clearly recognized effort or intention to learn. It occurs at a time when the subject is simply in a "mood" to reflect, is set to do something different. The period of preparation certainly precedes all insights, in cases of invention, of the discovery of new relations in the external world, and of new relations between the experiences which are lost in the distant past. So too, there might well be a period of incubation varying in length in every case of conversion. During this period the person toys with the idea, weighs alternatives, sounds out his own feelings and capacities, and allows—in a sort of passive way—his own self to await the outcome of the turmoil of events going on within himself. He might say, for instance: "I am not carrying out my obligations to my family and my social circle even though I seem to be doing very well at work. There is something lacking in my treatment of my wife and children; what might it be? Oh yes, it is probably the old fear that my wife is trying to dominate me—what shall I do? I must do something because the children notice my discontent and it may hurt them—what to do? I'll try—" Here is seen a kind of change possibly developing but surely incubating.

THE SLOWNESS OF CONVERSION: A NEGLECTED ATTRIBUTE

Since ideas are guides to action, the inner change which is always present in conversion must come before the outer or behavioral change. And the mental or total psychic change from within does not have to be sudden; in fact, it may well be very slow and gradual, extending over a long period of time. This will be true in all cases except those wherein there was obviously a special intervention on the part of God, as in the case of St. Paul. One reason for the slowness is that there will have to be a total reorganization of the inner habits and habit systems within a man, if a very meaningful sort of conversion can be made to take place. The process will be found to work itself out gradually over a time; there will be some preliminary exploration, as in most of the strivings which human beings experience; and the real change will be found to occur only after the preliminary or exploratory experiences are over.

Take, for example, the man who wishes to give up smoking. One might say that this is a conversion in the sense that there is a radical change of behavior involved. The man may have toyed with the problem of quitting smoking for years; there was no solution, no decision because of a lack of interest and motivation. He finds that he has given up smoking during Lent, Advent, many times in fact on a temporary basis; yet he has never said to himself, "This must be given up once and for all." In this case the external act of smoking is really of secondary importance, for what really counts in shaping the course of behavior is the inner resolution and determination. When he actually quits, it is presumably for a reason, such as pleasure or relief from tension. It is obvious from this example that if there is to be any real and lasting change, it will have to come from a motive within the individual and have to be bolstered up with some sort of stabilizing influence from within the person. Observers of his external behavior will merely be recording the direction which his inner guides to actions—his decisions—will have been imposing upon his observable behavior.

An example from real life might clarify and consolidate this discussion. An athlete once came to the writer with this problem: He must either quit athletics or quit smoking. This was the original problem, but it became more complicated as time went on. He was referred to a counseling center where he one day reported the fact that his doctor warned him of a serious heart condition. With this condition he must not only give up athletics but also run the risk of more injury to his heart if he kept up his habit of chain smoking. What could he do? He was given the advice that a new habit could be substituted for the old one, if he was willing to try to make the substitution. When asked what was his favorite food, he said that it was apples. So he was told that whenever an urge to smoke arose, he should think of his liking for apples, have a dish of delicious apples handy, and that then he could perhaps gradually substitute the habit of eating apples for that of smoking cigarettes. He agreed to attempt the substitution. In the early days he consumed very many apples, but he remained true to his earlier resolution: to change the habit of smoking into the habit of eating some desirable and non-injurious food.

Part of the motivation seems to have come from his liking for a particular person on the staff, but that is beside the point here. Actually, he gained new resources, a new sense of power from the experience that he could do this new thing; he saw its value, now not only in terms of avoiding a dangerous heart condition, but also in redirecting the course of his life and action generally. New reasons were added to his former motives for change. He not only completely changed the habit of smoking into that of eating, but he also understood himself better in the process.

IN CONVERSION THERE IS A STEP-BY-STEP PROCESS WHICH CAN BE SPECIFIED

Often it will be possible in retrospect to break down the total process of conversion into a few rather clearly defined stages or steps. While to do so is not essential in any way to the process as such, still it does help the investigator to make a full and accurate description. The stages referred to are the prelude or initial phase, the middle or crucial phase, and the conclusion or practical phase. Of course, without careful introspection on the part of the person converted, it would be impossible to isolate these phases.

The process may be illustrated again by the case of the person who wanted to give up smoking. Such a man actually did lie awake nights pondering what to do. His whole body seemed to demand smoking; his whole future good and healthy manly existence seemed to demand "no smoking"; he wished that he did not have the heart condition which made it bad for him to smoke: why were so many other persons no better than he capable of smoking with impunity? For some time he probably did not even tell his parents of his predicament. There came a time when he just had to tell somebody, and probably the counselor was the first to share the secret of his problem. When he actually came face to face with the problem, and was able to come to grips with the two alternatives—to smoke and run the risk of dying soon, or not to smoke and to be assured of better health—he had progressed a long way. This progress came about with the aid of his counselor, who was then instrumental in aiding him to see himself properly, and to accept the outcomes of his own decisions.

He must have reasoned somewhat as follows: He must get some substitute habit to alleviate the physical tension which was the cause of the smoking originally and of the continuing in the habit of smoking. The decision to substitute one habit for another and still get the desired outcome was probably the crisis or middle phase of his conversion. He was able to convince himself that he would be able to divert the energy which had been going in the direction of smoking into another action which was equally gratifying but yet not harmful. In the last phase, the conclusion or practical phase, he needed only to check on himself in some way to see that he was carrying out his resolution; to convince himself that not a single slip would be permitted, or else there would be a total loss of all the energy put into the process of preparing and initiating the conversion.

The factors and attributes sketched above were said to be sometimes present and sometimes absent in conversions. One common element found in every conversion deserves special mention and will be thoroughly discussed because of its special importance. It is the element of self-acceptance. If the change concerns a serious matter and therefore involves habits of long standing in a man, or if it would mean changing one's style of life or his dominant goals for action that were established from earliest childhood days, then it is essential that the man know himself and admit his real habits and tendencies, or else there can be no true process of conversion.

Obviously, the person who needs conversion will have to spend some time in self-reflection; the subject matter of his reflections will have to be his own problems and the possible outcomes of this or that solution to his problems. By this sort of reflection there will certainly be a clarification of the person's motives and a clearer perception of the reality of the self. With this new view of the self and appreciation of his needs, comes clearer and clearer detail in this or that area of the total personality but, above all, as the view becomes clearer it also seems to fade into, to cause, or actually to merge into fuller acceptance of the reality of the self now perceived. Joined to this self-perception there is also the clear view of the "self-as-could-be"; the other self that he desires to be. Whenever the self-acceptance includes the element of "I ought to be other" or "I could be so-and-so," then the stage is set for a redirection of action so that the "other" may actually emerge from the present actuality of the self.

A hint to better assure the conversion, besides clarifying the two selves by means of reflection, might be the following: Let the person desiring conversion try to formulate clearly to himself (and even to others) the expected change in action. Thus the sick athlete would say to himself, "I must save my health for my athletic prowess" or "I must save myself for a life of scientific invention." In so doing he puts himself in a state of readiness to stabilize his actions. This verbalizing of one's aspiration, ambition or resolution is found efficacious not only in the problem considered here, but especially in the case of so many other tasks which demand our attention every moment of the waking day.

Thus the preparation for conversion involves serious reflection upon one's own problems and conflicts; it also involves some attempt at clearly expressing these states to ourselves, or to others competent to help, if they are serious problems. Finally it involves as clear a perception of the self as can be had under the circumstances, following upon which there will be self-acceptance with desire to be other. If a man will not even admit he is in error and in need of change, who can ever hope to change him? It will assist in ways not clearly understood if the person trying to change will formulate, express or verbalize his inner processes and problems. The researches of Charles Curran and Carl Rogers on client-centered therapy seem to be pointing in the direction of some startling discoveries in this field. "What is it that mere communication to another person does to the emotions and feelings of the communicator?" they ask, and they seem to have one part of the answer ready, as Father Curran says: Communication under a warm permissive atmosphere releases energy which could seriously block the smooth-flowing and harmonious inner psychic processes.

3. *The Motives for Conversion*

MEANING OF TERMS

A motive in its most general sense is that which puts a person into action; or that which leads a person to a given kind of action. That which produces the action is called a power or an ability. The word "power" here has a meaning which is similar to its meaning when used to denote the source of energy or action in a physical instrument, such as a storage battery. In the latter case, however, both the energy and the motion denoted are in the physical or material order, which of course is not always true in the case of the motives for human action.

A motive in psychology is strictly defined as the reason why a person selects one action rather than another, this one rather than that. It is the guiding information which precedes the choice of an alternative, and is thus quite a different thing from the mere physical power or source of energy, or even the guided energy of modern physics. A person has the energy, a person has the power, and a person does the guiding and the acting, all at the same time. Moreover, in the case of a sustained action, the person not only initiates action along a given line, but he sees to it that it is continued, steered toward a given goal along the totality of the process. Thus a motive for human action is in a certain sense a source of energy and a source from which the outcome or the finished action actually proceeds; it is a cause of the action. A motive is more specific than simply psychological power or energy, in that it can be described as the power to perform this particular action rather than a generalized and diffusive energy or power.

Now the process of conversion can be analyzed from the point of view of its motives. The analysis will consider the motives for the beginning, the middle and the final stages of the conversion processes. Then will follow the motives for perseverance in whatever kind of conversion the individual has decided to make his own. The motives for perseverance will be the most enlightening, even intriguing, because of the fact that they so often drop away from the focus of consciousness and into the background of attention. They even escape from the immediate beck and call of the conscious agent, so that, in some cases, they well may be called unconscious motivators, inadvertent energizers of actions which have been previously set forward on their way toward a given goal or outcome.

WHEN VALUE IS KNOWN IT LEADS TO SPONTANEOUS ACTION

The first thing which seems peculiar to some readers is the manner in which human motives initiate the process of human activity. A rather universal rule with regard to motives may be

stated: As soon as there is clear understanding of the fact that
a certain object is valuable, then there is aroused a tendency
toward that object quite spontaneously, that is, previously to
reflection and deliberation. To illustrate: I perceive the quality
of cheerfulness in one of my friends, and I think it is a very
wonderful and desirable quality. If I pause even for a brief
moment to consider my own total reaction, I see that I have
not only approved of this quality, but I have actually begun
to like that person for it, to wish I were like him in that respect
and to want the quality for myself in some degree. I desire it
because I deem it valuable for me. This is an admission that
the quality, or any other similarly evaluated object, act, or cir-
cumstance arouses in me also a spontaneous tendency. One cannot analyze the initial stages much farther back than that. One
can, however, compare the process to one which occurs in the
case of intellectual insight. In the case of insight there is a
question of the mind's activity with regard to truth, objective
facts taken in themselves, apart from whatever value or beneficial quality they may possess.

The process of insight is traditionally studied in the case of
problem-solving, or of engaging in abstract thinking, in regard
to the solution of any difficult problem or situation. An example
might be the finding of a common element to such concepts
as that of cat, dog, rat, rabbit. As soon as one understands that
"animal" might be the common element or, better, "mammal"
he tends quite naturally to think of one more animal at least,
such as mouse or cow. This means that he has understood the
basis for grouping the previous four things and has gone on to
include another member of the same group; he has generalized,
almost without knowing it, or at least before adverting to the
fact that he has done so. Thus, whenever the truth in a given
case presents itself clearly to one's mind, he tends to accept it
spontaneously and to do something about it which shows that
he knows and accepts it. The intellect tends spontaneously to go
out after its proper object, which is truth, and it strives to
possess it in greater measure. This fact of experience is too rarely
noted, namely that as soon as the mind has evidence that a

certain position or judgment is true, it cannot help assenting to this truth.

Human powers are thus endowed with native or spontaneous tendencies to go out after their own proper objects, to attain their specific purposes. Truth is the goal-object for the intellect, in which it rests secure; goodness is the goal-object for the will, toward which it strives. The qualities of material bodies are the goal-objects for the various senses.

There are many other examples to illustrate the process of insight and the tendencies to action which it arouses. Suppose the problem now is to take a very general concept and to supply some subordinate concepts which belong under the more general one. Take virtue, for instance. Under this broad heading one thinks of honesty, truthfulness, charity; here the same tendency arises as in the case above, but the subordinate concepts are themselves just as abstract as the more general one, namely virtue. But to realize the fact that under each of the sub-headings, such as honesty or truthfulness, one might have numerous actions of men which possess these qualities, means to reason still further from the original concept of virtue. There is such a strong tendency for the mind to generalize from individual and concrete experiences to numerous situations that have something in common, that people even tend to over-generalize; they then commit the fallacy of judging about the many, or even all of a given class, just from studying a few members. The law whereby one moves necessarily toward that which is presented as true holds in spite of abuses of the law or fallacies in thinking.

Similar processes are going on constantly in one's mind whenever he thinks about such things as values. As soon as one perceives that an object is as a matter of fact an object of value for him, that it truly possesses goodness and not only external glamor, he tends to go out toward it, to strive for its possession. An object which might be considered here as illustrative is the cheerfulness which I witness in my friend. When I am convinced that this friend is truly cheerful and that the quality of cheerfulness is desirable in some respect, then I tend spontaneously to desire it for myself. This is again the law of will-action without which no consistent account of human volitions can be given.

Statements like the above are the expressions of truths which have from time immemorial been admitted by realistic philosophers. They have been summarized here in order to show the bearing of these truths upon the process of conversion. Once these spontaneous tendencies of the intellect and the will are admitted, the experiments of the famous will psychologist, Fr. John Lindworsky, of the Society of Jesus, will be better understood.

Lindworsky, a pioneer worker in the field of will experiments, extended and applied scientific techniques to the field of thoughts and volitions. He began his work in the University of Cologne around 1920 and continued it at the University of Prague until his death in 1940. His experiments have the straightforward purpose of examining the process of volition under controlled conditions. As a result of his studies, the above principle regarding the spontaneity of the will's act in regard to goodness, and that of the intellect with regard to truth, found exemplification in real life. One of his experiments was something like the following: The task is to understand the number series which begins as follows: four, nine, sixteen, twenty-five, ——; and then the following: two, four, eight, sixteen, thirty-two, ——.[1] When there is an understanding of the logical ordering of the numbers in either case, then the next number in the series will come to mind quite easily, as all observers will attest. Some little time may be required to study the problem, and some persons might even need a great deal of time, but if they are able to avoid blocks, emotional fears or number-barriers in their thinking, they will have arrived at the solution after some time. One could illustrate the force of habit by the above example also: We habitually think numbers by means of symbols: 2,4,8,16,32,——; and hence if the problem is presented in this manner most people solve it more readily.

Thus the mere fact of knowing that a certain relationship is true leads to an acceptance of it and even to doing something about it. There may be opposing tendencies, of course, and distractions from the task in hand and blocks; the origin and causes

1 J. Lindworsky, *Der Wille*, 3rd Edition, Leipzig, 1923.

of these too will be better understood by means of carefully controlled subjective observations. The co-workers of Lindworsky, and the followers of Michotte in Louvain, by means of experiments and with the aid of the Würzburg technique of fractioning the process of thinking, gave much more empirical evidence with regard to volition, some of which shall be sketched presently.

It was said that the mind discovers common elements in any class of objects, such as flowers, fish, men and virtue; wherever the element of value is also a common element the object valued sets up an attraction for the person who recognizes this value. This fundamental proposition sums up the background against which Lindworsky's experiments were performed and these explored very many angles that might throw additional light upon the process of human motivation.

The following statements should not be viewed as an attempt to settle disagreements of terminology used by various authors, but rather as an introduction to the present writer's use of certain terms and expressions. When any human power has arrived at its proper object it rests secure in the possession of that object; which means that it perfects itself by its operations. Thus, when one takes into consideration the fact that all human powers are rooted in one person—that is, they find their substantial existence in the reality of the person—he must also assert that these operations of the person, using his powers upon their proper object, perfect the whole person. They help him to a realization of the potential which is in him; they actuate some of these potentials, and thus they lead to the actualization of the self, the self-fulfillment. Notice the technical use of the words "self-fulfillment" or "self-actualization." The separate and distinct acts do not, each one in the same manner as the other, perfect the self in the same manner. Yet they all contribute to the totality of the experience, conscious or otherwise, of the total person.

In the practical order of daily living, everybody experiences from time to time certain things which will help to make clear what has been said about motivation. For example, it is said that men make resolutions to act when value judgments are present in consciousness. There was a good nun who recently lost her life in a disastrous school fire. She was quite generally judged to have been heroic. May her example be a stimulus to other persons to resolve upon a similar course of action under stress. Because the public judges Sister X to have been heroic, it also praises her action, shows gratitude to her, admires her, tries to be like her, it may be assumed.

But suppose for a moment that someone had seen her acting foolishly and timidly in the fire situation. Suppose that this witness had spread the rumor that the nun was ignorant of the rules for fighting fires and therefore she ought not to be praised but to be blamed. As soon as the judgment arises in the minds of the listeners, in which Sister X was suspected of being selfish and inefficient, the listeners would also cease to admire the nun and cease to desire to imitate her. This change of attitude and action seems traceable just to their changed judgment regarding the real value or goodness of her act in the situation under stress.

Human beings value heroism, but despise culpable ignorance and timidity in responsible persons. And these movements of the mind take place quite automatically while they are reading accounts of events such as the Chicago disaster. What motivates the mind of man to value so highly the qualities of altruism, heroism, zeal for the good of others? Men may not be aware of it, but the real motivator is the judged value of the human acts. If some writers think that they have a better answer to this question by saying that mere conventionality is the motivator, then the readers will have to go to the basic question, namely, what made society accept this convention? The only satisfying answer to this question seems to be that man is made to seek after the good when it is presented to him under the aspect of good. This is his nature, and because his nature is such, society is also respectful of his nature with its basic tendencies.

It appears now quite evident that there is a spontaneous movement in man toward accepting what is of value and rejecting its opposite; instances of these two tendencies appear on occasion in the daily lives of everyone.

THE JOINT-ACTION PHENOMENON

There is another phase of the motivation process which the German writers seem to emphasize, the phenomenon which is called "Mituebung" by Fr. Lindworsky, and which shall be designated here as the "joint-action" power of motives. Many factors operating here are similar to those the Americans call "transfer" phenomena. The law of transfer states that the improvement (or weakening) of one power leads to the improvement (or weakening) of another power, even though that other power has not been exercised. The law is, at best, somewhat ambiguous, partly owing to the fact that experimenters who tried to verify it were unable to isolate the power which was presumed to have improved without practice.

The law of joint-action is not confronted with these difficulties, since it does not deal with a spread of effect from one power to another. Rather it calls attention to the spread-effect within the operations of the same power. Stated briefly, it asserts that if one cultivates a value for its own sake, and not merely as a means to some particular other value, then there will be changed behavior in closely related areas of value, even without special practice or opportunity for action in those related areas. The process would thus seem more related to that of "response generalization" than to that of transfer, except that in the case of joint-action the things to which the generalization is extended are not necessarily stimulus objects that could be responded to. More often they are mental or abstract spiritual values.

If a class of values is deeply enough instilled into the vital organization of a person, it may be found to have extended the class to objects and instances which have not as yet been experienced. As suggested above in the mention of transfer, improvement in one discipline can be followed by improvement in another that is closely related to the first, so that, for example, skills acquired in mathematics are known to extend to the area of metaphysics. This transfer occurs, probably, because of the existence of common elements in the two disciplines. Similarly, as an instance of the law of joint-action, if a person builds up within himself a sufficiently strong appreciation of the trait of heroism, or of being devoted to a cause, then he will find that he will not need to have exercised himself in showing heroism in order to perform heroic acts. What he will need to do will be to get a full appreciation and realization of the fact that a given cause is a worthy one, and that it meets with his wholehearted approval. Then his zeal and enthusiasm will come into play just as if he had exercised them in similar situations previously. This is probably the explanation of the phenomenon of religious zeal, in which persons who have never yet been tried as to the strength of their heroic enthusiasm at once show this when the opportunity presents itself.

4. *Means for Assuring Permanent Conversion*

THE HIERARCHY OF VALUES

In regard to the whole question of conversion there is one positive statement which is the basis for a deep and lasting change: If one wishes to maintain himself in any changed direction of thought and action, and is not content with a temporary change, then it will be helpful to have a well-ordered set of motives, a hierarchy of values, to guide and support him along the way. What is meant by a hierarchy? The things around us do not all have equal value, are not all equally desirable; they lie on various planes or levels. For instance, improving one's mind by reading is one type of benefit possible for persons living in a free world. The opportunity to go on picnics over the weekend is another variety. Both of these activities could scarcely be engaged in at the same time. Each one has its place in the life of a man but at times to be specified in the schedule of each person's way of life.

Similarly, if a man is planning a change in his character, or a reform that would amount to a conversion of his whole way of life, he would take certain steps that would lead to this reform. He would not try to jump to an extreme change all at once. To try to do so would be trying to do the impossible; such might be the case with the individual who suddenly decides to become cultured, and then reads books and magazines far into the night, to the utter neglect of duties and family. The wise planner decides to take certain small and easier steps first. A loafer from a slum area would not be likely to take the step of becoming a Trappist in the monastery all at once. He would have to prepare himself by slow stages, test himself with regard to his ability to attain some intermediate goals first. These intermediate goals begin to be realized in succession, and to arrange themselves in an order, so that eventually a hierarchy or graded series exists. In each of the lower levels of effort there will be enough of self-satisfaction to carry the person on in that type of action, so that he can again set his goal and direct his efforts to something higher and perhaps more difficult.

When a person tries to maintain his new way of life, as happens in a conversion, he needs to set his goals in order, each in its proper perspective. Trained counselors and spiritual fathers can help him in this arduous task. Experienced counselors have noticed that the holier and more altruistic a person becomes, the more he realizes the true value of charity and love of his fellow man. Yet if he is expected to work and to deal with men and to keep a good balance in his own spiritual life, he will have to work out a plan whereby some time is spent in reflection, some in exterior works and some in healthy recreation. This is the usual manner of the ordinary run of men. Thus each of the classes of activity will come to have its own value, to stand out as a distinct goal; all their values will be arranged so that they will conduce to the highest value a man can achieve for himself in this life, the goal of self-perfection according to the divine plan. Hence, the converted person, in the effort to gain permanency of change, will utilize the same methods that have been useful in cultivating any of the human faculties. He will strive constantly for the value which he keeps continually in mind, from the first moment of his conversion onward through life.

GOAL SATISFACTION AND VALUES

There is a law of human action which states that action will not be continued in a given direction, or a goal will not be striven for persistently, unless there is satisfaction in the attainment of similar goals. The momentary satisfactions arising from this or that small goal-attainment are recognized as plain facts of experience as are the more enduring states of contentment arising from the attainment of a much sought-after goal or objective. One such desired goal might be a happy marital adjustment. Another might be peace and security in the choice of a vocation which involves serving others. There is a real need to emphasize the point of goal-satisfaction, so that no one will think that psychologists of religion are opposed to the pleasure motive as a stimulus to human action. What religious psychologists are opposed to is the doctrine of hedonism which has been prevalent among some thinkers at all ages and in all places. The hedonists state that the only motive for human striving, the only goal to be attained by their efforts, is sensory pleasure; the gratification of the bodily instincts which results in what they call happiness.

It is simply contrary to the testimony of serious-minded men to say that sense-pleasure alone motivates them. On the other hand, it is equally contrary to experience to say that the motive of sense-pleasure does not activate them. Day by day human beings need goal-satisfactions of all kinds and on all levels proper to their capacities; satisfying day-by-day experiences are needed if the convert is to be kept on his path; one might call them rewarding experiences if this term were not so heavily loaded with implications about a theory of learning sponsored by Thorndike. One might prescind from all theories and face the fact that after the first "thrill" of the conversion is over the convert needs some other incentive to which to turn. Then one could say that in his quest for self-perfection, he will obtain goal-satisfaction in the attainment of a set of distinct levels of achievement which are ordered with respect to each other. The reason that the hierarchy of goals and goal-satisfactions seems to help so much is that it becomes similar to a stabilizing mechanism within the individual. It at the same time balances the forces within him which are seeking outlets in everyday living, and it generates new sources of energy from day to day to replace those stores lost through the wear and tear of life.

What has been said, then, amounts to this: The arrangement

of one's goals in a system, and the consequent systematic series of satisfactions which result from attaining the various goals, help keep the person stable and firm in the new direction which he has sought to maintain since he experienced conversion. What probably happens is that the nice arrangement or organization of one's life according to a hierarchy aids the person in keeping the motives more clearly in mind as he meets new situations. He will find it very necessary to keep these in mind, otherwise he will lack both compass and dynamo, both the guide and the energy source for the persistent effort needed for perseverance. These various goals on lower and higher levels become short-term levels of aspiration; the person will set one of these as his ambition, attain it, and then go on to aim at something higher. For each aspiration or ambition that he attains, there is a corresponding kind of goal-satisfaction.

Progressive goal-satisfaction might be illustrated in the following manner: A person feels that he ought to give up smoking. He cuts down the number of cigarettes to three a day, then to one a day. Yet the thought that he might do better haunts him. He probably feels more satisfaction now out of each individual puff, than he did when smoking heavily. But yet there is the hankering for more, in between times. This disturbs him. He weighs the motives for quitting entirely; he thinks he could save more money for more worthy causes, such as providing for his children; his health might be better, etc. Finally he reasons that he is really not obtaining what he desired when he began to reduce his smoking. He feels even a little guilty about yielding to sensuality because of the heightened pleasure which he gets out of the delayed smoking. Gradually this person comes to realize, partly owing to the small bits of satisfaction gotten from keeping his resolution to limit his smoking and partly due to the influence of an over-powering motive to give it up entirely, that he must take the final step and throw away the matches and the ash-trays.

If he is to persevere in this rather radical resolution to give up smoking, he will have to keep present to himself, day by day, some of the reminders with which he began, that the task is worth-while, that some real benefit to himself and others will derive from his resolution, that he will be able to match the satisfactions lost by not smoking with others of equal or even of a higher value to him in his present state. Thus the persevering person is the one who not only gets satisfaction out of his actions and a great variety of these from actions on various levels; he is one who keeps the motives in mind which will enable him to continue suiting his actions to the attainment of that distant goal which he has set for himself.

A better way to understand this whole process would admittedly be to go through the radical experience personally. Then one could reflect upon his own processes and inner movements, keep a diary of his successes and failures, etc. The general pattern of such processes may be summarized briefly as follows: The goals for a conversion must be kept clearly in mind, together with the reasons for attaining them; this will be particularly important in moments of temptation, when there is an inner struggle to maintain oneself in the changed direction.

WHAT IT MEANS IN PRACTICE TO HAVE A STRONG WILL

The process of motivation has been sketched, and the necessity of having a hierarchy of motives in order to get satisfaction at each level has been indicated. The most pertinent question in regard to conversion now arises: How can one be assured of perseverance? Does it require some sort of will-power? How can anyone feel fairly certain that he is going to stay on the straight and narrow path?

A strong will is not conceived of in the sense of strong muscles or strong bones. Doctor W. Clark does a service to psychology in discounting such exaggerated faculty theories of the mind. Yet it remains a fact that *mental abilities* and *spiritual powers* do operate. And by these terms is meant simply the proximate source of energy for given kinds of actions. Without seeming to postulate the existence of independent faculties which are little machines or dynamos, it must be said that mental powers are not all of a kind, though they do all cooperate nicely in the production of mental acts. The power of sensing the form-qualities of an object is different from that whereby we appreciate the beauty of forms. Volitional or striving tendencies are distinct from psychophysical perceptual processes or motor strength.

It is enlightening, however, to note that there is a striking similarity between the operation of physical and mental powers, between all of the powers that exist in vital organisms. Whenever a power is used in regard to its proper object, as noted above, the power strengthens itself. Thus muscles grow by lifting weights; perception improves by constant and careful use; volitional acts make succeeding volitional acts easier and more prompt.

The rational powers of man similarly perfect themselves [2] and the whole man as well. When they function with regard to their adequate and proper objects, they give a special quality to the self-perfecting process; they strive for truth and goodness and will not rest until they attain these alone. But intellect grows and matures through use, as a man grows in the power of understanding, or in the attainment of wisdom. Voluntary acts perfect the habit systems in a man, so that he can overcome greater and greater obstacles. The talisman of success, then, in keeping our resolutions, may be found in that kind of strengthening of our highest powers which consists in keeping the motives for action in readiness when needed in concrete situations. This is the secret of success, the meaning of a strong will, according to the great psychologist, John Lindworsky. But the doctrine is very simple to state and not so easily put into practice. The process will be clarified once more.

It seems very reasonable to suppose that if one is striving for a certain goal, and knows what means are best suited to attain it, he ought to use these means, just because they are so suitable as guides to his goal. Now a motive for a human act is just such a means. It is the value or benefit apprehended in the goal-object, and conceived of as being a means to an end, for example, money for the attainment of power. When money is kept clearly in mind precisely by reason of its usefulness in attaining power, it will surely be a guide to many actions which

2 Ideas similar to that of Rollo May and Existentialists generally.

would not result if money were conceived of in some other way. So whenever one thinks of the goal which he desires, he must also be capable of remembering those means which lead to it, which he needs to use as stepping stones toward it. And if he does gain such facility in thinking out loud, as it were: "This will get me there," whenever he thinks of "There is where I want to go," then he is having his motives available, ready to activate him. Then one's will may be said to have strength because it is operating so as to lead him where he wishes to go. There is nothing mystical or mysterious about strength of will; it is merely the readiness of a mind to have efficacious motives available under all kinds of stressful situations. The persevering convert will surely need such a will.

This point may be illustrated again with the lad who wanted to quit smoking and decided to substitute an apple for a cigarette whenever the urge to smoke arose. He thus implicitly decided to have the image (or idea) of himself eating an apple quite ready on the fringe of consciousness to direct him to the desired substitute act. Such a ready motive could keep him directed toward his goal, namely the avoidance of smoking, which seemed so desirable and even necessary for his health. So if he can be assured of having the "apple" image ready whenever he is tempted to smoke, even if he should be sitting among a group of persons who are all smoking, he will win the struggle; if the image of self-eating can supplant that of self-smoking, his value-motive will be available, ready for use; this is what it really means to follow resolutions with a strong will.

What are the means for keeping the motives ready? Apart from grace and miracles it is simply the habit of attending to the effectiveness of one's motives, so much so that they appear to one as quite spontaneously "motivating" even under the most severe stresses and temptations. The point is not subtle but it needs to be considered deeply before its full import will strike the reader. It can be of immense help to those who wish to guide adolescents through their period of doubts and struggles. They might be particularly impressed with the need of keeping their spiritual "muscles" fit through regular exercise.

Many a young man or woman, in time of retreat or meditation, thinks himself unusually strong in spirit, yet fears that when he gets back into his old environment again, temptation may be so strong that all his efforts at reform will have been fruitless. These persons should try to dispel their fears by realizing that human beings are preeminently creatures of habit, whether these be good or bad habits. The real strengths of the ego or self will show up in the time of trials, and they will be developed in time of prayer and retreat. To worry about future lapses is as fruitless as to worry about what one would do in a panic situation. Actually, during the first moments of panic disturbances, man is fully bound by his reflexes, since he has no time to deliberate. Then he wishes most assuredly that these habits and reflexes be the desirable and suitable ones. Adequate motivational systems will be of great assistance in bringing about these desirable habit tendencies.

In panics, as well as in times of great stress, one wants to have guiding motives ready and available, but one also needs to have fundamentally adequate habit systems so deeply imbedded in his total personality structure that he sets his goals, strives for them and reaps the satisfaction from them as one flash-like integrated act. These systems will be so harmoniously integrated with each other that the total self experiences an indescribably unique kind of contentment in the strong vital activation of the total self.

Let it be noted that in this whole scheme there is ample room for the functioning of forgotten motives, sometimes designated unconscious. Such will be likely to manifest themselves in impetuous rather than deliberate acts. Yet both forgotten and recalled motives contribute to the execution of any self-initiated deliberate act. Except for those who are emotionally ill, compulsive and fully unconsciously motivated behavior is not the rule. The psychopathologists describe such systems of motivation in their proper places.

What, then, will be the most efficacious type of motive for a lasting conversion? It will be that one, or those selected ones, which keep the person gratified, contented, in the choice of the means which he sees and continues to see will be necessary for his total future happiness. He must be maintained each hour of each day in his new direction. He must be locked in the proper course by some sort of control, one that has been engaged in his service from the first moment that he experienced his true conversion. An aid to this locking of the controls will certainly be the keeping of his systems of value on distinct levels. For instance, if he wished to learn an act of motor coordination, he would practice as he learns, and his progress would give him a sense of accomplishment which is good on its own level. Yet this kind of satisfaction is really not comparable to that which is obtained from mental learning, such as learning to understand a logical argument. A still higher level of satisfaction comes from exercising one's ability to solve difficult and abstract problems.

Yet all of these together do not equal the satisfaction and contentment which a person experiences who has had the thrill of conquering a difficult and selfish habit. Each value, when kept at its proper level, guides and motivates at that level; all the levels together build up the total self-satisfaction known as self-assurance or self-respect; they become part of the meaning of life for a person who has experienced them. They nevertheless keep their distinctive satisfactions at the various closely related higher and lower levels. There is an hierarchy of relatively gratifying goal-attaining experiences that contribute to the total ego strength.

The above perhaps sounds logical enough, and quite easy on a purely theoretical level. In practice, when one has been instrumental in bringing about the conversion of a person, it so happens that knowledge of the whole life history of the person is helpful in guiding him. If the counselor shows a genuine appreciation and acceptance of the person of the convert, he can be a most powerful source of motivation and strength for the striving person. The counselor will find it perhaps useful to suggest the use of memory crutches in helping the convert to remember his motives at the proper time. The crudest of such mnemonic devices cannot fail to be of service if it attains its end.

For example, in the case of the school fire which took the lives of so many Chicago children, there was a man who kept working in the building, helping to remove as many children as he could, knowing all the time that his own two children were somewhere back in that ruin. What motive spurred him on to such heroic deeds? Certainly it was not a narrowly exclusive familial love for his own children. He was really sacrificing, in intention, his own life that others might live, whether they were his own offspring or not. The writer likes to think of his case as an instance of the joint-action of motives. He was imbued with the great thought of devotion to others in danger of their lives; it mattered not who those others might be. He must have reacted at first rather spontaneously to whatever value he saw in saving the lives of those other children. Another man in the same kind of situation might have panicked, rushed off and done nothing, or madly demanded the salvation of his own offspring. The manner of the organization of a person's motives, and their availability at any given time, largely determine the outcome of his actions in very stressful situations.

Motives are, after all, thoughts about the value of things; so whatever is effective in guiding the thinking toward relevant images will also be of service in getting the desired action.

It is becoming more and more fashionable in psychology and psychiatry to speak of the body-image, and if any human striving individual can profit more by thinking of himself as a body-image than as a good old-fashioned self-in-action, let him do so by all means. It is also style to refer to the competitive motive as being very valuable in securing action. Theorists in group dynamics have made us very much aware of the subtle forces that get action from groups. They now prefer the cooperative motives to the competitive ones as efficient action-getters.

Nevertheless, there is one kind of competition which can and does strengthen motivation without at the same time leading to the detriment of any other person. For want of better words, it shall be called striving to excel those whom one wishes to excel; or competing with self-chosen competitors. Here one is striving, not so much against others as with them, letting them help him set the goal. An example might be the competitive spell-downs with language vocabularies often found in the upper-grades. There we have inter-group competition in which each class seeks supremacy for the whole group. But we also have within-group striving, in that Person A of one class wants to outdo Person B of the same class. Here it will be noticed that A does not bother much to compete with C or D, because they are not up to the level of A's ambition. A reserves to himself the privilege of selecting the one he will vie with, and such a kind of motivation is known to improve the achievement of individuals as well as of groups. The custom of staging such competitive learning situations in our schools may serve to show what is meant by selective competitive motivation. It seems obvious, also, that such a striving for goals which all will be sharing in common can make for more persistent striving without at the same time resulting in any kind of undesirable or selfishly motivated behavior.

The setting of the goals or standards toward which one strives determines the effectiveness of much of our striving, just as it does for the high-school pupils in the spell-downs. And everyone may do well to strive to emulate and to excel those other persons who are outstanding in the valued traits and in the virtues, without acting in any way selfishly. This is because when one person gains in virtue, spiritual value, or perfection, he does this without taking anything away from the other persons who might be striving to perfect themselves similarly. In fact, such a person may even be helping others unintentionally toward greater perfection, by means of his own silent example.

5. Supernatural Means for Conversion

SUPERNATURAL MEANS ARE NECESSARY BUT NOT SUFFICIENT

The opinion of learned divines in the Christian tradition is that true and lasting conversion must be aided by supernatural means. The truly humble person realizes that his own efforts are feeble, that he must strive continually to better himself, but that he also must rely upon divine help if he is to be secure. He must labor, as Ignatius of Loyola says, as if all depended upon himself, but he must pray as if all depended upon God.

It is not to be denied, in spite of our lengthy explanations, that a sudden illumination and transformation, like that of St. Paul or others, can sometimes occur. Yet these very persons who are so highly favored by divine help are the first ones to insist that there is a need for some action, some predisposing, on the part of man himself. By means of faith and prayerful meditation upon God and upon His relation to man, any man can predispose himself toward receiving divine help. This is actually known to be a fact and moreover God has promised us this. These special helps will be considered in another section.

SELF-HELP IS ALSO NECESSARY

Even though St. Paul apparently experienced his remarkable conversion in an instant, his inner soul had undoubtedly been prepared for days in advance for the special action of God, though he had been the deadliest enemy of the God of the Christians and of all that Jesus stood for. Priests and ministers have witnessed some remarkable conversions, and so has Mr. Graham. Many of them seemed to be sudden. Those which the writer personally encountered have related certain events from a rather long period of their earlier life history; these events had surely turned the tide of their lives in favor of the new way, even though they did not realize it at the time. There is an axiom in theology which will apply here, no matter whether the conversion generally is considered to be sudden or not. It runs as follows: Grace builds upon the natural dispositions of a man at all levels; it does not destroy them. So it would seem that until there are means adequate for the detection of the inner and secret dispositions in a man, the effects of grace cannot be separated from the effects of human efforts. When a man acts in such a way as to prepare himself for divine graces, the workings of psychological laws in the human mind during the process may still be investigated.

In order to determine what is possible or what is impossible for the human nature to perform, the philosophical dictum is used: From the actuality we learn the possibility or potentiality in any concrete case. After a man has tried all means that seem possible for raising himself up to the divine, he must still humbly await the divine call and acceptance. God is above nature even though He respects the causality and achievement proper to those natures which He has created. In this chapter however, we have examined the feeble efforts of men in striving toward a higher life, a participation in the divine. Ultimately it will only be revealed in the Beatific Vision just how marvellously incomprehensible are God's ways in dealing with the acme of His visible creation, the never-ending marvel known as man.

SELF REPORTED CASES

The Case of Phyllis

"The story of my conversion is the story of God's patience with me and of God's answer to my prayer. I have to start back in my childhood. Because of the training my mother and father gave me just ordinary training, one of the foremost things was church every Sunday—also during the week when it was possible. We went to church every Sunday, we went on Sunday evenings and occasionally on Wednesday for prayer meeting. My father always took us, and mother was there when possible, but many times she missed because of small children. So it became a duty, an obligation and a joy. This we tried to follow through without actually realizing it, as children, and even as teenagers growing up.

"But before W and I were planning to be married, Fr. X gave instructions to me, as is always done; and because I wasn't in tune to the instructions that he was giving and he realized it, he asked me to bring W to the instructions with me from then on, because we must complete the necessary instructions before the marriage; this I did and W and I went, I suppose, five or six times after that. And he talked to us as an earthly father would talk to his children. And he told us the important things that must be remembered if our marriage was to be really a union: that we must not end the day on a quarrel but quarrels must always be resolved. We must respect each other in his particular religion, and make it our responsibility that the other fulfill those obligations. This we did to the best of our ability. So as life went on and we had Sandy, W and I each went to our own churches, and I took Sandy until the age of three, and at the age of three I felt that she was beginning to get to the age where she should go with her father to church, because just going to a little kindergarten in a Protestant church with a baby-sitter, so to speak, for the hour was not enough.

"I paid very little if any attention to it because I felt that he should do the job, and he was doing a good job. So in our life, there was very little, practically no discussion of religion. I know there must have been lots of times when W felt that he would like to have all of us together, and I know I felt the same way, but nothing was ever said. I sang in the choir for years in the church and I enjoyed it, but we always made excuses that we never became active in our churches because the other one was not there, so I wouldn't do anything of a special nature during the week nor would he, because we worked together as a family. So we were lacking, both of us, all through the years but God was very patient, as it turned out.

"I felt very antagonistic against anyone in the religious life; I refused to call the priest *Father,* and call the sister *Sister,* I just didn't call them by any title or name at all; but God took care of this as time went on, and indoctrinated me slowly. Sandy went to school, three years to parochial school, and during this time I met a few, very few religious. During the high school years—public high school of course—I didn't meet any.

"But actually when we were in the store ten years ago, we were open on Sunday morning and I wasn't able to go to church and it began to bother me greatly because I knew that it was our duty to be in church every Sunday. And so, since it was just physically impossible otherwise, I asked W and Sandy if I might go to church with them so I could at least read my bible and be in church on Sunday morning. This I did for several years, really for three years almost; during this time of course I didn't realize that little things were filtering through to me. When Sandy decided to go to a nun's school for college, I didn't have quite the stiff feeling with the religious that I had had prior to that. So when I met the sisters at ——, I began to relax and to enjoy being with them, and I was able to call them Sister.

"During this time we had lots of fun, of course, with the religious; we had a lot of little chats, and little tea parties and such. So with the Mass on Sundays and being with the sisters on occasion, I was beginning to feel a little at home in the Catholic church. But it wasn't until a year later that it really got down to specifics. Sandy had a friend, D, and they went to summer school at the U, and each day I would take them to the train and pick them up in the afternoon when they came back. So they had time on the train to have many little chats and they talked about all types of things. Being a Christian Scientist, D had many very odd views, according to Sandy, on religion as well as just daily thoughts and actions and judgments. And so after a while she would come home and discuss these things with me and say: 'Mother, I just can't understand D feeling this way about thus and so'; now I can't remember a single one of those things that we were so surprised at about D's feelings, but since those things occurred day after day we decided—and I don't know whether it was Sandy or myself—but we decided that we should investigate. So we took our Bibles, she took her Catholic bible and I my Protestant. And we sat on the floor in the kitchen during the hot summer evenings; and we checked these things. And each thing we could check, we would each look them up and Sandy would read the passage, and I would follow it. And I began to be a little surprised, because I felt that these two bibles were quite different; and in every passage that we looked up there was not a single difference, not even an *if*, or an *and* or *but;* they were the same.

"This really shocked me quite a little bit. I thought, my, this is most peculiar; because I felt certain that there must be a great difference in the two bibles, and so therefore a great difference in the two faiths. And so by checking the bible—perhaps it was only three or four nights, I began to feel a little uncertain, I was not as solid and strong in my particular faith as I had been before. Since I did believe in prayer and I did pray, I felt this was the only thing to do. So I did pray to God that if I wasn't on the right road, He would let me know. I don't know how long I prayed this prayer, it must have been two or three months, that I prayed every night. I felt confident that I was right, but if I wasn't, I must know about it. I just couldn't go on this way if I was wrong. On Oct. 22nd, when Sandy came to us and asked us if we would give our permission for her to enter the convent, naturally it was somewhat of a shock, because we hadn't discussed it before, and we didn't say very much. But, in my mind, I felt a little ashamed because, instead of thinking of her, I had thought of myself. I thought, "Oh my, this is God's answer to me." And it took something really great and big to be an answer for me. When we took Sandy to the train on Sunday evening, and the next morning, since we had had very little sleep, all three of us being a little wakeful each night wondering about the future with Sandy, Sandy's happiness and our own, W asked me to stay in bed that morning and not go to the store.

"So I did that but, as soon as he left the house, I got up and telephoned Father X and asked him if he would please give me instructions. Of course he was a little bit surprised and, when I explained Sandy's request, he felt it was the normal thing to feel, that I was doing this as a convenience. After all if she was to be in the convent, we just couldn't be that separated, so it would be far more convenient for me to be in the church—all three of us together. I told him of what had gone before, and how I had prayed that I was on the right road. So I think it took the instruction night after night to make him realize that it wasn't just a whim with me—it was something truly that I wanted, I wanted to learn and I wanted to know and I wanted to do what I felt God had sent me the telegram to do.

"I took my instructions from Oct. to Jan. and we had a sort of a crash course, we had about three nights a week of really intensive instruction; W sat in on the instructions and they were actually lecture courses, because I didn't feel that I had any questions to ask—it seemed very clear to me, and it just made me feel good all over. I was baptized Jan. 17—and Sandy didn't know anything about it. When she came home at the end of January for her eight days before entering the convent, I told her then that I was in the church and that we now could go to Mass together. It was a great joy to her, and I can't describe the thrill, the feelings, and also the sorrow that I had missed so much of this before.

"God was good to me. He was very patient, and He waited

and finally let me find His hand, and I am learning every day how better to hold on to that hand. I still have so much more to learn. I could go through these instructions I think every year—they meant so much to me; and there is so much of it you forget. I am so grateful for the grace of faith that was given to me. And I so hope, in some little way, that I can maybe help somebody else receive the same grace.

"I know, Father, I have probably left out so much; but it was really such a simple thing when you look back on it. There was just the matter of living, loving, listening and letting God pull the strings. You know this little book I got in church Sunday, 'This is your tomorrow and today,' I didn't know what kind of a turn it was going to take; well it did take a turn all right. It really is a spiritual reading book, it's wonderful; it's about a Trappist monk whose brother is dying of cancer. And the Trappist monk sends him these letters, to help direct him, to show him how to live gloriously and joyfully the last days of his life, as a real inspiration to those around him. It's really a terrific book and you will have to read it, Father."

This mother was obviously drawn to the church partly by the example of her daughter and the strong love she had for both her husband and her daughter. She shows the real value and efficacy of prayer, and the effects of deep faith and trust in God as a preparation for the gift of faith. She also lets the reader realize most powerfully that her change of heart followed almost spontaneously from her good dispositions. These were, first of all, her removal of obstacles to grace by agreeing to allow her daughter and her husband to follow their own inclinations without interference; and, secondly, her great charity and kindness to those around her. Another predisposing factor for her conversion was her willingness to talk over her problems with others, peers as well as superiors.

The story highlights the fact that life-long misunderstandings exist in the minds of many non-Catholics about the meaning and content of the bible, and concerning the mind of the Catholic church regarding the reading of the bible. When she finally found out for herself that Catholics are not forbidden to read the bible, and that the Catholic bible is NOT totally different from that of the Protestants, then she had removed the biggest obstacle in the way of her conversion. Of course she had also to become curious about what the bible contained before she could have studied it so intently. Again her curiosity was occasioned in large part by the questions raised by her daughter in her talks with the schoolmate.

It might be doubted whether or not the mother ever would have seen the truth and accepted it had she not *prayed* so devoutly and ardently. The content of her prayer was simply marvellous. She wanted help and she spelled out, so to speak, the kind of help she wanted from God. In the very simple yet elegant prayer she asks, like a trusting little child, that God would help her to see the light. She expresses her dilemma in very clear words like this: "You know, God, that I had always thought I was in the right in my religion, and now you must help me to see if this is really so, for I cannot go on in doubt."

Her unabashed descriptions of her repugnance toward the titles of "Father" and "Sister" are also quite significant. When this little feeling of hostility has been overcome, she is well on her way toward better communication between herself and those around her, and doubtless she feels already that she is becoming more catholic at heart.

Lastly her case shows the necessity on the part of priests and nuns, for great prudence and caution in dealing with members of other religions. But, above all, it shows that a person who is active and sincere in her own belief and diligent in the search for truth will be more likely to take the question of the truth of religion seriously. The very seriousness of the desire to learn God's will cannot but help bring about wonders of grace for a person of this kind, whereas one who is quite indifferent about his or her own religion, whatever it may be, will not be moved to engage in a serious search for the truth in her beliefs.

The Case of Cyrillus

"...But the above isn't the real reason I'm writing you at this time. I believe I have come to some type of a real turning-point and wanted to tell you about it, since you were involved for so long.[3] Besides you are the only one I can talk to about matters like this—and for this I feel very fortunate. I also hope you have some time over Thanksgiving when we could talk. Please don't feel I'm trying to reestablish a therapeutic dependency. The last time I saw you I forgot to tell you of a dream I had just a few nights before. For months I had been feeling very guilty about never having developed any teaching materials on scrupulosity for your program. I didn't want to face you and tell you that I didn't. I had not had a single dream for months, but had this one a couple of nights before I knew I was going to see you. In the dream I went to see you, but all I could see was the back of your black coat, collar and head. Then there was something about a transfusion. You turned around and it wasn't you as you are now but as a much younger man—in mid-thirties. Then I awoke and asked myself what it meant. The immediate answer was: from "father" to "brother." There was a sense of relaxation and the fear was gone. I guess what I'm asking is to interpret what follows as from one who has a selective and mature dependency rather than a total neurotic dependency on you. I know how responsible we feel when we know the listener is hanging on our every word and suggestion.

"You may remember way back to 19—, when I first went to you, I had the feeling that Catholicism wasn't all that it should have been for me. With somewhat more clarity now I can explain what I vaguely felt at the time. It seemed then that all it was was Mass on Sunday, confession, avoid the 6th, fast and abstinence on the appointed days. All those things we find in Moral Guidance by Healy, S.J. The senses were to be denied—any pleasure was wrong or merely tolerated in the real Christian order of things. Perfect we must be, but imposed from without we should drive ourselves down the route of the purgative, illuminative, unitive. The whole business was cold, austere, uninviting and just didn't seem to square with facts: that we were physical also, and that all of us were quite imperfect

3 The letter was addressed to the instructor, a man of 60 years, who very permissively watched this soul find his way back over the labyrinthian ways.

limited beings, and the solutions of life's problems were not quite as simple as they were made out to be. I think this is the way I felt then. This in 19— despite the joy I felt at reading in 19— (four years earlier) the *Principles and Foundations*[4] and 'finding out' that the material and human world wasn't all bad. In fact the *P and F* were probably my passport back to the 'world.' A few weeks ago I was thinking how presumptuous it was for me to go in in the first place (to religious life). But that is getting ahead of the story.

"If the past eight years have had any meaning it has been finding my way back—rather out of this somewhat sterile enclosure. And I believe I have made a real turn in the road.

"Where to begin? I don't remember when I began doing this, but for several years, whenever the anxiety used to get bad or some problem was bothering me and I thought I was losing perspective, I would go through a little formula: God created man; man sinned and the gates of heaven were closed; Christ came as a redeemer with the Gospel. What is this 'good news'? It seemed to help to put my little problem into perspective and to reduce the anxiety. It was also a new way of asking my question of 19— (8 years ago) or a little after: What is Christianity? At that time I sensed that it must be something more than what it meant for me and what it seemed to so many of those around me. You may remember my inadequate expression of the feeling that there should be something to 'internalize'— that would be a basis for everyday living.

"As time went on I would think about each section of the formula and of course when I would use it, it would have more meaning. Then late this summer I read a section in *Love or Constraint* by Marc Oraison in which, in a few pages, he made clear for me something all of us have heard a thousand times: that we should be sorry for and avoid sin because it breaks the bond with God rather than because of the fear of hell. In this section he wrote of God's love for man. Well every night for some time—and it's difficult to put dates on this—before going

4 He refers to the *Exercises of St. Ignatius* which he made as a novice in a religious order.

to sleep I would think about this fact. Then gradually—or I suppose one day—it all made sense. Out of His Love God did create man. After the fall man must have been fearful and waiting. Then the redemption in which God became man. This then is the most important point in history for us, and it presents us with some important questions. This fact should be the source of our joy, and we really can't keep quiet about it. I'm finding it a little hard to express this all well and perhaps it isn't the place.

"Well, since that time a number of weeks back, this basic insight has been the starting point for a whole series of reflections regarding the past, present and future—if we can reflect about the future. The fragments seem to be coming together.

"Please don't think I've 'flipped,' or am flighting into unreality. I feel very involved in my job and am attentive to it. I cheer on the football team and am even having my old friend Mary (high school friend) out for next week-end. In fact I still have my old faithful friends: mild neurotic symptoms. I feel I could write pages on the feelings I have been expressing and their relation to the neurosis. There is a greater feeling that I am in command rather than my symptoms, and that if they go away, fine; if they don't, all right.

"While I feel I understand what really drove men into the desert or off to the missions, I feel I have to give expression in my own way, recognizing realistically my limitations as well as talents.[5] It may or may not be much different than I'm doing now. One very encouraging thing to me was the intense desire to receive communion last Sunday, and this hasn't happened in a long time.[6]

"I'm sure that the proximate cause has been the somewhat lonely life I've been leading out here, but I sensed I needed it

5 He refers to his intense desire to "return to religious life" (although he was declared unsuited time and time again by doctors). He had as a second choice, desired to make "Catholic Action" on the foreign missions his life's vocation—he is now 36 years old.

6 During his period of intense doubt and scrupulosity, he has rarely if ever gone to communion.

when I was at ——. But that's a whole new train of thought and you can tell I'm all wound up and could go on for pages.

"I will look forward to seeing you over —— if you aren't going to —— or elsewhere.

"P.S. Please excuse the paper. After reading this very inadequate expression of my feelings in these past several weeks, I'm going to put this in the mail box tonight or I won't tomorrow."

And a few weeks later. . .

"The above is one level of reasoning and deals with subjects and feelings I am familiar with. (The 'above' refers to his feelings regarding success in his new job—which he compares to a game, saying that the anticipation of the outcome, the use of one's skills and knowledge, make it seem like fun; but that, when it's all over, the prudent person says maybe it was just all a game, and maybe its healthier to look on it this way.) But then—or rather now—I can shift into a whole new system and begin to deal with things I am not too familiar with—and, frankly, I get confused and anxious, anxious in kind of a spiritual sense. I think about these things and it's almost like meeting a stranger.

"The process can be stated by thinking about the God we learned about in natural theology—without the need to even recall the demonstrations; this God who exists outside of time in the ever present now. This powerful God Who by His will sustains the world, Who created the atom and designed an evolutionary system. This God Who created us—or me—in His image and likeness. And of course the question comes up of why me, and every one else? Why did this mysterious, all-intelligent, powerful, self-sustaining God create us? And only through a somewhat clouded reason and feeling can we say that it was because of love.

"Then the Fall, when man was buffeted about and alone in a strange world; where paths were not marked too clearly, where the Jews—symbolical men—were in a way frustrated in what they sensed was their destiny as men. Then this God, this same God, came down as man. And through the events of

His life redeemed us and brought us the words on how we, as free men, must cooperate to achieve our destiny.

"Out of the above skeleton I can spin in my mind the ideas on which to base the patterns of the 'new world'; the ways to go about it, the re-definitions, etc. Of course I have ideas almost about everything! The bits and pieces of things I've read over the past several years come back, and I want to fit them together. I want to relate them to the things I learned earlier. I get excited when I read Guardini, Oraison, and de Chardin.[7] I get the feeling I want to just walk out of my apartment some morning, lock the door and seek the 'new life.'

"But even as I let myself go and write like that, I know that it's the easy way. People today just don't think like that and do these things. The above is the 'stranger' speaking that I mentioned earlier. And the record—my record—offers little foundation for the aspirations. My academic record doesn't bespeak a good mind; my working life is somewhat mediocre; I'm only a few drinks away from all the old ways; no publications, poor memory; scruples; some emotional malfunctioning, etc. This is the person I am. Even when I recently 'found' these new thoughts, I felt I should do something, just to prove their reality. I thought of giving up liquor, but told myself it now didn't play a big part in my life, and wouldn't really be a sacrifice. Then cigarettes— but I discarded that because I'd be giving these up for fear of cancer. I hit upon the idea—bright ain't I?—of going to Mass in the morning, not so much for the difficulty involved in getting up, but for the spiritual benefits. You know how many times I've gone the 250 feet to do this? Zero times.

"So I keep asking myself what is the best route for me? At times I feel it is only by making a clean break with the present way. I have never mentioned to you, I believe, a kind of phantasm I've had for a number of years. I don't know whether it was a dream originally or not, or how it came about. I see myself in a kind of a bleak desert writhing in dust, trying to rid myself, I guess, of the past and the guilt. It always seems to be in the

7 Subject has always enjoyed reading such highly controversial authors.

southwest U. S., and I said: 'See,'—but I don't mean see really—because it is too closely attached to some feeling.

"A few months ago I was reading somewhere about the desire of all men to be re-born, and I associated that always-readily-available phantasm with that. By a 'clean break' I don't mean to go into religious life, but do something that would be more in harmony with the deeper value system.

"The other times—and these two may not be mutually exclusive—I feel that only a human love will help me rid myself of these psychic problems, thereby enabling me to proceed on the spiritual-intellectual level. This, in a way, I sense. I can't throw Rosenheim's analysis (the psychiatrist) out completely, for I feel he is competent and honest. Theoretically—taking into account a word I know little about: sublimation may be the solution—it may sound inconsistent, but perhaps not. (Substituting new and socially acceptable goals for basic needs).

"I write all this because I think it helps me, but also I wanted you to be sure of your 'data,' i.e. your picture of me. While I recognize that you use 'conversion' in a technical sense to include any radical change, thus imputing nothing to me about worth or lack of it, I still felt a bit strange to see my words come back under that heading. I don't know your framework really, so after you read this, I'll let you judge whether you still want to use it."[8]

Case of Bertha

"It was early morning hours on April 1, 1928 that I came into this world—not as the majority of babies come—but as the

---

8 Comments: The subject here obviously does not wish to admit that he ever deliberately lost the faith of a Catholic, though his doubts and seemingly "irrational" behavior would lead an outside observer to judge that he was no longer a believing or practicing Catholic. He continued to struggle with his doubts in an heroic fashion for many more years. At the time of this writing he is fairly secure in his beliefs and constant in his practices. It would seem that the war experience might have been critical, both in precipitating his doubts and in facilitating his conversion. Fundamentally a good home life seems responsible for his success.

minority group which we might term 'unwanted.' The only way that I know this is that it was told to me by my Dad and my paternal grandmother. And there must be some kind of truth to their statements since, at the age of three months, when my parents were divorced, the courts relegated to my Dad the legal status of guardianship. I would visit my mother for a couple of weeks each summer and then spend the rest of the year with Dad. I don't really know my own feelings about my mother. In some kind of a way I loved her and yet I didn't really know her. Also, I don't feel that my mother had my real interests at heart because she would permit me to do anything I pleased. From this standpoint I'm very grateful to my Dad. He was very, very strict with me and I knew that when he said a thing that was it! But I loved him! He never had to spank me but twice—that I can remember. He usually only had to 'look' and that was enough to make me cry. I idolized this guy. I cannot recall any evenings as a pre-schooler when Dad would not sit on the couch each evening after supper, put me on his lap, and then read to me book after book. And sometimes Dad would tell me it was my turn and I had to read to him. He had infinite patience. After hearing *Peter and the Turkey* so many times, I practically knew it by heart. Where I would stumble on words Dad would patiently help me sound them out. The result of all this was that I read before I started first grade and this posed a problem for my teacher. She thought I was sneaking my primer home for extra help because I could read all my stories.

"My school years through the first four grades were probably typical of those of any other youngster. I loved to go to school, I loved to learn new things, but then I also loved to get back home at the end of the day. I felt that I belonged, that I was loved, and that, in general, it was good to be alive. It was also during these early school years that Dad was dating a school teacher. She never made a visit to our home that she didn't bring me something; usually it was books. I naturally thought this was the greatest. It doesn't take much to thrill a kid, you know. Monday night visits were looked forward to, since it meant an added collection to my tiny tot library.

"Before I move into later years there is one more point about my Dad. Even though I never really had to want for anything, Dad was going to make sure that I wasn't spoiled by all this. Therefore, when I asked for some things, I would at times get a 'no.' And with the things I had, if I didn't share them with the other children of the neighborhood, I would find that they were no longer in my possession. I almost lost my tricycle by selfishly wanting to ride 'first.'

"I could write many, many more incidents before coming to this fifth-grade level but I suppose they would be irrelevant. At any rate, somewhere around the end of my fifth grade, Dad remarried. I'd spent all these preceding years with Dad and my grandmother. Now that Dad had moved into the new home which he built I was anxious to be with him again. When their honeymoon was over I used to call home each evening and ask when I could come to live with them. My step-mother always had excuses. The pillows hadn't come for my bed yet. I tried to tell her that I never used a pillow. At any rate, I believe that at the time I was too stupid to realize that she never wanted me to come and live with them. She was, and is, a very selfish woman. She doesn't really know what love is—and maybe I don't either—but at least I know that it is meant to be shared and it is meant to grow. Came the day that I did move home, and living wasn't too bad the first year except that I didn't really live normally. I shared no family life. When I came home from school I had to go upstairs where I had a bedroom, den and bath. These were my living quarters. For breakfast, I *stood* at the kitchen sink to have my fruit juice, toast and milk. My lunch I ate in school and for dinner in the evening I could sit at the table with Dad and the *thing* he married. (I'm sure you caught the sarcasm and that's what I wanted.) Whenever she decided that I should be punished she would put some food on a tray, place it on the bottom step of the stairs, and then holler up that the tray was there. After eating the food I'd replace the tray on the step and remain for the rest of the evening in my room. My time was also regulated. In fact, it was regulated from the time I got up until the time I went to bed. I was limited to very exact minutes for making my bed, cleaning my rooms, brushing my teeth, and caring for all personal needs. I didn't dare to be a minute off schedule.

"I mean it when I say that *EVERYTHING* was on this schedule, even to when I used the lav. At a certain minute I had to turn on my radio for the morning news, and it had to be turned off on the minute. My study schedule was arranged down to the exact number of minutes I had for each subject. All written work was checked by 'it' and if an 'i' was not dotted exactly in the center I did the work over. If I didn't get all A's on my report card with sometimes an exception and a couple of B's might be allowed, I could go to no school activities. I had a terrible time studying because I always had to worry about the mark I was going to get. What I learned didn't matter. Just so I got that Almighty A. Even my wardrobe was scheduled. I had shoes and socks to match every outfit I had and she made the schedule for the week. I was told in detail what to wear—blouse, sweater, jacket, skirt, dress, shoes, socks, etc., etc., etc. Naturally, being thus penned in, I was beginning to hate life, even though it could be tolerated. When the beatings started this was getting to the end of my rope. For any reason that she could make up, I would get a beating. My Dad never knew of any of these things because, after the first year of their marriage, I *never once* talked *alone* to my Dad. She was always there—afraid she'd miss something. Anyway, about these beatings I felt so embarrassed because I would have to strip off *every inch* of my clothing, lie on the kitchen floor on my stomach and then she would beat me with a yardstick until it would break. (Dad worked at a lumber company and the yardsticks were *thick*.) Many was the day I went to school with bruises and welts on my back and there was no one I could turn to. Not even my best classmates could I tell, because I would never want them to know that I had this kind of a home—excuse me, I meant to say *house*. There's quite a difference!

"In my 7th and 8th grade years there were several incidents which may be worth noting. For one thing, I entered the annual spelling contest held for the schools in the county. I won in the school and went to the sectional, won in the sectional and went to the county. I was thrilled and very happy that I'd gone to the finals. When the final contest came, one after the other went down until myself and one other girl were left standing. I missed on the word 'superfluous' and came out second place winner in the county. I was still thrilled because I still felt there'd been a tremendous amount of competition to overcome. So I went home with my teachers who'd been with me, and couldn't wait to get in the house and tell the news. What a shock I was in for! When I said *second place* this 'thing' raised the roof. What a disgrace to go that far and lose out!!! 'Why don't you think and use your head before you open your mouth?' Guess this is what you call deflation.

"The second incident which happened was that I entered an elocution contest. My monologue was 'Ma and the Auto' by Edgar A. Guest. Again I'd gone to the finals. When the decisions of the judges were final, a fourth grade boy took first place and the Jr. High girl rated second. I hadn't learned yet. I was still very stupid because I went home, just feeling on top of the world. She, a former teacher of English, was humiliated to the depths of her being. I should have been ashamed of myself—the idea—letting a *fourth grade* boy beat me!

"I didn't even know how to clean house. When I'd clean she'd do all in her power to find dirt if she had to scrape under the baseboards with a bobby pin. And this would be an excuse for beating me because I *lied.* How was this a lie? Well, I'd be asked if I finished cleaning and when I answered in the affirmative, this dirt inspection would begin. And I always knew that, no matter how hard I tried, I'd never succeed because she'd always find something. Since I said I'd cleaned and she found dirt, I was a liar. I hadn't cleaned at all.

"This was about as far as I could go. I could stand all this no longer. I didn't want to live, but I was afraid to die. And I was petrified of this woman. It was sometime within these years—I was about 12—that I decided to run away. I decided in school one day that I just wouldn't go home that night. After school I stayed for a baseball game and when it was getting near 5:00 and a green Buick pulled into the school drive I was on my way; I didn't know where and coudn't have cared less. But I was scared! I didn't walk on the highways because I didn't want to get picked up by anyone—stranger or acquaintance. Note that I didn't say *friend* because I didn't have any. I walked through cornfields. It was cold—sometime in April I believe. I was hungry, tired, alone, and just wanted to be dead. Curled up behind a tree I tried to get warm but I couldn't; I only cried and kept walking; went to the highway and walked until I came to a bridge by the lake. This lake was a part of the Country Club to which my Dad belonged. I looked over the bridge for a long time and really wanted to jump and end it all. Something wouldn't let me. I just wanted to desperately but couldn't. Then I walked under a viaduct where the railroad tracks ran. I wanted to stretch out and wait for the next train. But again, I couldn't. Something wouldn't let me. As I headed back on the highway a car stopped and two fellows got out. They asked me if I wanted to ride, but I just told them to move along. When I saw that they were determined I started running and if I ran in a Marathon today I could never run like I did then. I was so far ahead of those guys that they gave up. But I was scared to go back on the highway. I just kept wondering what was going to happen to me.

"After what seemed like hours I was back on the highway when a car came by and stopped. A familiar voice said, 'Get in.' I argued and was determined. But there were two Boy Scouts in the back of the car and when I saw that they were ready to get out I knew the fight was over. I was too tired for any more resistance. I was taken to the house where the 'witch' greeted me with 'Well, it's a good thing you got home now. If you'd waited five more minutes we were going to call the police and the only thing that kept us from calling sooner was that I was afraid my mother would be listening to the radio and I'd never want to have her know that this is what I married into.' Naturally, since this was a very small town, everyone knew that I'd run away. This was terrible for the family name and I was supposed to go to school the next day and face the other kids. What happened in school that day no longer rings a bell. But the fact that my STEP-mother had to defend herself was another story. She composed a letter which I was supposed to read before an assembly at school. I don't know why she changed her mind but she did. Instead, she made me write copies of it to all my aunts, my teachers, friends, everyone I knew and she did the mailing of them. The letter was telling everyone what a wonderful home I had and how unappreciative I was. I just had everything a girl could ever want—clothes for practically every day of the year, my own little apartment, every material thing anyone could ever ask for; but I was ungrateful. I had parents who were truly concerned for my welfare and that's why they were trying to help me now, etc., etc., etc., ad infinitum. After all these people had received the letters, I still had to face them, go to school with them, meet my teachers day after day and thinking all the time what a rat they thought I was.

"It was in these years also that I found I had a dirty, filthy, rotten mind. I'd been told by this Simon Legree that if I had any questions on sex or anything at all that I wanted to know I should just come to her. I toyed with the idea for a long time before I decided to give her a chance. An incident happened in school and I took it home. When my question was asked, I was told that I was a dirty, filthy, rotten girl and that my Dad was going to hear about this. At this stage of the game I knew I'd never again in my life bring up the subject of sex but I also knew that I was going to find out everything there was to know. This wasn't so much that I was really after the knowledge but the fact that I was going to prove to myself that she couldn't keep me from gaining any knowledge I might want, and that I could find it all out without her help.

"With the passing of each day I was becoming more and more hateful toward this woman, but I never dared show it. It might seem surprising but in all the beatings I got, I never cried. I just hated! And I was reaching the point where I was about at the end of my rope. By the time I was 13 or 14 I wasn't going to take any more. Maybe it would have been more drastic had a few more years been added to my age. I don't think I'd have been as docile if this could be called docility. I say this because at one time when I was getting one of these frequent beatings in the kitchen I was very very tempted to pull open the knife drawer and stick the meat carving knife right through that woman. And I thought about putting poison in her food. If I could have found a poison that would have killed her immediately I think I would have used it. But I figured she'd get sick first, a doctor would be called, they'd pump her stomach, she'd get well, and my life would be good and wrecked. I just kept trying to hang on and telling myself that someday I could get away from her and that she wouldn't be over me forever.

"It was in the second half of my Freshman year that I was actually permitted to sit downstairs in their living room and have the fortunate news told to me that I would have the good fortune of going away to a private boarding school. I knew that this was just her way to get rid of me and she *confirmed* this when in the course of our conversation she said she didn't want me to think they didn't want me at home. Who did she think she was kidding!! I just wasn't that stupid. They told me that I could go to a School for Girls. It was supposed to be very exclusive with many activities. You also had to keep up your scholastic average. I was angry because I knew her motive in wanting to send me away but, on the other hand, I was happy because it meant getting away from her tyranny. It must be the way guys feel that are let loose from prison after spending 75 years there.

"Before beginning any of the events at ———, I might make a comment or so regarding the practice of religion. From as far back as I can remember in my childhood, I went to church (Christ Evangelical & Reformed) and Sunday School every single Sunday. In the summers I would attend Bible school in the mornings, remembering only that we received milk and graham crackers about mid-morning. On Sundays this meant about two hours of worship. Each night before going to bed I would kneel at my bedside and say my prayers. This was the extent of my religion. When I'd leave church on Sundays I'd feel like it was one duty performed and I'd be back next week. As for thinking of God during the day—well, I wondered about Him at times but never talked or prayed to Him. That was just for Sundays and before bed.

"And now to the school. It was the second semester of my Freshman year. When I arrived I was greatly impressed by the picturesque scenery. The Freshman cottages were little white wooden, two-storied homes. The homes of the upper classmen were brick structures and mansion-like. These were all in a circular formation around the campus. In the center of the circle was a large wooded area and a very beautiful campus. Tremendous, and away from tyranny! Since I had never lived so closely with anyone my own age it was decided by 'dictator' that I should live in a six-girl dorm. Five of us were Protestant and one girl was a Catholic. And never forget—it was impressed upon me that this was a very *elite* school. Now I'm wondering just what this term really meant. It was here that I learned of things that I never dreamed could really exist. Oh well, maybe they could—among *uncivilized* people. I do not believe there was anything left undone there. And I was overwhelmed. I was shocked, I was disappointed, disgusted, and disillusioned. If this was what elite meant then I wanted no part of it. God had nothing to do with all this. I never connected sin with any of this because the word 'sin' was rather foreign to me. I just knew that decent people didn't live like this. Never did I take part in any homosexual activity, though I was asked, but neither did I come out of that school unscathed. Draw your own conclusions. I was beginning to hate the place. However, the semester went by rather quickly and I returned back to the 'hell hole' for the summer.

"The middle of the summer came and this brought with it my letter of invitation to return to —— for my Sophomore year. I did not want to go back but I had no reason to offer and besides I didn't want to live in this house either. I wanted someone to talk with, but I had no one. Mrs. Legree limited my time and my visits to my grandmother; I could never talk alone with my Dad. And even if I could have seen him alone I would never have dared bring up the subject of sex. Not after already having been told what a rotten mind I had. Outside of Dad and my grandmother, there was no one else that I could trust. I seemed completely alone and there was no one to whom I could turn.

"In September, I returned to School and into a quad. This was no help. Things were as bad as ever. I did not want to stay.

I only wanted so much to talk with someone but no one could I trust. I know that one had to be invited to return to this school. I didn't want to be invited back and I didn't want to be expelled. I started out by getting a nice red '34' on my report card in business arithmetic. You can just imagine how this went over at home.

"I may mention here that I was home for all vacations and one was just as bad as the next; on one of my visits I had my head cracked with a hammer and thought I was going to bleed to death. I had twin beds in my bedroom with quilted spreads. This one morning she told me to go and get her the hammer. I did and when I brought it to her she started hitting me over the head. She said I lied because I told her my spread was on straight and she said it wasn't. She kept hitting me until the head of the hammer flew off and hit the banister over the stairway. The blood was pouring out of my head and down my white blouse and powder blue shorts. Then she grabbed me by the hair and pulled me into the lav where she stuck my head under the cold water spigot while hitting my head against the faucets. To this day my Dad does not know about this. It happened near lunchtime and she knew my Dad would be coming home. This was one of those days when my food was served from the bottom step. Anyone who needs proof for this can examine the scar on the back of my head.

"It was now second semester at school and all my discontent was growing. Besides the homosexual activity that went on there it was nothing to walk the paths of the wooded area and find contraceptives thrown among the leaves. I was confused, mixed up, and felt completely destitute of friends. I made my decisions-as to how I would go about not getting invited back. No one may go to town on a school day without a permit from the dean and she will only give you one a week. I went to town two times in one week with no permit either time and happened to run into the housemother both times. She asked me if I had a town permit and I told her 'no.' The following week I was called to the dean's office where I was questioned as to whether I'd do this again or not. I told her that I could make no promises. From here on out, to make a long story short,

I was not invited to return to that school. This really brought hell down on the entire household. What were they going to do with me now? I was a disgrace to the family. What were they going to tell the relatives and friends? By now, I was embittered, resentful, and hateful because I had no one to turn toward, and they seemed to have everyone on their side. I could not stand the beatings any more and I did not intend to live at home.

"On one occasion my Dad took my part. Not that he was really trying to stick up for me. He was merely telling the truth. You see, each night I had to get on the scale, nude, and with her at my side. If I was one pound over-weight, she cut out the food the next day. Well, it so happened that one morning there were two cookies missing from the cookie jar. At breakfast she asked me about them. I told her that I did not take them but then as usual—I was a liar. Dad happened to hear this and came into the kitchen. He said he'd eaten them before going to bed the night before. She thought he was taking my part, and then said, 'Either she gets out or I get out.' Dad turned to her and said, 'You don't get out.' I looked at both of them and with gritted teeth said, 'Then I'll get out.'

"This is when I planned my second run-away. I had been saving my money for a bicycle. When I went out to work in the yard that morning I took the money along and hid it behind a tree in the front yard. I decided that I'd leave at midnight. I really hated the whole damn world and I was going to prove to everyone that I could get along without them and that I simply wouldn't let them wreck my life. My first plans were to leave at midnight and set fire to the house. Since Mrs. Legree had to have the most expensive of everything we didn't really have anything cheap in our house. However, I also figured that if I set fire to the house I'd never get to run away because I had to go 12 miles to get a bus. I couldn't even have gotten a quarter of a mile away. They'd have smelled smoke, the house would not have been destroyed, and I would have been caught. Since it was the most important that I get away, I decided that I'd just go out the front door and leave it wide open hoping that someone would come in and steal everything they could possibly steal.

"This is the plan I followed through. I did get up at midnight, took my suitcase, picked up my money and started on my way. I had to make 12 miles before seven in the morning since that is when they would get up, and if I wasn't at breakfast on the exact minute, she'd be there to see what I was doing. I walked and I ran. Cars would stop to pick me up. Trucks stopped and offered their transportation. All were declined with the excuse that I'd been baby-sitting and was just going to the next house. The dawn was coming up but I was almost to my destination—the Greyhound bus terminal. I believe I made it around ten minutes before the hour of seven, I bought my ticket for ——, and was on my way. When I arrived there I went directly to the home of one of my roommates, but what a disappointment I received. I wasn't there more than five minutes when a police car drove in. Jane's dad knew the policeman and told him that he'd bring me over to the station. When we arrived at the police station the officer was waiting for me. He told me to follow him up the steps and that my parents would be there to get me in a few hours. There was a long flight of stairs to climb and he led the way. In wending our way to the top he stopped in the middle of the stairs, turned and looked at me, and then asked, 'What's your name?' With all the defiance and belligerence I could get up I answered, 'If you're so smart you figure it out.' He just looked at me and said, 'You're not really tough or hard. You're just a hurt kid.' This was all I needed and I burst into tears. He took me to his office and gave me a stack of magazines to read. Who could concentrate on magazines at a time like this? When he left, I went to the window. There was a rain pipe running right down the side of the building. I decided to slide down this and run again. I just wanted to run and keep running until this maniac of a woman would let me alone. On the other hand, I was tired and so very depressed. It seemed I could do absolutely nothing without getting caught and I was picturing a policeman directly under that rain pipe ready to catch me when I hit bottom, gave up that idea but knew it wasn't the end of my fighting. I was going to keep on until I got out of that house. I even begged that policeman to let me live in jail or put me in a prison because I wouldn't get beaten and hounded like I did at home. It was drawing near the time for my parents to come. Again my plans were made. They would sit in the front of the car as always and I'd be in the back. When the car stopped for the first red light I would jump out of the car and be on my merry way again. And they could continue in another chase. But things didn't work out this way. They put me in the front seat between them. Another idea was shot.

"All the way home the only thing I heard was that I was pregnant and that they were taking me to a doctor. I don't think I could have hated that woman any more than I did and this really clinched everything. To accuse me of being pregnant was the end, but I must say she did give me an idea. We did not get home until late evening and they didn't say much more that night. But the following day she called some *woman* doctor in the neighboring city. It was here that I went for a physical. I hated this doctor because she was a woman; I wasn't going to have any woman examine me, and I was also angry because Legree was at her side. What a disappointment she got after the physical! But like I said, she still gave me an idea.

"I had a cousin who was just seven months younger than I. Her father was dead and her mother worked, so I went to her house one evening and told her all my plans, that I was going to get pregnant because this would be the best way to really ruin the family name. Having felt my life was already doomed, I wanted to do everything in my power to make their life perfectly miserable. This was the perfect way. And again to make a long story short—I could not carry out these plans. I just couldn't. Besides I kept trying to tell myself that I wouldn't always have to live under this woman. If I did anything like this then I would wreck my life. And at no time in my life did I really want to be bad. I wanted to be good. I wanted to love people and do kind things for them. This is the only kind of example I ever had from my Dad. He was always doing things for other people—always, always. And there was a thrill and deep sense of satisfaction in knowing that you'd done something to help make someone else happy. I didn't really want to ruin my life and I didn't really want to hurt my Dad—just the other thing.

"Again a problem faced the family. What were they going to do with me? I didn't worry about it. It was their problem. I just knew that I was going to run away again and again and again until someone would step in and say that I didn't have to live at home. Dad conferred with the lawyer who was a personal friend of the family and who had helped get the divorce for my Mom and Dad when I was three months old. Dad had told him that he didn't want a court case out of this and didn't want me to have any kind of record. He said it could all be handled privately but that we should call a particular woman in the children's court. After going to see her she felt that a social worker should come in and work in the home. For Mrs. Legree this was just an unheard-of thing. She wasn't going to have people pry into her affairs. Besides, it's bad enough to have three people living in the house let alone others coming in. You see, we had always had plain carpets on our floors and every little thing would show up. When someone walked on them they naturally showed the imprints. So, when people would leave the house she'd get out her broom—special one for this— and would sweep over the carpets so that they never looked walked on. And even the cushions on the chairs were picked up and fluffed so that they never looked like they were used. When she dusted she used a yardstick to measure on both sides of the lamp to be sure that it was exactly in the middle. I just can't live this way.

"To get back to the woman from the Children's Court. I'd overheard some of their conversations and knew that they were planning on sending me somewhere again. I didn't really care where as long as I didn't have to live at home. One thing was certain, I could never get anywhere that could be worse. I heard them talking about schools in two fairly large cities, and I heard something about giving me the choice between the two. As soon as I heard this I ran to my globe to see which was the farthest from home and my decision was made. When the time came for them to decide they never asked me and their decision was not the one I made. It was then that I was told I would be going to the school run by Franciscan Sisters since it was an accredited school and there would never be a stigma connected with going there. My choice would have been the Good Shepherd's since they were farthest from home but, so they said, this wasn't where I really belonged. I wasn't the kind of girl that belonged in a Good Shepherd home. Accordingly plans were made for the accredited school.

"Before I go on to the incidents of my 'new home' there were a couple of things which I forgot to mention. I knew from my Sunday School classes and most of all from the example of my Dad that we must never hate people. It just wasn't the Christian thing to do. We can never read what is going on in the next person and therefore we cannot judge. And I was really impressed by this in my Dad. I really don't think my Dad had any enemies. He was good to everyone and would do anything for anybody. He was tender-hearted and couldn't bear to see someone else suffering. He was constantly doing something for someone. I can remember going home from school and telling Dad of some poor kid who never got any candy in her lunch and didn't have any money to buy any. Result: the next day that little girl would have some candy bars. Just anything to bring someone any little amount of happiness or joy. He'd feed the tramps that came to the door, give them clothes, just anything. Nothing was ever too much if it meant happiness for someone else.

"At this 'elite' school I'd attended I took a course in clothing. I liked clothes and I liked pretty things and I was anxious to make things that I could wear. But I just kept thinking about how I didn't dare let myself hate the woman my Dad married. After all, our Lord didn't hate the people responsible for His death. In His dying moments He could only find forgiveness. So to tell myself that I had to be a good Christian was a problem because I felt hateful to this woman and yet I didn't want to feel this way. And I believe that I can sincerely say that I tried to overcome these feelings but they just persisted. Anyway, in the entire clothing course I made three things for myself and all the rest of my sewing was done for this woman. She liked beautiful things too and I'd pick my materials from her favorite color—orchid—and make things for her to wear. She simply could not appreciate anything I did. I just felt it was a lost cause.

"One more point. Before I ran away from home the second time and when I felt there was just no use in living I still had God on my mind. I was in church every Sunday from before the time I ever walked. My Dad and Grandmother took me. Then when I could walk, my cousin Carl and I would walk to the church each Sunday. All those years of church and Sunday School didn't really teach me much about God. The extent of my knowledge of religion was that there was a God. He was supposed to have loved and died for all people. We should hate no one because God loved them all. God was a loving Father who didn't want His children to hurt or be hurt. And then we always got how much He specially loved children. Mary belonged to the Christmas story and that was the end of her. For sixteen years of living, this is about all I could tell you of my faith. So, after I'd taken all the beatings, etc., that I could possibly stand, I was sure that this loving God we'd heard so much about wasn't really loving at all. If He loved children like He said, then He'd never let all this happen to me. If He was the all-powerful Person He was supposed to be, then He could change all these things if He really cared. I decided to tell Him that night after my regular prayers that I did not ever again intend to pray to Him. And I well remember the things I said. It might go something like this. Incidentally, the night I said all this I was kneeling on a chair, my arms propped on the window sill of my bedroom window as I gazed into the star-twinkled sky with my heart heavy.

"'I wonder if you're really there, God. I wonder if You can really hear me. Do you know what I'm telling You? Do you even care? I can answer that. You're not a loving Father and You don't care. If you're really there, how could You let all this happen? Yet I know that someone had to put all those stars up there. All this stuff in the world had to have a beginning somewhere. I don't know who it is, but I don't think it's You. In fact, I don't believe in You. I don't think You really exist at all. And yet, if You don't exist, how can I be talking to You? I don't really know if You're there or not, but just in case You are, let me tell You this. I hate You. I hate every bone in Your Body. You're mean. You can be so complacent in Your heaven, but You don't care what happens to some of us down here. So why should I even bother to talk to You? Well I won't any more. You'll never hear from me again. I hate You, I hate You, I hate You. So long God.'

"The crazy part of all this was that the next night I was back on my knees with the same ritualistic prayer—'Now I lay me down to sleep, etc.'

"The day of my arrival at M —— in August of ——, the social worker rang the doorbell and we were greeted by Sr. H. I hadn't said much on the couple of hours drive to the school just because I had nothing to say. I felt that I was being punished for something I never did. I felt my parents should be the ones to be punished. This just wasn't justice. However, at the same time, I was glad to get away from that woman. I felt let out of a cage. As Sister let us in the door the very first thing that struck my eye was a statue of Mary in the center of the hall. I looked at this nun—never saw one before—and then at the statue, back to the nun again and said, 'Just don't try to teach me any of your religion because I don't worship statues.' She explained that they didn't either but that just as I had snapshots to remind me of those I love so they had statues to remind them of these holy people. It made sense but I'd just never heard of it that way before. We then proceeded to the parlor. I sat across the room from her because I didn't trust her. She was just too darn nice. These were the kind who tried to rope you into their religion and once they had you there was no escape. They put you into dark dungeons and beat you with whips (might have been a change from yardsticks). Then this Sister said she was sorry but they just would not be able to give me all the comforts and luxuries I had at home. This did it. Again, my bold front was gone as I broke into tears and said, 'I don't want comforts and luxuries. All I want is happiness.' And Sister responded with 'Well if that's all you want, I think we can give you that.' That was music to my ears, but I still wasn't going to trust anyone.

People were not sincere. They were always finding ways to corner and trap you just to gain their own selfish ends.

"Day after day went by and I was most observant. These women wearing brown baggy things and white clotheslines really intrigued me. They were different, but I couldn't figure out what it was. Most of the girls who went to the school felt like they were put into prison and confined. I felt like I was let out of prison and could go wild. These nuns just let me do anything I wanted. She just said that she believed the girls should make their own decisions as long as they were not morally wrong. She felt that, even if their decisions may not always have been the wisest, it was good for them to get their noses bumped once in a while too. Guess this was learning. Since some of the girls—in fact most of the girls—felt they were being jailed, they weren't always nice to the nuns and this just killed me. I really got to love these people. It was always a mystery to me how they could give up homes and children of their own to take care of brats like us. Not considering the heavenly reward, there surely was nothing for them to gain by all this. Those nuns were so kind to me that if they told me to go hang by my feet from a 30-story building I'd have done it. I'd do anything for them. It took me a long time though before I realized that they were even a little bit human. I didn't think they slept, ate, cared for any personal needs, just nothing that we humans do. I wasn't even sure they were flesh and bone. I thought they were all an offspring of angels or some heavenly body. And they never got mad. The kids could do absolutely anything, say anything and they'd just humbly take it all. It was hard for me to understand and I really couldn't make much sense out of it. It was a mystery.

"In religion classes I sat, pretending to hold my ears shut. Since you had to have some credits in religion to graduate from a Catholic school, I had to go to class but was told that I didn't have to believe it if I didn't want to. Well, I didn't want to. We all had to attend Mass on Sunday but we were told that we didn't have to follow the priest. We could say our own prayers. So, before I got to any religion classes I'd seen what a Mass was like. I wanted to laugh out loud but then, in another way, I felt sorry for these poor foolish people. They didn't know if they should sit, stand, or kneel. And how ridiculous for a man to wear a lace slip! And then they used some 'stinky' powder at the end of Mass to drive the devil out of us. It was all very mysterious. So, due to pure curiosity, I was really listening in those religion classes because I was hoping to find out what all their superstitious beliefs were. Lo and behold! Everything they said really made sense and I was filled with questions by the millions, and couldn't ask them fast enough—but not of the religion teacher; I wasn't going to let her think I was interested. After school I'd go to my directress and ask her everything.

"By the end of two weeks in this school I went to see Sr. H. to ask her permission to take instructions. This had to be without my parents' knowledge, but she said they didn't have to know. So for my two years there I attended private instruction classes each Saturday morning. By the end of my first year there I just felt I could never wait another year before entering the Church, but the school had a rule that no girl there could come into the Church unless there was Catholicity in her family. And I could understand their position but I didn't like it. So I figured I'd devise my own way of doing things.

"The summer between my Jr. and Sr. years I pleaded to work during the summer. Sister couldn't see any point in it since I had absolutely no need of money. Dad sent me an allowance and I just had everything I needed. But I pleaded trying to tell Sister that I just wanted to be independent and know that my money was my own. She said if I could find the job I could go to work. So to the Employment Agency I went and to work a week later. I got a secretarial job in the office of one of the large department stores. I never ate lunch. I spent the first couple of days visiting a Catholic Church which had perpetual adoration.

"From there I planned further. I became acquainted with a woman in a religious book store and asked her if she knew any priest who would baptize me and she recommended a priest friend of hers from one of the Catholic hospitals. The following noon found me on a city bus enroute to the hospital. What a disappointment when I arrived only to find that he wasn't in. But, I'd try again tomorrow. However, I didn't have to wait until tomorrow for that afternoon a priest walked into the office looking for the woman for whom I worked. I idolized priests and nuns and would run blocks out of my way just to talk to one. I went right up to this priest to ask if I could be of any assistance and to ask his name. When he told me I just said, 'Thanks, God.' I made an appointment for the following day, and when I went to see him I told him of the rule of the school, but also how I wanted so desperately to be received into the Church. He said that, since the school was under the auspices of the Catholic Charities, he couldn't do this without some authorization but that he would come out to the school and talk with the sisters. He did but I knew it would be of no avail. We went to the chapel to pray, but I just couldn't. This was the only thing that I wanted in all the world and nothing else mattered. He said he'd lead the prayers and I should answer. But when my turn came, all I could do was cry. And all this was making me more determined than ever. I went to daily Mass while in attendance at the school. How much I wanted to receive the Sacrament!

"So many nice and wonderful things happened during these two years at the school but I guess I cannot write everything. This would never get finished. I went home for holidays and could never wait to get back."

This girl obviously was being slowly but surely drawn toward the Catholic church as to a refuge, a haven from suffering, a true home at last. She had suffered 18 years from parental mistreatment and utter lack of affection. Meantime she kept up her Sunday devotions but her faith in God must have dwindled to a new all-time low just around the time that she entered the new school.

Her subsequent history is one of persistent battles, not only with her parents but also with the authorities in the church of her choice. The latter would not take her into their fold because of her dependence upon her parents for support. The former continued to make threats of disowning her forever, if she should join the Catholic church. Finally during the summer of her graduation from high school, she got a good job, boldly told her parents of her decision, and bid farewell to her proud but unyielding parents, never, as they then said, to see them again. The step-mother actually never did accept the fact of the girl's conversion. The father did, some 15 years later, seek to contact the girl and assured her of his continual love and admiration of her.

7 necessary means for religious growth: penance and suffering

INTRODUCTION

WE HAVE considered the process of conversion as one in which a person learns to accept himself, but together with the need to make a change of some kind. As a result, it is equally important that he be willing to accept the new kind of self, the self he will be after the change. There is, of course, always the continuity of the self throughout the change and, because of this sameness, it was possible to have motives guiding and strengthening oneself throughout the process. The basic fact that a person needs strength gives the cue for discussing penance and self-denial. While grace and sacraments undeniably aid materially in conquest of the higher virtues and in arriving at a more perfect self, still it is permissible to seek out the natural psychological manner in which self-conquest aids in perfecting the self.

The term *repentance* will be used to indicate that a change has been made from a less perfect way of life; then penance and self-discipline would be at once a means leading one to the change, predisposing him to the same, and they would be also powerful helps in assuring the continuance of the change. The change, it should be recalled, might be in some externally observable action, in an interior motive or act, and in all possible combinations of these. With the recollection of the totality and unity within the functioning of all the powers of a man, it is seen that sometimes the change would involve virtually all of the powers of the man in some way at least. It is, then, not inaccurate to state that the man is changed totally when he is converted, and that when he prepares for the change, or persists in it, his self-conquest is, in some sense, a conquest of the total self rather than simply a victory over an undesirable aspect or inclination of the self. The same might be illustrated by simple examples, such as the overcoming of a habit of swearing. Spiritual thinkers have already written admirably on the value of mortification, and one thing they never fail to stress is the fact that some mortification or self-denial is absolutely indispensable for perseverance in the spiritual life. Perhaps the reason for this can somehow be explained as in the following paragraph. The explanation will not be restricted to the self-initiated or self-sought type of penance and suffering. It will rather include the total composite of the inevitable sufferings and hardships which a man will have to undergo by the very process of living. These too may have some psychological bearing upon the development of that ego-strength which is necessary for healthy adjustment and which is also an added support for the growth of the more perfect total human being.

MEANING OF PENANCE

Penance may be defined here as the acceptance, deliberately or otherwise, of some hardship for the sake of some good. The necessary ills which confront human beings in everyday living will be included under the heading of penance or of penitential acts. Obviously what would be needed to justify such an inclusion would be the intention to suffer such hardships. Hence penance is similar to suffering though different in scope. Suffering is taken to mean the experience of sickness, trials and hardships. Inevitable ills and hardships stemming from the very fact of human existence are included; in addition, there are sufferings which one deliberately imposes upon himself for a motive. This discussion will include all such voluntary and involuntary sufferings; penitential acts which result in sufferings are included as, for example, fasting; yet it is not our purpose to limit the discussion to such forms of self-conquest as cause bodily pain.

There is a kind of penitential spirit which is entirely distinct from the mere inflicting of bodily pain.

It will be apparent, as the discussion proceeds, that in any of these experiences of suffering the individual person can and will in some manner be developing tolerance of some sort for a modicum of affliction and may, in addition, add to his power of sustaining sufferings by a special kind of religious orientation and motivation. Moreover, there must be a clear distinction made between that kind of suffering which seems to be sought for its own sake, as in Yoga and other phenomena dealing with tolerance of pain, and the kind which is but a means to some higher end or purpose. In either case, it might be noted at the outset, the thing known as suffering, considered as a privation of suitable perfection, is apt to be looked upon as an evil.

To avoid becoming entangled in the endless debate regarding the purpose and nature of evil, the sufferings considered in this chapter will be looked upon as being, of their very natures, *means,* which are capable of being used for some other end. That is, suffering here is not at all to be considered either good or bad in itself. It is studied psychologically only in its possible role of serviceability to the total man, of becoming a cue or foundation stone for the development of other psychological states which are both healthy and sound. Sufferings and pains are not, then, to be treated as ends in themselves, nor as being mere negations. Pain can be found to have a purpose even on the biological level, namely, to signal danger. But pain and suffering are here portrayed as being capable of serving man also in his aim toward building up a strong and resistant total personality, which can be healthy on the purely natural plane, and which can, in that case, also be elevated to higher degrees of perfection by means of the other aids consequent upon religious exercises and voluntary intentions.

SUFFERING AND PAIN COMPARED

In psychology, pain is classified with the sensations, because it arises by a damaging stimulation to any living tissue, by cuts and by bruises, by electric shocks, and by too strong stimulations on any of the sensory organs of the body. Thus some pain will be the inevitable lot of a sensory organism, and as a general rule, people tend to avoid pain as much as possible. But, it could hardly be asserted, as have some theorists, that in deliberately seeking to experience pain, a person would always have as a motive self-blame or condemnation for some one of his acts. Of course, it might happen that the accidental experience of pain could be connected with some pleasing sensation, such as touch, and then a kind of inversion of the order might take place, and the person would seek pain rather than try to avoid it. This is entirely in agreement with the statement that pain can be treated as in itself neutral, but as serviceable for some goal. That goal might even be one of self-condemnation, which intention might come to take possession of the mind of the person to such an extent that he forgets all other motives. This would be the morbid sense of self-blame which may be found among mentally ill persons. But it does not follow that all human beings engage in the pursuit of suffering and voluntarily inflict pain upon themselves solely because they have committed the unpardonable sin, or because they have masochistic tendencies. Penance through pain and suffering can contribute to the elevation of the human mind toward a higher kind of life than that of the sense. This goal is accomplished by joining the thought of suffering to that of strength, and by accepting forgiveness for our failings with the need to make a better response the next time there is a trial; the improved response can be prepared for in advance by vicarious and voluntarily self-inflicted pain and suffering. When pain is accepted in this spirit it leads to the strengthening of the total person, and for this reason it is deemed essential in the lives of the saints.

That a person adds to or subtracts from the amount of pain connected with everyday experiences by his own efforts can be verified by comparing children with adults. It is a fact of experience that older persons suffer more from the very same kind of damaging stimulus than would an infant. This, experts in sensory psychology tell us, may be due to the fact that the adult adds to the magnitude of the pain because of expectation. Again, the effect of attitude and attention upon the actual experience of pain is shown by the fact that the adult may even experience a cut in a finger happening so suddenly that no pain at all is experienced; this will occur only in case the attention of the person is so diverted to other things that the stimulus is not noticed at all when it strikes. Therefore the intention and inner state of the individual determine the total outcome of the experiences of suffering and pain.

EXPECTATION AND PAIN

The mere existence of pain and its evaluation by a human being may involve many other features, associations and complications than sensory ones. Adults quite commonly experience fear, anxiety and insecurity at the prospect of pain. This emotion is connected with the reasoning given in the first chapter: from birth each man knows that he is going to die, that he must suffer, that he needs some support to carry on against all the forces which will continually oppose his progress and threaten his very existence. Pain and suffering may also lead to fears and depressions, although there does not seem to be any intrinsic reason why depression should follow more from pain than from any other kind of unpleasant experience in life. Just how a man will react to the prospect of suffering is largely a matter of his own inner attitude and preparation. It is true that the great mystics learned to tolerate enormous amounts of pain. Did they enjoy it as some would believe? The answer would have to come from the mystics themselves. While they were going through the dark night of the senses, of the soul and of the spirit, they obviously did not enjoy it. Perhaps the expectation of the cessation of pain is a source of satisfaction. This consideration again involves the goals and motives of a person. Ultimate happiness is surely the strongest and most persistent of all human motivation systems. Applied to the question of suffering, it means that one can diminish the intensity of the experienced ills now and add to his strength to bear up under them by keeping constantly before his mind what he may expect after the trials are over. This is the psychological basis for the fact that pain strengthens the ego.

Certain reminders can be beneficial in acquiring and preserving the right, healthy attitude toward pain. These reminders can console sick persons, and help them to tolerate or even lessen their pain when they are ill. They will lead the thoughts of the sufferer to use aids which only each individual will recognize as best for him to help him attain some of the goals of suffering. There is the model which is Christ. There is also the motive that distraction can lessen or relieve the pain. Finally the sufferer usually is encouraged to learn that, by facing up to pain, his tolerance increases and this adds to his total ego-strength, his readiness to face new hardships.

Sufferings and trials of various sorts do not always conduce to ego-strength. Sometimes they generate doubts, diffidence, and distress; even worse, when the light of faith is dim, hope dwindles, and a person can slip gradually into a state of depression and desolation. Probably those who apply themselves a good deal to religious exercises will feel these mood swings more frequently than others, although they are certainly not their ordinary experiences.

As a result of the above and similar considerations, most spiritual writers and some authors of psychologies of religion today specify three kinds of religious experiences, ranging from the most intense and warm feelings of union with God ever-present, down through the ordinary, monotonous, dim and dull awareness of the realities of faith. In each level of religious experiences there are wide ranges of experiences of the value of pain and suffering. The deeply religious person can and does show a willingness to suffer without becoming morbid or a "sick-soul" in the sense of William James. Extremes of suffering and mortification, self-imposed for a higher end, rarely lead to morbidity. Contrariwise, it would only be at the risk of great misunderstanding that one would attempt to identify "healthy-mindedness" with the absence of suffering and of mortification. Yet several authors in the field try to do just this.

The important feature of suffering, then, is the motive for it and the manner in which it is borne. As far as the value of accepted or self-inflicted pain is concerned, for increasing one's total perfection, for bringing him closer to the ideal of the self which he is trying to actuate—this will depend upon his total system of motivation. After a person has somewhat immunized himself, through patience and tolerance for pain, he finds that he is able to accomplish things which would have been impossible for him without such preparation. There may or may not be a biological foundation for this strengthening; there surely is a psychological foundation. Because the life urge is so strong within men, any discomfort calls out a tendency to avoid what causes discomfort, and to flee from that which causes harm. That is equivalent to the biological basis for the kind of strengthening discussed here. As for the proof of its existence, one must read the writings of the sufferers themselves and then accept them as true; both the biological and the psychological resistance to invading forces which would upset the well-being of the organism stems from the basic quality of life itself, namely, its urge for subsistence. Some spiritual considerations can be added to those already given to show the value of suffering for strengthening the ego. When a person has followed the commandments from early childhood, and has gone through life enhancing his own religious life and increasing in the perfection of his higher spiritual life, he is indeed motivated on the highest plane to be able to incorporate trials and sufferings into his scheme of behavior. Examples of voluntarily inflicted penances and mortifications can be listed showing that even young children grasp the true meaning and value of suffering, as for example, St. John Bosco's description of St. Dominic Savio:

> In regard to the mortification of all his senses, I shall restrict myself to a few incidents. In winter-time he had a novel way of treating his hands, for he was subject to chilblains, and these he exposed to the cold and wet as much as he could, so as to increase their size and painfulness; he even pricked them to make them smart the more. He thought that he was thus imitating, in a small degree, the wounds inflicted on the person of our Divine Lord. His companions assert that in the very cold weather he went along slowly to school, so as to be exposed to the weather as much as possible.[1]

1 St. John Bosco, *The Life of Dominic Savio*. London: Salesian Press, 1914.

The attitude toward pain seems to be a kind of indicator of the amount of strength that one has available for meeting emergencies. Could this be the explanation for the fact that people quite commonly think that toleration for discomfort strengthens against further suffering? That it even immunizes from further pain somewhat after the manner of an antigen in biology?

PAIN AND REPARATION

There are psychologists who seem to think that all forms of self-blame lead to morbid guilt feelings, self-condemnation and all manner of unhealthy complexes. Still others think that any person who is willing to suffer with Christ, or for another human being, must be afflicted with a delusion that he is the Messias. A word here may do much to clarify the situations which lead to statements like the above. It is obviously one thing to blame yourself because you accept the fact that you injured someone else. It is quite another thing to feel blame for something, you know not what, nor how you came to be in such a state. The former can be a healthy activity on the part of any human being who realizes that he is not all-perfect; he accepts blame for some specified acts of his which had an effect on others. For other acts he also accepts praise, which he knows to be due to such acts. When a person remains aware of his own need for both praise and blame, when he reflects on his own strengths and weaknesses, he is not likely to be morbidly accusing himself of the unpardonable sin, of being the missing murderer, etc.

Similarly, when a loving mother identifies herself with her child, and sees the little one writhing in pain, she too participates, by reason of her strong identification, in the real pain of her child. Such vicarious suffering with and for another is the natural consequence of being social entities. It is a far cry from that kind of delusional process wherein the patient in his own estimation actually is the Messias. Having become the Savior, he feels a real need for a self-punishment which would make reparation for the sins of the world. The trouble here is that he is also the old self. This is the split which is avoided in the healthy-minded sufferer we have been describing. The normal self-immolator, the man who elects to do penance, to suffer hardship that another may benefit from the act, never quite loses sight of the fact that he remains himself too. In other words, there is a normal process of identification with another, in which self is not dissociated. Psychiatrists and religious workers could both well afford to aim at keeping the religious person an intact self, while he goes on with his rigorous acts of mortification and reparation for others.

The above sketch of the dangers inherent in religious dedication ought to help clarify another point. The thought of suffering, far from being a negative something, is a very positive benefit. Through suffering, or the anticipation of suffering, the zealous person, well-grounded in faith, hope and charity and in the practice of religion, welcomes a life of hardship and suffering, not for itself alone, nor for the mere prestige of being able to boast about his great tolerance for torture; rather he accepts pain and privations for their positive value. This value consists, first, in a strengthening of the ego of the person suffering; and then in its being a stepping-stone toward greater and greater perfection, greater dedication of the self to the cause of the Creator, greater annihilation of the self so that the cause of Christ may prevail, that all men may be brought to God for their own justification and final salvation.

There is a faint beginning of this desire to accept suffering engendered in the children of Catholic parents, who learn when they prepare for their first Holy Communion that it is their duty to share. They know, perhaps vaguely at first, that this willingness to share includes the easy and the hard, the good and the bad. They know this too when it comes time for their Confirmation, and the sharp blow on the face delivered by the bishop reminds them of suffering. Their strength will grow apace with every exercise of choice. The self-discipline which they will see urged upon them at every level of life has its effect gradually; the end result should be, in the divine plan, an individual purified in the Blood of the Lamb, strengthened with the Bread of Angels, ripe for heaven as his own much hoped-for destiny. If at times the hardships imposed by religion seem almost unbearable, due to the endless sacrifices, confessions, etc., then a man needs to reflect upon the meaning of suffering and mortification. Catholics get ample reminders four times a year, and more conspicuously at Lent and Advent. Their group participation helps strengthen their motives, and their very use of sacraments and sacramentals, prayer and ritual remind them of the need to diminish self. Religion without self-conquest and self-immolation could hardly endure.

REASONS BASIC TO THE NEED OF SELF-IMMOLATION

Every human being is endowed with a basic tendency to sustain himself in existence. Any threat to existence is warded off as effectively as possible by an inadvertent or even unconscious act. Many names have been given to this tendency. There seems little need to postulate the opposite tendency, namely, to put oneself out of existence, a death instinct. Some theorists demand this instinct so that their systems will not lack that harmony possessed by the theories in physical science, and they assert that where there is a positive attracting force there must also be a negative or repelling force to balance it. Cases of self-destruction have been observed in animals, yet no human being can ascertain the motives for their actions. Human beings persist, when normal, in their desire to resist any force that would put them out of existence; when they fail to throw off the invading organism, death may be the result; but if they can they do resist. On occasion, there is self-destruction which arises either in the morbid mentality, and is thus scarcely voluntary, or is the result of despair or some other positive motive such as spite. Yet striving to maintain oneself in existence, to be healthy, and to experience a basic sense of well-being are admittedly experiences of everyone.

Under panic situations, one's striving may be so violent that he actually does bring injury or even death upon himself. This seems to be due to the fact that, in the first moments of panic, one reacts purely reflexly, and thus does not foresee the consequences of his act. Hardly anyone would admit, when he has almost killed himself during a panic that he actually sought to harm himself. His whole impulse is to go, to act somehow; not having time to initiate voluntary movements, he actually does harm to himself and others very often. This merely shows that the life-urge is strong and even blind.

If then there is an urge to survive and be healthy, there is also a tendency to improve oneself; this is related to the instinct mentioned in children, to accomplish things, and to get joy out of creative activity. So if an instinct impels one to stay alive and to perfect himself, this means that there will have to be redirection of his efforts when he has gone wrong, or when he has initiated habit systems which do not lead to the perfection which he seeks. Having detected such habit systems, one blames himself for them and tries to change them. Thus that amount of self-discipline which will be needed to reinforce the change will be a minimum that is required. In other words, there is a basis in human nature, striving for subsistence and perfection of self, for one's doing something of violence to himself. There is need of directed effort to bring about any permanent change. Such self-direction is not easy and one prepares himself for the same by self-conquest, exercising himself in the power of self-direction.

EFFECTS OF MORTIFICATION

What does mortification actually do for a person psychologically? This is not easy to answer. For one thing, it reminds one of his own state of imperfection, of his need for striving for further perfection. It sets his mind in the direction of being willing to make effort; and there is also the knowledge that this effort will profit the individual in adding strength to the total ego. It ought not to be said that the aim of suffering is to mortify the passions. The passions are good in themselves, being tendencies to their own proper acts. If they have been disordered, or have acquired strong tendencies which are at odds with the higher strivings and goals of the individual, then they need re-ordering, re-integration. Whatever other purpose may be served, it should not be claimed that one can kill the passions by means of mortifications and acts of self-denial. By means of self-inflicted sufferings and voluntary acceptance of hardships, a person exercises his power of self-direction, of bringing the passions into the desired harmony with other powers of man.

The psychological basis for mortification is the fact that man possesses higher and lower powers which must be kept in their proper order if the whole man is to be made perfect. There is the fact of original sin, which gives rise to a still more disordered condition among the powers of human beings. The passions are even more rebellious than they would otherwise have been, simply because of original sin. The need for self-conquest is therefore based upon the fact of a diversity of powers in man and the historical fact of a deordination having been acquired following the acts of man.

Union

TRANSITION

In faith one accepts a truth on the authority of God; in hope one relies on His promises, His friendship; in love one learns to share, to give up that which he treasures, to make others happy. One must submit to some kind of discomfort all through life, by the very fact that he is losing power with increasing age.

In the experience of conversion one sees himself needing a change, and, accepting the fact of imperfection, he strives for greater perfection. In penance he tries to strengthen his ego in spite of the deteriorations due to age, so that the "new man" may not weaken under stress. In love and union with God one confirms and consolidates all his efforts so that God lives now in him in a new and intimate way.

In every human striving there is an element of love. The loved object, a person for example, gives direction to striving, and by so doing it helps to integrate one's efforts. Thus the striving for a goal which is desired and loved, the process of being directed by this loved object and of being integrated in one's efforts in regard to the loved object seem to be all inter-related. Love is in some way an initiator of action, a director and a harmonizer. Even Sorokin, a purely naturalistic writer on love, claims that love on its highest level is a going out of oneself, a relinquishing of selfhood, a union with another, which helps to make the lover at the same time unselfish and inwardly integrated. After describing the great altruists, Ghandi and Assisi, as to their observable behavior, he seems to say: this is what love can really do for a man.

Natural love is merely the attraction one feels for any object, regardless of the reason or motive. St. Thomas says that the initial attraction will always be aroused by some goodness in the object. The person being attracted is not always aware of the real nature of this goodness, while he is aware of the motive for his love, namely, the love of God Whose image is the creature. From revelation and reason it is known how valuable sacrifice is as a proof of love for another person. The natural attraction one feels is not a denial of the supernatural; rather, both are harmoniously interrelated. In the most perfect love of God one eliminates the self motive entirely, and that could hardly be done without the aid of supernatural graces. This discussion will proceed as much as possible on the purely natural level. Just as there is a natural religion, a natural love of the good, so there is a natural love of God and a natural striving after the perfection of self through the love of God and the neighbor. The supernatural does not destroy the natural; it perfects and sustains it. This holds true in regard to all the virtues; there is a natural goodness, charity, justice and love. These natural virtues are the foundation upon which the infused supernatural virtues can be built.

Thus in trying to describe the highest form of love and union to which human lovers attain, union with God and fellow man, one is not committed to the task of saying just what the causes are and how they operate at each level of human development and striving. In their behavior, people act as if love united them to one another, as well as to a higher reality or Person.

LOVE AS AN INNER INTEGRATING PRINCIPLE

After an attraction is set up in one for an object, for instance, a particular person, then his actions toward this person take on a new character. This person is select in the sense that he occupies one's mind and his attention more than other persons. Because he is so much in the focus of one's loving attention, he is able to exert a pressure, or a pull upon the other; he makes the other want to go out to him, both personally and with tokens or gifts which speak for one personally. Thus by means of the direction which is taken by one's affection for this person, one's efforts and aspirations are integrated in a new way around the attributes of this person. One is made to move, imperceptibly at first, more in his direction. The same can occur with regard to loved inanimate objects. If one likes coffee rather than tea, then the mere suggestion of coffee arouses a secret movement inside him toward coffee, not toward other beverages. Love as liking is at the bottom of all striving because of the nature of human wills. They spontaneously go out only after the good in objects, nothing else.

The primary inclination arose because the good was loved, that is, it attracted one to it. One was pulled, and it did the pulling. One was pushed in the sense that he could not help being pulled as soon as the value appeared. This double aspect of love is easily overlooked. It is not just a push from inside. The inner aspect of the movement indicates the gyroscope or director; nor it it just a pull—the outer aspect signals the goal or good to be striven for. This outer aspect also gives direction but only insofar as it is interpreted by the inner organizer, the evaluator, which is intelligence. Now the meanings of those two terms, subjective and objective, can be grasped as applied to motivation. The good outside one as perceived by one is the objective motive or value. The particular quality of this good which always attaches to one's own individual thinking about that object is one's subjective motive, his conscience guide.

With this explanation it ought to be easy to see how the love-process can both direct striving and integrate it into a meaningful whole. If both the push from within and the pull from without are focused on the same object, then there is little cause for tension or discord. But if the inner bent is toward one thing, say communism as an easy way of life, and if the outer pull is exerted by Christianity which attracts because it is a rationally conceived right manner of living, then one may experience conflict of motives. It seems obvious, from the example, that multitudinous causes for conflict exist and that man will gain inner peace and harmony of living only insofar as he can face and resolve most of these conflicts. Conflicts, then, relate to and belong to our natures simply because of the fact that we may be striving toward opposites which cannot both be reached at the same time, or because we are not directed toward any one unifying valued object at all, but rather strive randomly, in a sort of chaotic fashion, for any first-noticed kind of good. In both cases, that of chaotic striving and that of seeking to enjoy contrary goods at the same time, one will do well to distinguish the real source of the disharmony, the beginning of a kind of disintegration. That will usually be found in a push from within toward one object, say coffee or Jane, and a pull from without initiated by tea or Joan. One easy remedy for the conflictual situation would be to substitute a third object, neither coffee nor tea, which would then have a more unifying effect upon our desires, for instance, cocoa; or some third person, rather than either Jane or Joan.

Love is a powerful motive because it permits happiness to be shared. Love has such a strong power to push and pull partly as a result of the fact that it is a principle or source of action generally. And it is a cause of action not only by initiating activity, but also by guiding the whole course of the action and by integrating the part processes involved in the love relation. The battery of an auto acts as energy source for turning the starter as well as for supplying a flame to ignite the gas. It does not ordinarily direct the flow of energy; a distributor does that. The man at the steering wheel picks out the road. Love in an analogous way does all these things, and thus it is both an energizer and a satisfier. When one considers love in its character of energy producer, or activity drive, or push, then it is a motive or a moving power. Love or the love object could just as well be called the anticipated outside attraction, the motive considered as an incentive; more accurately it is the goal toward which one strives. The loved object motivates striving only insofar as it is apprehended, interpreted as having something of goodness about it. However, the actual attainment or possession of the object itself is the goal of the striving. The known good features of the goal object which attract one toward it are the motives; and when motives are strong enough, they may impel one almost to achieve things otherwise impossible.

Systems of human motivation are rarely simple; rather often they are subtle and almost always complex, manifold, or heterogeneous. Their complex character may now be described. The approval one expects from others in his immediate family group serves to motivate him. If one's family likes cocktails before meals and he wants to be accepted by his immediate family, he also develops a liking for cocktails before meals. The approval of one's national group motivates him. If his fellow citizens consider it stylish to wear slacks, he tends to think likewise. Finally, motives spring from one's own inner self-determination. Thus one secretly likes to enjoy his cold shower every morning in spite of possible social disapproval. Yet in all such activities the real problem of love has not been considered.

When an object of love is a person rather than a drink or a garment, then there is a reciprocal relation set up whenever you as a person act in response to the other person. If the other likes sherry and you do too, then you both have something in common. If the other loves you greatly and you like sherry, the other also tends to move toward sherry. This is the reciprocity referred to in personal relations. If, finally, you show that you are very happy in the other's presence only, or for the most part, then the other is happy just because you are. This is a kind of spiritual sharing which tends to unite persons more and more to each other. It does not require wealth or fame in order to experience this sharing. It requires only mutual appreciation and understanding, one for another. This social aspect of a man is one that is not easy to describe. Sorokin does not get at its real essence in his treatises on altruism, for it is a deeper kind of personal relation than he thinks. It tends to carry people on, so that they want to share with one another not only joys but sorrows, not only work but play. It is a potent source of human motivation, the sharing of human happiness, yet it is not quite the ultimate. No other person can completely fill the need each one has for shared happiness. Each one needs an ultimate. Each individual tends to create one, whether it be the service of man in humanitarian projects, or love of God in true satisfying union and bliss.

However strong the motive of human love may be, there still remains the fear of its coming to an end, the danger that some-thing might arise which will spoil the relation. Supporting indeed is the love and union while it lasts. What else can a poor human being hope for? Religion can give him an answer. The undying and fully requiting love of our divine Friend, Creator, Redeemer, and Sanctifier, is promised to each and every one of us. This love motive predominates over fear of the justice of God, for the same reason that love in human relations is often a more powerful motive than fears and doubts. Yet both fear and love seem part of the complex motivational schemes which sustain the actions of men. Love rather than fear would predispose men to go on sharing their assets with their fellow man. Love, and never fear, can be the basis of a permanently abiding friendly relation between one person and another, between God and creature. For love of God, man can strive all his life, because he is endowed with a need and desire to go back to God, and he will not rest until it be accomplished.

ALLURING BUT IMPERFECT MOTIVES MAY BLOCK

Motives for action are far from being perfect. One easily satisfies himself by means of lesser values, since they give him temporary contentment, partial happiness. One of these is the motive to share all with some other fellow human being. If this person should happen to die before you, then your motive dis-appears and you are helpless, hopeless, momentarily lost.

Another motive which allures a great many people, one which has and always will have many admirers, is the motive of wealth. Who has not seen the lives of otherwise well-meaning individuals suddenly ruined by an inordinate pursuit of wealth? The pages of history show what miseries can be brought into the lives of men when they substitute a love of wealth for a love and sharing with human beings. The blockage in human strivings which comes from being attached to the money-motive seems to arise because of the difficulty in sharing. Fiction tells us of miserly characters, Scrooges who really felt that money was a part of themselves so that they could not share it. Rather they should have known that love demands reciprocity, and that in real love the sharing of oneself with another gives greater joy than sharing wealth. Money cannot give back anything but money, while in human love the lovers share their whole personality with one another.

Could a striving for social approval, for power and fame, be an ultimate motive, one which secures perfect happiness? Again, it is a powerful motive for action, but its reward, the satisfaction, is purely temporary. Apart from the close inter-personal and deep understanding and appreciation for a dearly loved person, there is no enduring social approval short of that given for divinely sanctioned behavior. Today some behavior may be all the rage, tomorrow it is condemned; as, for example, style of dress, or language, or political bent. Are there any goals which can be thought of which human beings strive for that are guaranteed to make them happy and secure? Money and fame are transitory, to be sure. Peace of mind can be permanent for the man who trusts in God. The real value of gaining a fortune and of preserving one's good name is obvious. They can both be used to further the happiness and contentment of others. Only when these goals become ultimate do they become obstacles to further progress in self-perfection. When they are sought beyond all bounds, they cripple and cramp the personality. They are now ends rather than means for human happiness, easily sidetracking a person who seeks true and lasting happiness in religion. They even block the weakling in his very pursuit of a happy human relation. The person so blocked may be in serious need of expert counsel and direction.

PARTIAL SELF-ACTIVATION EASILY ATTAINED

The strivings of a human being tend to make him stronger and more perfect. They build, as was said, the self-structure and ego-strength by means of actualizing human potential. Each power or faculty will be perfected when exercised upon its proper objects: the eye by vision, the intellect by reasoning, and so on. But notice that the only faculty of man which is of and by itself directed toward the good is the will. Man's striving for separate and distinct goods in this life, his employment of his volition in the choice of satisfactory means for gaining immediate objectives, such as success in his work—these acts perfect the superior part of man and hence mean much more for humanity than acts, for example, of sensation or feeling. The actuation of the self obtained in the healthy use of any faculty is a partial attainment of the goal of human perfection. These partial attainments add to our strength, but they need the guidance and confirmation of a fuller and more complete kind of self-actuation. Such self-actuation does come through love, since this is the combined action of intellect and will and has reverberations throughout the total emotional self. By the use of all these powers man perfects his total self, but only by the correct or morally good use of the same does he prepare himself for ultimate total happiness with God.

LOVE AS COMPLETE SELF-ACTUATION ALONE GIVES STABILITY

To recapitulate, love can start a process of striving,[2] it can direct the course of action, and it can be the fruition or complete possession of the sought-for goal. If only immediate goals are sought, partial happiness results. The only ultimate and completely perfect grasp of happiness for men is in a permanent and fully stable possession of the joys of the Beatific Vision. This goal is the one God sets for all men, and He supplies ample means for our attaining it. The eternal joy of heaven in perfect possession of our love object is subject to no danger of loss, no fear of cessation.

Human loves, one for another, might be capable of attaining all the qualities described above with the exception of permanence. Nevertheless, with increase in the sharing of all goods between two people, there is a kind of stability in their strivings,

2 See footnote at end of this section.

one person leaning more or less upon the other. Religious psychology would encourage lovers to share more and more with each other, and thus to gain greater stability and security in life; but it also reminds lovers of the necessary insecurity of such an arrangement. After all it was designed by God for the fuller growth and perfection of His children, who were destined to go through a period of trial and probation before being allowed that ultimate crown of glory.

The means for assuring more perfect possession of love in and with God, our Father, are first the removal of disordered affections, i.e., repentance and permanent conversion, and secondly, the building of a higher and higher tower of self-strength and perfection in the choice of acts of unselfish virtue and self-conquest. Such deeds and habit systems within one go far toward stabilizing his love relations to his fellow man. They guarantee ultimate attainment of God's love in its ultimate perfection, because man has God's promise that this will be the case.

If certain recent developments in human social organizations have pointed to the possibility, even in this life, of sharing something of the eternal blessedness of heaven by means of altruistic sharing among human beings, the point is clear; men do need and strive for more shared happiness in the company of each other.

If man's natural powers are sufficient for him to gain some security in love and sharing with his fellow man, then he ought to use them for that purpose. Yet he ought never to forget that, in addition to his natural powers and talents, religion offers him priceless other aids in the way of sacraments and rituals. Moreover, it can be shown that for every specific kind of faculty which man possesses there is a corresponding new faculty on a higher plane given him by sanctifying grace, a new life principle which grows and develops within him.

The thought of how much stronger one's ego would be when permeated with this new life of grace, when ornamented and equipped with these new faculties, should also motivate toward love and the fulfillment of man's destiny.

THE FOUR-FOLD WAY OF ATTAINING UNION OR LOVE

Most people have read about the Ignatian Retreat or the book of the Spiritual Exercises; or they have heard about it, since it is referred to very often. These exercises are a set of rules and spiritual guides to a reform of one's life and they are sketched here briefly only as an aid to understanding the process of conversion, of growth in self-perfection and in total ego strength. The author of these exercises claims that if man performs the exercises in the prescribed way, if he cooperates with God and works at his problems seriously, when he comes to the close of his retreat, he will have experienced a true and genuine conversion. The exercises were designed so as to be made in 3 or 30 days, but each candidate was to go on making the exercises until he experienced conversion.

What would be the sign of the conversion? First, the person would have to go through a purgative way. Purgation entails the clear awareness of a man's dependent relation upon his Creator, and a deeply felt desire to amend his ways, wherever he has not lived up to God's expectation of the creature. Purgation, of course, is achieved by meditation on one's sins and on his ultimate end, which is God. In the course of meditation on the end of man and his right use of creatures, the retreatant strives, with the aid of grace, to purify himself from his sins and imperfections, to realize deeply his own littleness, with full recognition of his true value, in the sight of God. He tries to understand precisely what God requires of him and to evaluate his own actions in terms of following the Divine Will in all things.

The second stage is called the way of conformity. It consists in meditating upon man's model which is Christ, in learning to know Him, the Leader, more intimately, to love Him more ardently and to follow Him more closely. The life of Christ, of course, as seen in the Gospels, is studied intensely. Christ becomes one to whom we must conform, whom we must follow, if we want to attain our end in life for sure. The humility and poverty of Christ are chief topics for meditation.

The third way is the sorrowful journey in company with Christ through the various scenes of His Passion. Here the retreatant considers the role of suffering, especially in the life of the God-Man and, by means of a deep appreciation and empathic identification with Christ, his Redeemer, he is able to confirm the resolutions made in the first two ways and to look forward hopefully to the future. Through imitation and consideration of his Model, Christ the Redeemer, with all the perfection inherent in the human-divine nature of Christ, the retreatant grows in strength in order to make a real reformation of his own life. In the fourth week the exercitant contemplates the joys of the Risen Savior and strives to experience some of the true joy of the followers of Christ. In so doing he not only confirms his resolutions to do better in the future, but he crowns his efforts by reflecting upon the reward which is heaven. However, in a special final contemplation he prays for the gift of true altruistic love in which he could sincerely say to Christ: "Take and receive all my liberty, my mind, my will, my memory."

The dominant point of the Exercises is reached when the exercitant can say that he is really willing to suffer whatever Christ wants him to suffer in his attempts to save his soul. The desire to put one's ideal as high as it can be, through consideration of the Divine Model, gives strength through the thought of suffering, hope through friendship with Christ, and finally love and joy through full union with Christ and the Blessed Trinity in heaven. The climax of the Spiritual Exercises is seen in the fourth week, the week of joy and crowning. Here man joins hands with the Risen Savior, forever in glory now, forever his Savior and Redeemer, never to part company with the Beloved by any deliberate fault or evil deed.

For a fuller treatment of love and union as related to the intellect and will, the reader is referred to the writings of Frederick E. Crowe, S. J., appearing in *Theological Studies*, published by the Jesuit Seminaries in the United States.[3]

In the Volume for 1959 there appeared an article entitled "Complacency and Concern in the Thought of St. Thomas."

---

3 Our greatest appreciation is here expressed to the Rev. James J. Doyle, S.J., professor of ascetical theology at West Baden College, who generously referred the present writer to these texts.

Here the author clearly distinguishes love as striving, that is the Greek EROS, from love as AGAPE, or the love feast of the Christians. With precise and neat speculations he shows how misleading it would be to emphasize the active or restless side of will life, the processes leading to an end, to the exclusion of the passive or quietistic aspects, namely the full possession of an end.

Father Crowe in this article constantly refers to other writings, especially of Fr. Lonergan, which have as their chief purpose the fuller clarification of the relation between the higher faculties of the human mind on the one hand, and the theology of the processions in the Blessed Trinity, on the other. It is reassuring to the modern psychologist of religion to notice that the so-called "dead mysteries" of religion and the "defunct theory" of human faculties are still being investigated by serious and competent theological observers, with a view to better understanding and appreciation.

8 means of growth (2)

THE psychology of prayer is concerned with the efficacy of prayer, the value of prayer and the motives of prayer. Many authors have noted that the fear motive, or the "selfish" motives, often serve to initiate or to motivate processes of prayer; thus, they say, it can hardly be considered a really religious, that is, morally good, sort of activity at all. Rather it is the mark of a regression to childhood, because in prayer a person crawls to the Almighty Father on hands and knees. This cringing and obsequious approach to the Father God is nothing more, they say, than a return to the father figure of early childhood; the return to the father is always in order to obtain some favor. Or if prayer is not such a regression to childhood, it is at least nothing more than a reaction motivated by fear and carried out almost mechanically; it is a routinely practiced performance of some rite or ritual by which, in a sort of magical fashion, the person who prays tries to compel the Deity to conform to his way of thinking and desiring.

All these criticisms of the person who prays and of the prayer itself overlook the crucial distinction between praying to get something from God, and praying in order to give or to share something with Him. Some of them also do violence to the fact that, to some degree at least, prayer encompasses and involves, as it were, the whole person of the one who prays; it does not consist merely in the activity of mumbling a word or a phrase, nor is it simply a ritualistic practice. And prayer to the Christian is not to be classed with the magical practices of the primitive, nor with superstitious beliefs and practices found in some other religions. In such practices the "magician" attributes divine powers to all kinds of toys, inanimate and animate objects, without any concrete and tangible evidence that these objects have such powers. The Christian is even taught from earliest childhood studiously to avoid delving into the realm of the unknown by means of fortune-tellers and palm-readers and the like. The reason for this is, obviously, to lead the mind of the Christian to the One True God and away from idols and false gods of all sorts.

College students, high-school students, and other groups have been systematically questioned by certain investigators[1] in order to find out why they think they pray. On the assumption, of course, that some people at least can and do truthfully answer the questions as to why they pray, and as a result of counting up the numbers of the different kinds of responses, the following conclusions can be drawn.

Some students pray because they think that prayer will bring them close to God; this motive is the most frequently given in the study cited. Other persons pray because it gives them solace in affliction; this motive is the one next most frequently reported in the research. Finally, some persons pray because they want to obtain some favor, to receive some benefit or cure. Very few of the respondents seemed to be aware of the fact that prayer may be of at least a dozen different types or varieties, depending upon the avowed purpose or motive with which the prayer is performed. Nor were these different types of prayer mentioned by the investigator, so that it was to be presumed that most respondents would take the questions to refer to vocal and not to any other kind of prayer. The reason for making this statement is the fact that the present writer asked two dozen college students of his acquaintance why they prayed; then he immediately asked them what they meant by prayer, and to the man they all agreed that they had interpreted the question to mean

1 Unpublished study by a Loyola graduate student.

vocal prayer. And most vocal prayers fall into the category called prayers of petition. A study is under way now to find out what motives people will give for engaging in the act of mental prayer, or of simple contemplation of mysteries of the faith. It is fairly obvious that these latter types of prayer do not lend themselves to serve the purpose of petition as do the ordinary printed vocal prayers.

One widely publicized attempt has recently been made to test the efficacy of prayer, that is, vocal petitionary prayer, by empirical means. A brief description of the study will be given. William H. Parker and Elaine St. J. Dare[2] carried out what they call a controlled observation of the effects of prayer, first taken alone, secondly taken in conjunction with therapy sessions, and finally the effect of therapy alone without prayer. The minister and the psychiatrist worked together during the whole design of the experiment. They selected three groups of patients, equal as regards the degree of involvement in illness. With one group of fifty persons the minister and the psychiatrist together engaged in prayers and (group) counseling sessions weekly over a period of six months. The stated purpose of the prayer combined with counseling was to improve the adjustment of the patients and/or to effect a cure. With a second group of fifty persons, the psychiatrist alone used therapy and counseling. With the third group of persons, the minister used simple prayer of petition, the request being, of course, that the patients would get better. In all three groups there were weekly sessions for six months. The results showed that the first group, who had experienced prayer and therapy together, improved 75%; the second group, having received therapy alone, improved 60%; whereas the third group, called by the investigators the simple pray-ers, showed no improvement whatever.

One is inclined to make several criticisms of the method used in this investigation. Space will permit of only one, and it is the following: The fact that zero improvement followed from the activities of the simple pray-ers might easily have been deduced from the fact that the prayer sessions were described as

2 In *Prayer Can Change Your Life*: Prentice-Hall, 1957.

mere routine sessions in which no one took the initiative; the patients merely mumbled their vocal prayers, which had probably grown over a period of time to be practically meaningless to them. At any rate, prayer can scarcely be expected to be efficacious unless the person praying puts some meaning into it. The first two groups in the above experiment could surely be expected to have kept their minds on the task in hand because of the continual activity of the therapist and of the minister.

At any rate, if the experiment proves anything, it shows the importance of joining the natural aids given by the medical profession to those made available through religion in order to secure the most beneficial results from prayer of petition. Those persons in group three who prayed automatically or routinely might well have been guilty of the fault mentioned above, namely, that in a purely magical fashion they expected to force from God a favor which they had no other way of obtaining. Such attempts at compelling the Deity smack of the regressions to primitive levels of development so often mentioned by comparative psychologists in recent times.

Much more will be said about prayer under the heading of worship which is the supreme form of prayer. It is characterized mainly by the fact that the pray-er is here engaged almost entirely in the supreme act of giving to God that homage and respect which are His due.

If vocal prayer is the focusing of our mental sights upon the beyond while conversing with the Deity, it involves a pointing or directing Godward of our highest faculties of intellect and will. Mental prayer involves not only this pointing toward God of one's highest faculties; it includes the act of engaging memory, imagination, and feeling in regard to the same divine object, divine truths, or whatever is the subject matter of the prayer. Contemplation is the combination of all the acts already mentioned, with the addition of a studied calm, a fixed gaze or direction of all powers on all levels capable of being directed by the act of voluntary attention toward the object of mental prayer. Much more will be said about these forms of prayer in the next part of this work.

In the next section the higher forms of prayer will be considered, especially since they have received so much attention from writers who are bent on showing that such higher experiences are in reality nothing more than abnormal psychic phenomena. It is the contention of the present writer that critics of this sort simply do not know the facts which they are describing, and hence cannot be held accountable for their deviant views. Be it said here that in the ordinary form of contemplation practiced by religious and priests throughout the world, the sum total of all the human faculties are brought to bear upon the task of forming a very real and close bond of mental union between the pray-er and the Person of God.

Undoubtedly different types of religious persons will engage in widely different forms of vocal and mental prayer. The hermit or the monastic person traditionally practices contemplation. The active priest and preacher will lean more toward the vocal or the ritualistic forms of prayer. In all cases there will be found a common denominator, namely, that the human being is trying to express in some tangible way the fact of his dependence upon his Father God, as well as his desire to be and to remain friendly with and very close to God. In other words, prayer and meditation are psychologically fruitful in helping man to satisfy his deep need for attention, recognition, and response. Prayer also helps man to satisfy his need for security, because it inclines him to seek for help in his trials from that infinite source of goodness and mercy which is the Divine Being in Himself. He is reminded of this Goodness whenever he considers that God has a plan in life for each individual, that every person, however apparently insignificant or forgotten, has a place in the divine scheme of things.

WORSHIP AND THE SACRAMENTS

The pagans have their gods, and the Christians and the Moslems their one God. Perhaps the great diversity of Deity-concern will bring a sneer to the lips of the all-knowing scientist. Yet he will often not be averse to such "ritualistic" performances as trying to measure and predict human behavior by means of an estimate of the frequency and voltage in the nerve fibers.

It is true that the scientist is able to provide a good analogy between nerve impulses and servo-mechanisms and feed-back circuits and between servo-mechanisms and behavior mechanisms; so is the psychologist of religion able to show some analogies between signs of physical health and vigor on one hand and the means of grace, prayer and the sacraments, on the other. But to press the analogies so as to imply identity or even common natures between the spiritual and the bodily would be as absurd as to claim identity between the electrical mechanisms and the mental mechanisms. The analogies help the human mind to grasp some aspects of spiritual reality.

Worship and adoration are the highest acts of prayer of which the human being is capable. Worship means to bow down, to prostrate oneself or otherwise symbolize that one is paying homage and respect, and not merely lip service nor mere physical submission to the Divine Person. One can adore only God, but most prayers readily move from one to another of the divine attributes, during the course of one's meditation or acts of adoration. The bows might be either of the knee or of the head, or of both, and such bowing become a conscious and deliberately produced sign that a creature knows where he stands with respect to his Creator and that he wants to come into or to remain in the best kind of friendly relation with the Deity Whom he recognizes and respects. An act of faith is the clearest sign of the recognition one makes of God; the act of worship requires that a person put his whole being into the recognition. Rituals and church practice from the earliest days of Christianity predisposed the faithful to pray, not only with their lips, but with a real contemplative grasp of God or by means of a search for a closer union with God. This search will then at times resolve itself into an affective union rather than a merely cognitive one. In such an affective union with God, the worshiper knows God through a sharing of himself with God and, in the contemplation of the goodness of God, he brings himself nearer to God. He finds that God is intimately present within his very self and that he himself is immersed in God. This new kind of sensing of God's presence may turn into a special kind of mystical experience which will be discussed in the following section.

Sacraments are, psychologically speaking, physical or visible signs that God is dealing in a special manner with men. Every sacrament has a purpose, a specific benefit which it is to confer upon men. Thus, at last the crucial complaint made so often against the sacramental system is seen: Man must be a selfish and self-seeking kind of being to allow himself to be lured into the practice of using the sacraments. However, on the contrary, it is affirmed that to conclude that one is selfish because he uses the sacramental helps provided by God is utterly and entirely a fallacious sort of argument. If God made man in such a manner that certain aids are necessary for him before he can come back to Him as his last end, then it is not only not selfish to make use of these aids, it is actually another sign that man is trying to conform as much as possible to the Divine Will in his life. It would show human submission to the Divine Will in a special manner if people made free use of these aids in the manner Christ intended when He instituted these sacraments. It should never be forgotten that the sacraments were instituted by Christ for the benefit of men. They serve to encourage one's reliance upon God's help, but at the same time they fulfill the divine plan in regard to man, since God wants him to use them, or else he cannot be assured of coming back to Him. Here is a brief sketch of the manner in which each of the seven sacraments aids man in fulfilling his duties as a Christian.

Baptism gives one entrance into the Church, Confirmation strengthens him for bearing trials and difficulties, while the annointing of the sick person in Extreme Unction consoles him. And Confession, with its firm purpose of amendment, signifies one's willingness to do better and to repair the evil done because of his transgressions. Holy Orders and Matrimony give the special helps and courage needed to perform the duties of a minister or of a parent. Going to Holy Communion and hearing, and/or offering, the Holy Sacrifice of the Mass means a culminating bond of union between the human and the divine. It is the supreme act of worship which was initiated for mankind on Calvary's height. It is a sacrificial act in which the Victim and the High Priest are one and the same Divine Person, Christ, the second Person of the Blessed Trinity. In this sublime offering, the Christ, Who entered into glory through suffering, descends upon the altars of man to stay there very near us throughout the day and night; to be a solace and strength, a hope and joy; there He is man's changeless Friend personally and realistically, for the purpose of drawing him unto Himself, to take away once and again the sins of the world, and to help each one singly and lovingly to put on God in that manner in which He Himself has instructed us. He who receives Christ receives God, and he who puts on Christ puts off himself to be one with the Divine as much as possible in this life.

Sacraments are God-designed instruments whereby, according to God's plan for men, God's providential scheme of things, God reaches down to man, renewing His once-redemptive act ever anew. This coming and staying with man on the part of God serves the purpose of lifting man up, of bringing him closer to that mystical affective union sought by all the saints—of perfecting his whole being in the mutual act of love. Man begins even on earth to be incorporated in the Divine; man continues to grow and to perfect himself in this divine union which will be perpetuated in the timeless span of the eternal joys of Beatific Vision.

What specific goals are reached, it may be asked, by prayers, and especially the superb forms of prayer associated with sacraments? The answer is not far to seek. Prayer and communion with God bring man closer to God and keep him there, while man tries in his own feeble way to carry out the plan of Divine Providence in his own regard, and while he works out the will of God in the service which he is expected to render by the free use of his highest faculties. Even if prayer were to move a man a little closer to the Source of all being, the Divine Nature, the God Who is seen reflected in creation everywhere, it would also tend to serve the secondary purpose of bringing man closer also to his fellow man; for he sees God reflected in a special manner in that creature for whom God chose to become human, in every human being for whom Christ died, in every person whose dignity was such as to move God to redeem him. The stranger to whom one gives the cup of water is the image of God, our Father, Redeemer and Sanctifier.

Prayer, worship, and sacrifice, in addition to the sacraments, also express man's real and fundamental need of God. The plan of Divine Providence whereby men are commanded to pray, yet urged to give God a voluntary service, shows God's "need" for man; rather it should be said that it shows His design through which He wishes man to come back to Him when going astray and to abide with Him in a closer bond of love and sharing with Him, our everlasting Friend.

In each of the purposes for which prayers and sacrifices are offered to God, the psychologist should see a kind of token which symbolizes man's greatest good. In each and every one of these prayers and sacrifices there is an activation of man's faith in the meaning and purpose of the universe, of life in general, of one's own being in particular. Each also gives security and stability in a changing world. Each adds assurance and hope that God will not abandon man since He promised to be with him always. Each cements that love and affection between God and all men, between men and God. Each encourages not only a give-and-take, but more, a real sharing, a communion of minds and hearts, a sharing of the most treasured of all gifts, the total surrender and binding back to God of one's very self in the oblation one makes of himself in prayer and sacrifice.

Above all, these prayers tend to make and keep man humble, because they remind him of how much he needs help, how dependent he is upon the Divine Life Itself. They help man to keep an abiding sorrow for sins and purpose of amendment, which is necessary because, no matter how elevated he may be by virtues and special gifts from God, still he is His creature, and will have to keep sacred the trust He places in him until the very end, knowing it is always possible for him to abandon his virtuous ways. Though one retains a capacity for sin, he strengthens his resistances to evil by purposes of amendment and especially by propitiatory prayers, offering to make good what has been amiss in his life. Add to this the express desire, so often found in a man's prayers, that he may go through life persevering in a state of close friendship with God, despite his faults and defections; and there will come spontaneously to his lips that most heart-rending prayer of King David: "Out

of the depths have I cried, Oh Lord, make haste to help me."
May it be deeply engraved in the hearts of suffering humanity!

There are two other purposes that are both served by prayers
and sacrifices offered to God, and these purposes are as altruistic
and self-immolating as can be conceived. One is to thank Him
for Himself—for being to man what He is, for man's being able
to serve Him Whom it is an honor to serve. This type of prayer
can scarcely be called self-seeking; it can and often does lead
spontaneously to the prayers of supplication and petition, as
an example, for the favor of never being mean and ungrateful
to God. One other sublime petition might be to beg God that
He would make one a little more worthy of his supreme destiny.
Worship and adoration expand and perfect man's nature and
elevate his desires above mundane and transitory delights. In
prayers of petition and thanksgiving the soul communicates with
divine and heavenly beings and such sharing tends to saturate
the mind and heart with the divine goodness and light.

The man who is truly humble and suppliant before such
a God as this will know what to ask for so as not to be selfish.
He will know and instinctively feel what the best way will be
for him to fulfill the Divine Will in his regard. He will go to
God in adversity, remain there in depression, in desolation;
he will find no true rest until he is permitted to go back to
God, through that portal he so often viewed at the end of life's
journey; thoughts of the portal of death will not deter him
from his loyal service and the practice of prayer. On the contrary,
they will stimulate him to prayer and generosity of service.
He knows, and feels secure in the knowledge, that this is the
only way that is open to him to come back to God the Father
from Whom he was born, by Whom he was saved, for Whom
he was destined to live.

DEDICATION THROUGH VOWS

If man needs both stability and consistency in his adaptation
to a changing world, and if no one outside himself is really able
to produce in him that stability which he needs, man must do
something about securing it himself. The vows of religion aid

a person to establish himself in a stable and consistent way of life. His teachers and monitors can give some examples of how to behave consistently, can urge him to follow rules of right living, to acquire some stability or strength in meeting the difficulties of life. Yet in the last analysis each man must learn by and for himself how best to stabilize his own energies, how to harmonize his own strivings, how to gain the feeling of self-worth from the knowledge of his own accomplishments. Nevertheless, in order to do this a person needs time and serious conscientious effort. Habit, it is known, helps man to economize on effort. The mind needs little cooperation in an act or skill which has become automatic by means of habit.

Virtuous living can also be made somewhat automatic. Striving for perfection can become stabilized through the use of firm and fixed direction of will toward the desired goals. When a person pronounces a vow, he gives to his will that constant direction which insures stability; his strivings, from now on, are channeled, as if he hemmed them in with walls; his ideals are now directed; his acts of the virtues will now be easier because of the facility given by habit, and the continuous direction given because of the vow or promise. These actions will not now need to be explicitly and formally directed on every occasion, since a permanent set or disposition has been acquired by means of the vows. The actions tend toward the desired goal, the purpose and motive of all the striving, through a kind of automatic process.

This briefly is the thinking of spiritual-minded persons in regard to the taking of vows, the making of resolutions, and the making and keeping of promises. With vows, the ordinary virtues can be practiced more easily and smoothly. A person with vows is freed from the need to attend to each of his separate part acts. He can go on to higher goals, to the attainment of richer and fuller satisfactions in the complete dedication of the self, and to the service upon which he has entered. The added facility given by vows is somewhat analogous to the added ease in performing movements of motor skills which can be acquired after lengthy practice. The skilled acrobat does not need to concentrate on the delicate movements involved in, let us say, juggling. The precision of his movements is initially determined by means of purpose aided by practice.

Similarly, a vow gives stability but it also presupposes a large amount of purpose and foresight on the part of the one who takes the vow, and practice in performing the desired acts. He must be able to evaluate himself beforehand as to the likelihood of his being able to keep the vow. This act of self-evaluation, again, is beneficial toward the attaining of facility, stability and balance.

The three vows traditionally taken by religious are designed to aid in stabilizing all of man's strivings. They cover practically every posible field of effort, every area of goal-striving known to man. Each of them will be considered succinctly.

Poverty habitually turns man's will away from the love of money and worldly possessions, thus freeing him for other pursuits. Obedience turns his will away from the love of power and the tendency to prefer his own choices to those of other persons; in obedience one's own will is killed so that he now lives a higher life. The vow of chastity turns the will away from the desires and entanglements consequent upon satisfying the instincts of propagation. Through chastity the leanings of carnal nature are reoriented, slanted toward other goals than sexual or purely carnal, sensuous gratification. In chastity the cravings of sensory nature are never condemned; rather they are channeled into paths which will enable the person to become more stable and efficient in the accomplishment of more difficult tasks, in the gaining of his highest goals, the perfection and sanctification of his whole person. Thus all the areas, all the basic needs of man, that of recognition and power, that for acquisition and property, that for personal sensory gratification, are redirected and set toward new goals. These goals are the service of God and self-dedication to helping others. Such a redirection can hardly be thought of as limiting a man's strivings, or dampening his efforts. It must rather be considered as a special way of enabling him to get the most from his efforts, for the purpose of making his life most meaningful, for the total plan of divine

providence, for the benefit and mutual happiness and contentment of all mankind.[3]

The vows of religion are safeguards for the religious person.
They do insure a stable orientation of the individual, and they
do help him or her to remain constant and persevering in the
pursuit of religious perfection. This is not to say that they will
free the religious person from interior difficulties, or that they
can be kept from day to day without strain and hardship. It may
be interesting now to outline certain of the difficulties which
the younger persons encounter in their attempts at leading the
life of the vows.

The listings which follow are based partly upon the writings
of religious persons, and partly upon the declared statements
of religious themselves. In the latter cases the responses came
from the interviewed persons quite spontaneously. The main
purpose of the open-ended interviews had been to find out how
the religious and the seminarians felt with regard to their living
out their vocation, the stresses they experienced and the demands
their vocation made upon their energies, and their present
methods for handling their problems. There was no attempt
on the part of the interviewer to explore the whole field of
possible problem areas. On the contrary, the non-directed per-
missive-interview method was used. There was some "steering"
of the responses in the sense that, by the end of the interview,
a fixed number and kind of questions had been answered. But
answers to one question led naturally to the next question,
so that, for the most part, the whole interview was non-directive.
There was strict anonymity, and the seminarians seemed willing
and even eager to communicate their problems to the psycholo-
gist-interviewer.

PROBLEMS OF THE COMMUNITY LIFE

When a young man or woman goes away from home to become a religious or to study for the priesthood, he obviously
makes a sacrifice of much that is dear to him, the dearest things

3 See note at end of section.

in the world, perhaps; he leaves home and breaks ties of love and affection which have been years in forming. He can do this only because very strong motives attract him, and such motives are always in some way linked with the love of God and of his neighbor. His whole natural self has for years become identified with parents and loved ones in the home. Now he or she must transform these bonds of affection into spiritual bonds. He must live with utter strangers at first; he must do all this for the love, for the *greater glory* of *God*. He knows this is supposed to be his motive, from all his study of religion and from contact with God through prayer. But all this requires strong faith, and he may begin at times to wonder if he can really endure the life, if he really had a pure intention and a sufficiently adequate motivation right from the beginning.

It is not at all strange that these young persons begin at times to notice their loss and to feel very keenly the strangeness of this new form of life. It appears to them as artificial and even at times unnatural and even unbearable. Similar feelings were had by the enlistees in the armed forces when they had to go at about the age of 19 or 20 into the community life of the army or navy. Their success was dependent, as we now know, upon the kind and efficiency of their motives in the same way that the success of seminarians is dependent largely upon their motivation. We are assuming that in both cases there is the required amount of talent or native ability to accomplish the required tasks.

With the seminarians, however, in contrast to the service men, there is a special set of circumstances, or we might even say causes, for stress and strain. These causes stem from the fact that the seminarians and religious know that they are expected to enter into a state in which their ambition is to strive for perfection. There is no limit to the ideal they are striving to imitate; it is none other than Christ Himself, the model and master of the hearts and souls of men. The candidates for the priesthood, as well as the religious, have absorbed this teaching about their model and master from earliest childhood; they have become keenly aware of the fact that they can never hope to make others holy unless they themselves are holy. They have learned this not only from sermons and spiritual reading; they have perhaps actually experienced it at first hand. They know therefore that they must, they are expected to strive continuously for the perfection of all the virtues, yet they feel very helpless at times, very human; singularly weak and even totally incapable of going on with the struggle for this elusive thing called perfection. They are subject to fits of discouragement, to bouts with depression. They are tempted to inconstancy, to lower their ideals, and even to give up their vocation entirely and to go back home again.

If a boy or a girl in such a situation can match the inclinations to give up and go back with equally strong desires to buck up and go forward in the generous surrender of the self, in the service of God and the other, then he or she may be able to surmount the difficulty. They will grow in spiritual stature just because of the conflicts they have experienced. They will increase their spiritual strength by reason of the hardships, and they will perhaps become better ministers later on, just because of the difficulties, the feelings of isolation from home and the bitter pangs of home-sickness they have suffered. It is not surprising that they look toward modern science at times, with the hope of finding ways of alleviating their sufferings. They seek ways of making their self-oblation less burdensome and trying, less disturbing to their equanimity and peace of mind. Yet, to the knowledge of the author, there is not in existence any remedy for homesickness in the repertoire of scientific books on psychology. There are no fool-proof remedies for the isolation one experiences on leaving home or for loneliness or homesickness. There is, however, the wise counsel of religious educators down the ages. It tells the novice in the spiritual life to develop so much ego-strength, so much inner poise and personal security, that he is able to fight effectively against the demon of discouragement and loneliness. This means the candidates must build up reinforcements of character, buttresses of power sufficient to ward off threats of any kind to their vocation. But under periods of stress the candidate will be in special need of a good counselor; a spiritual adviser who can keep the confidences and trust of the subject, and yet who can at the same time steer the person safely over the momentary obstacles.

PROBLEMS RELATING TO THE VOWS

As stated before, the vows give stability of purpose; but they also place a certain stress upon the person who pronounces them in perpetuity. The stresses are no different from other psychological stresses experienced in difficult undertakings. If there were none of these stresses the church probably would not have approved the life of religious and the clergy so wholeheartedly over the ages. From this approval it does not follow that the church means the religious life to be the cause of mental anguish and of psychic disturbances. She means to teach us, as cultural history and biographies of many persons clearly indicate, that the curbing of man's natural desires and the elevating of his goals above the purely natural, out and beyond that of the licit satisfaction of native impulses, will be conducive to the greater good of all concerned. For one to dedicate himself or herself to the higher service of God and of his fellow-man, no better natural means exist than to exercise oneself in self-denial and self-discipline. Careful study of oriental and occidental history will give testimony to the truth of this statement. The same sources may be appealed to in confirmation of the fact that no man easily makes a complete sacrifice of himself. We know there must be sacrifice in the self-immolation of the vows, and hence we know that a person will not take vows, intending to keep them in their perfection, without placing some restraint upon his or her natural urges and inclinations. Poverty must be expected to put a restriction upon the free use of this world's goods; in place of these a man will experience freedom from competition for wealth and power. Obedience will be expected to cause some feelings of self-depreciation, self-humiliation, and it may even mean submitting to the whims of a naturally obnoxious superior; but the sequel of this will be freedom from worry about the outcome of many of one's choices. Chastity must indeed mean a guarding of the senses, an avoidance of frivolous stimulations; but in its wake will come a quiet and serenity, as well as a freedom from the cares of family living.

Then should we say that the life of the religious and the seminarian is an escape from reality? Rather it is a withdrawal from the sensible world, coupled with the approach into a new world of spiritual comforts and consolations, into the peace and contentment partially described by the Gospel writers. The scientists of today have sometimes observed and called attention to the distinctive kind of person produced in the seminaries and in the religious life. They say his composure and calm remind one of a kind of person whose inner strivings have been harmoniously balanced with one another, one whose contacts with the external world are effective and seemingly gratifying and rewarding, so that the whole life of such a person reminds one of that Utopia of which mystical writers speak wherein every human desire is perfectly satisfied, every need fulfilled.

PROBLEMS RELATING TO LONELINESS

Some of the workers in the Loyola Mental Health Project were surprised to hear that seminarians and religious suffered from loneliness. These research workers had probably built up a different concept of the community life. They had perhaps thought of religious life as being particularly designed to prevent any such thing as being isolated or lonely. But when one becomes more familiar with the kind of life which these persons lead it is only natural to expect that feelings of loneliness will occur at times. The persons spend long hours in silence, in serious study, in meditation and prayer. The routine of their daily existence might even be said to predispose to loneliness. The rule is generally that one does not speak out of times approved for recreation. He speaks only when required to speak, as it were. When he might need to speak most in order to relieve his feelings, he remembers he is not supposed to speak. This state of affairs has been in existence for centuries, and will go on for many more. There is no real psychological danger in having these feelings of loneliness so long as the sufferer does not deliberately engage in prolonged periods of day-dreaming. Even day-dreaming is not dangerous unless it is engaged in as an escape from real life, from responsibility for duty, from hard and undesirable tasks. The danger in the latter cases arises from the fact that one would gradually lose contact from the real world and come to live in a little world of his own, the world of make-believe.

The seminarian who approaches his spiritual adviser with the complaint that he is lonely will find a sympathetic listener. No man can feel completely unlonely so long as he is exiled here on earth away from his eternal and wished-for home. Human companionship may lessen the feelings at times for a while. Being active with many and varied diversions may take the edge off the lonely feeling. Worldly distractions may camouflage the deeper feeling for a while. None of these natural solutions of the problem of loneliness really gets at its inner core. Natural remedies will, of course, serve to tide one over until some more solid grounds are found for dispelling loneliness and for learning to feel at home with others.

Certain natural distractors will at least support the person until such time as he may be stronger, or the mood may pass away. When the person is particularly susceptible to mood swings, he should be referred to a good physician who will know what to prescribe. When the moods and depressions are slight and transitory, each of the seminarians can learn to make the best of the trials; to use them as stepping stones to greater self-abandon to the service of God and fellow-man. When there is steady growth in holiness and when the person has found his own proper solution to the problems of loneliness, then he will have found that he is a better man because of the strivings. No natural means alone will be able to make him immune for all time from future bouts with the demon of loneliness and discouragement. Much more will be said about this in Chapters IX and X.

At the suggestion of Fr. James J. Doyle, special reference is here made to *Life in the City of God*. Carpentier (original; English translation published by Newman). The author is also indebted to the workers on the Loyola National Mental Health Project for the use of taped interviews with seminarians. See especially *Religion and Mental Health*, a publication of the Academy of Religion and Mental Health. N. Y. 1960.

9 the way of ascetics

IT IS not the purpose here to dispute or to defend any definitions of the terms *asceticism* and *mysticism*. What is meant in this treatise by these terms will be stated clearly, and then other definitions can be compared with these. A clear description of mystical phenomena will be given without going into great detail about the different schools of mysticism. The purpose in bringing these phenomena into a treatise on the psychological processes related to religion is to describe and categorize them with respect to their psychological import. It is by no means to establish a complete philosophical system of asceticism, much less to expound a theological system.

Asceticism means the ordinary religious experiences of the ordinary person, of whatever kind they may be. The meaning will be clear if the three elements are recalled which are essentially connected with the idea and practice of religion, namely, the creed, the code and the ceremonial or ritual.

The religious experience which is most widely and frequently discussed by non-Catholics is the experience of conversion. For them this is a keen sense of the presence of God, in Whose presence and with Whose close cooperation the person feels himself saved. It is a change of life's direction which is deeply felt and is accompanied by some assurance that it is to be permanent. For Catholics, conversion implies at least this; but in addition it includes the compunction following or preceding a good confession, and also the abiding sorrow for sin which the Saints possessed as the result of meditation on divine things and of the special grace of God.

There are as many kinds of religious experiences for the Catholic as there are opportunities for change. This is because for the Catholic conversion implies the increasing assurance that one is saved, but in addition the saved person is urged and impelled to keep his mind on his own weakness as well, to remember his own dependence on grace, without which his efforts would be fruitless. Thus, conversion savors more of sorrow and firm intention to make amends for the past than it does of assurance of the friendship of God. Of course, indirectly the Catholic knows and feels the fact of his friendship with God, but his assurance of its continuance is obtained by the continuance of his abiding sorrow and deep remorse for sin.

Mystical experience, on the other hand, refers to contemplation, visions, raptures, ecstasies. These are far from the ordinary experiences of the unreflective religious person, for they are the result of special gifts and aids coming directly into the mind of God's creatures, and are not the mere resultant of the intense prayerful activity of the one who prays. In a very true sense every grace, actual as well as sanctifying, is a gift. When it is admitted that the supernatural life of the soul itself is a gift, it is then true to say that the additional mystical experiences of certain people are also gifts in a special sense. Ecstasy is a mystical experience, and it is the main one to be discussed in this section. The reason for emphasizing ecstasy here is that the scientists and critics of religion have so often belittled it, comparing it with such abnormal psychological phenomena as hysteria, psychoses, and obsessions.

To summarize the differences between the ordinary religious experience of God possessed by the Christian and that of the mystic, this may be said. God may be experienced by the ordinary person as something beyond, though related very closely to man. He will be conceptualized and discussed mentally, and it will be possible, as the result of these speculations and arguments, to make positive statements about Him which express the human way of looking upon the Divine Nature. He will be visualized as a Person Who possesses the most admirable of all qualities, above all a love for man which can be reciprocated. The ordinary ascetic respects, worships, and loves God, and therefore also desires to be with Him in the experiences of His real and abiding presence. The God of the person who devoutly meditates upon divine truths, is one with whom any man can enter into a great variety of cognitive and affective relationships. Some or all of these specially individuated personal experiences of the Deity can be and undoubtedly are had every day by the person endowed with an ordinary amount of reflective ability.

God may also be experienced as something quite outside and beyond man, yet at the same time permeating one's inner consciousness in a specially intimate way. God's presence is sensed as beyond and within at the same time. He is "around" and "within" one at the same time. This means more than the mere fact that one assents to the truth of His existence as infinite perfection. It means more than that one desires to serve God as His devoted son and loving servant. It means that His presence is immediately sensed and felt. It is more than a firm belief in His presence with assurance of His friendship and love, more than a mutual communication between friends. It is a newly realized form of presence which serves to make a person's acts of faith more real than those of sensory perception. It gives to belief some of the dynamic qualities of ordinary perception. When God is known and loved through the medium of images, concepts and all those other conscious concomitants of religious experiences, there is activity known as ordinary prayer or asceticism. But when God is known and loved, in addition, by some direct psychic process, by an immediate realization of the Divine, then this is mystical experience. There is a difference in intensity between the two experiences, but there is also a difference in the quality of the experience which is felt in consciousness.[1]

1 A. Poulain, *The Graces of Interior Prayer*, St. Louis, Herder, 1949, Chaps. I, II, III.

THE FIRST LEVEL OF MYSTICISM, THE PRAYER OF QUIET

Historically, spiritual writers have held three views regarding mysticism, which are here mentioned in passing in order to highlight the significance of some well-known abuses of mystical experience. One view holds that all ligature in prayer, all suspension of any sensory activity found in mystical prayer, is an extraordinary gift, freely given by God, in addition to the graces necessary for one's state of life. Such gifts cannot be striven for and ought not to be desired by anyone, since to receive them is utterly extraordinary, and a pure gift or favor quite outside the scope of ordinary spirituality. It would be rash, says Rodriguez (*Christian Perfection*, Chap. IV) to pretend to have it. No one should seek to rise to it unless God Himself raises him. To do otherwise would be presumptuous and would merit even the loss of ordinary prayer.

Such a view borders on an inspirational view, in assuming that mysticism belongs in a class under the doctrine of "inspiration," according to which man receives direct communications from God, entirely at the discretion of God. Because of this strictly supernatural characteristic, this first view should be relegated to theological discussions and has no place in psychological clarifications.

Another view, which has been known through the history of religious thought as Quietism, maintains that a man becomes mystic merely by removing the obstacles which hide the Divine within him. Man, by a positive sort of removal of his imperfections, attracts the real inwardly felt presence of God to encompass him and, as it were, compels God to bestow mystical experiences upon him. This is a view which reduces the phenomenon to a level to which every person may aspire with confidence of achievement. This statement of the problem of mysticism brings the psychologist into the picture, for it is his special role to deal with the whole gamut of natural experiences, even with those of the mystics.

The middle-of-the-road view regards mystical experiences as legitimately desirable by all, and yet at the same time maintains that God can and will give a new kind of grace or gift to certain worthy persons whenever and wherever He so chooses. To bring out the point of difference between these two last views will require a description of the contribution which is made by ordinary ascesis toward the acquisition of real mystical experiences. Stress will here be placed on the efforts and psychological processes which are deemed to be important in the serious striving of a normal individual for the higher life of mysticism.

It is to be noted that even Buddhist and Neo-Platonist mystics agree with the doctrine of Christianity, in saying that man must, by his own efforts at least, be responsible for the removal of obstacles to the higher mystical experiences. It is clearly one thing to say that this removal is a condition *sine qua non* for mysticism, and another to think that, once this condition is placed, God is compelled to grant the gift. If the removal of obstacles alone were the essence of the mystical experience, there would be no difference between a Plotinus and a St. John of the Cross.[2]

The quietists of the 17th century fell into heresy, which led to numerous other aberrations still recorded as abuses of religion.[3] This was largely because they said it was necessary only to remove the obstacles to divine grace in order to secure the highest mystical experiences. Their view led them to strive and to seek by their own efforts to compel, as it were, the Divinity to entrance them, to enlighten and illumine them, and this long before they had completed the removal of obstacles, before there was a subduing of the passions by moral ascesis. Thus absurd practices developed, the excesses of belief and the delusions, the obsessions, and so forth now so well known to all historians of this period.

The genuine prayer of quiet, more commonly called the prayer of simple regard, as practiced by the Christian mystics, may be

2 Howley, John, *Psychology and Mystical Experience,* London, Kegan Paul, Trench, Trubner & Co., 1920, Part II, Chap. I.
3 Armstrong, A. H., in his 1953 book *Plotinus* has written authoritatively on the relationship between mysticism and Neo-Platonism, showing the distinctive characteristics of each.

described and exemplified from the life of St. John of the Cross, or from that of St. Theresa.[4]

The prayer of simple regard involves a discourse, though less varied and less apparent than in non-mystical meditation. It leaves more room than ordinary ascesis for sentiments of love, praise, gratitude, respect, submission, contrition and so forth; there is room also for practical resolutions. The speculative deduction of one truth about God from some other truth is, however, partly produced by a kind of intuitive glance at the Divine. Thus, negatively, this prayer is characterized by relative lack of speculation and, positively, by a relatively greater degree of affection and resolution. The affections show less variety than in ordinary prayer and are expressed in fewer words or sometimes not expressed at all. Positively, then, there are also these characteristics in the prayer of simple regard: a thought or sentiment returns incessantly to occupy the mind, entering easily and without disturbance. The dominant thought is not continuous, however, but it returns frequently and spontaneously for the most part. This prayer is really one slow sequence of single glances cast upon one and the same object.

Such prayer of simplicity differs greatly from Yoga and from Buddhist quietism. In these techniques there is sought an escape from the "wheel" of conscious existence; there is little emphasis on seeking the newer and fuller experience of the Divine. Yoga techniques resemble those advocated by certain modern psychologists, in the effort to get rid of undesirable habits. They call this process auto-hypnosis. Such efforts at auto-hypnosis are so prevalent, and are such a marked feature of Eastern mysticism, that American psychologists are beginning to investigate them by experimental means. Like hypnosis, this auto-hypnosis may involve a sort of dissociation or splitting of consciousness; thus it may lead to undesirable consequences, both for religion and for the health of the mystic. In Yoga, as well as with some Sufis, the ascetical practices, the *nothing*[5] of con-

4 Poulain, *Op. Cit.*, pp. 293 ff.
5 The writings of Charles Spearman, noted British psychologist, also

sciousness, is sought. There is not much evidence of the positive
search to find God, or to fill the gap or void of consciousness;
the aim is mostly to escape from the self rather than to approach
and possess the Deity. With other Sufis the process results in
an emptying of consciousness, not only for its own sake, but also
for the purpose of filling consciousness with the Divine Reality.
In this, then, non-Christian mysticism comes very close to that
of the Christians.[6]

HIGHER LEVELS OF MYSTICISM: ECSTASY AND RAPTURE

In discussing the prayer of quiet, it was noted that the error
of the early Quietists consisted largely in that they believed that
they could find God experimentally, that is, feel His immediate
presence by merely removing the blocks, by creating a mental
blank as it were. Now the higher aspects of mystical prayer will
be sketched more fully, according to the notion of Christian
mysticism. These higher phenomena will be shown to differ
psychologically from the psychic processes of the sick minds of
abnormal people.

In all mystical experience there is an immediate awareness
of God. It is, however, a unique kind of approach to God. The
writers all speak of the negative idea of God, and show how
this idea differs from the positive one possessed by ordinary
persons. The terminology is a little confusing, because, philo-
sophically speaking, every man must arrive at his natural notion
of God by ways which involve some kind of negation. That is
to say, the Infinite cannot be conceived positively as infinite.
He must be thought of as possessing perfections; and in each
line of perfection there is no assignable limit. This is the meaning
of the "way of negation" whereby the philosopher arrives naturally
at the truth of God's existence.

With the mystics there is a different meaning to the word

contain frequent references to a technique whereby trained introspectionists
will be able to arrive at a nothingness of conscious content, an awareness
of pure awareness.

6 See John P. Howley, *Op. Cit.*, pp. 265, 184, 185.

"negative." It now refers not only to the way of arriving at the notion, but to the notion itself. Certain attributes are negated which human beings ordinarily have, because of the nature of human mental powers. The human intellect in this life depends on images for the elaboration of concepts. Theologians say that the process of representation, by means of and through images, is exactly what does not happen to the mystics when they have a concept of God. Their idea of Him is negative, in a new and fuller sense; namely, it is not the result of any kind of abstraction from created images of things; it is not the product of generalization from particulars, conceiving all possible perfection and then denying any and all limitation to these perfections. Rather, by a process experienced only by mystics, and described very vividly by them, their minds rise to the widest and most general concept of being almost immediately; this being is at first created, then the Infinite, and finally the ABSOLUTE and the ULTIMATE. There is no relativity in their concept and no comparison and abstraction.

Their wills transcend the data of their own experience, their own relativity of knowledge, their own limitations. St. John of the Cross writes:

> For this reason, then, if anyone is moved to love God by that sweetness he feels, he casts that sweetness away from him, and fixes his love upon God, Whom he does not feel; but if he allowed himself to rest in that sweetness and delight which he feels, dwelling upon them with satisfaction, that would be to love the creature, and that which is of it, and to make the motive an end, and the act of the will would be vitiated; for, as God is incomprehensible and unapproachable, the will, in order to direct its act of love unto God, must not direct it to that which is tangible and capable of being reached by the desire, but must direct it to that which it cannot comprehend nor reach thereby. In this way the will loves that which is certain and true, according to the spirit of the faith, in emptiness and darkness as to its own feelings, above all that it can understand by the operations of the understanding; its faith and love transcend all that it can comprehend. St. John of the Cross, *The Living Flame*, London, Baker, 1912, Letter X, p. 162.

What he seems to be saying here is that in mystical prayer the will directs its act of love to God not through any tangible object but directly. Also there is certainty in this love, there is truth even in the deepest darkness and emptiness, but according to the spirit of faith. This with love transcends understanding. The mystic not only experiences the supernaturality of these acts, but he becomes attentive to the fact that they are passively supernatural. He does not need to know first, then love. By means of his special gifts from on high, he first loves, and in so doing he finds that his knowledge is perfected. Secondary effects of mysticism, such as visions of God, levitation and ecstasy may then put in their appearance. By the will-reaction the mystic perceives the presence of the negative idea of God, the Absolute. Such mystic experiences come and go suddenly and apparently without the person's consent.

The ordinary thinker can only express the absoluteness of God by a denial of the limitations of being represented to consciousness. Thus the ordinary person arrives not at all at the concept of "God in Himself." Most of his concepts are tinged with the reality of creaturehood, making God one with creation under the broad heading of being; thus, an element of pantheistic thinking, a certain identification of oneself with God exists for him. In order to transcend the relative and to conceive God as distinct and yet one with creation, one needs to flee from all representations of created things.

But this would be against a tendency to return to and to utilize phantasms in all our individualized thinking. Thus the mystic's negative idea of God as Absolute has, by a special divine endowment, no remnant of such personal sensory experience in it, not even the image of the person himself. The mystic's idea is more like a love than like a knowing, more a feeling than a picture. Instead of needing to know before he can love, the mystic, by means of his special gifts from on high, first loves, and in so doing he finds that his knowledge is perfected. Then follow the secondary effects of mysticism: vision of God, levitation and ecstasy.

Again, St. John explains how the idea is not attended to in

consciousness before the reaction of the will, but how it becomes daily visible in that very reaction of embracing love. We quote:

> It is, therefore, plain that no distinct object whatever that pleases the will can be God; and for that reason, if it is to be united with Him, it must empty itself, cast away every disorderly affection of the desire, every satisfaction it may distinctly have, high and low, temporal and spiritual, so that, purified and cleansed from all unruly satisfactions, joys, and desires, it may be wholly occupied with all its affections in loving God. For if the will can in any way comprehend God and be united with Him, it cannot be through any capacity of the desire, but only by love; and as all delight, sweetness and joy, of which the will is sensible, is not love, it follows that none of these pleasing impressions can be the adequate means of uniting the will to God; the means are an act of the will. And because an act of the will is united with God, and rests in Him; that act is love. This union is never wrought by feeling, or exertions of the desire, for these remain in the soul as aims and ends. — St. John of the Cross, Op. Cit., p. 161.

No amount of abstraction can bring it, no distraction can drive it away; there is a union of mental acts with each other and with God. Intellect, will, God's love seem all one. Mystics rarely reach this kind of sublime union without passing through various stages of purification known as dark nights, as is amply testified by St. Theresa. We quote:

> Daughters, I assure those of you whom God does not lead by the way of contemplation, that, both by observation and experience, I know that those following it do not bear a lighter cross than you; but indeed you would be aghast at the different kinds of trials God sends them. I know a great deal of both vocations, and am well aware that the sufferings God inflicts on contemplatives are of so unbearable a kind that, unless He sustained such souls by the manna of divine consolations, they would find their pains unsupportable. St. Theresa, *Way of Perfection*, London, Baker, Ed. 1911, Chap. XVIII, Par. 1, p. 112. Quoted by Howley, *Psychology and Mystical Experience*, p. 239.

Traditionally mystics are said to pass through the dark night of the senses, and the dark night of the soul. But these details of mysticism, though very interesting, are not pertinent to this study. Rather a very brief account will be given of the differences between hypnotic and similar phenomena on the one hand, and true mystical experiences on the other. In making the distinction we shall again have to rely upon the reports of the mystics and their behavior.

Let us take ecstasy for example. It will here be taken to mean a mystical experience in the full stage of union of such intensity that the normal sense relation of the soul with the outside world is completely suspended. The subject perceives nothing of the surrounding environment, is frequently incapable of movement, and cannot terminate the ecstasy at will. Ecstasy has a positive as well as a negative aspect, namely the union of intellect and will with God and the deficit of sensori-motor experience. When the state is over, the subject feels great reserves of new moral energy and is stimulated to greater and greater efforts in the spiritual life. Thus the tenseness and apparent strain under which the person seems to exist during ecstasy do not deter him from carrying on his ordinary activities after the mystical experience is over.

Were this phenomenon to be compared with that of hypnotism and drug-intoxication, certain similarities and differences would appear. On the one hand, in the trance of hypnosis as well as the ecstasy the person is able to speak; in both cases there is apparently a dissociation from the immediate environment and a heightened responsivity to certain stimulations (suggestions) exclusively. But apart from this the similarity ends. Authors who are regarded as experts dispute about what is possible and what is not possible under and after hypnosis, especially in regard to the transfer of the rapport from the hypnotist to another person. Certain details will be sketched briefly, which are known for sure about the ecstatic.[7]

In the first place, the one who experiences ecstasy is improved

7 The literature in this field has become so extensive that it is impossible to do justice to it in this chapter. A good authoritative summary appeared in Arnold, M.D., Intern. J. of Clin. and Exp. Hypnosis, Vol. VII, No. 3, July, 1959.

by the experience in the sense that he has more decisiveness, more resolution, more energy and perseverance in keeping his resolutions. He does not become enslaved or dependent upon any other person. He becomes more united to God, the source of his new strength. Secondly, during the ecstasy itself the person is intensely active and not passive; he will on occasion begin to speak, but not very clearly, about what is going on. And when the experience is over, he is somewhat confused by it all, not being able to describe in clear and conventional terms just what has happened, but there is no amnesia for the events. On the contrary, they are very deeply and indelibly imprinted upon his mind, so much so that they will never be forgotten. This element of depth in the case of the mystical experience is talked of with recurring and almost monotonous frequency in all the reports of the mystics.

It is curious that the person who is in the trance cannot be aroused from the state by the ordinary noises and stimulations, nor by being spoken to by the ordinary person; but, in response to the command of a religious superior, the person leaves the trance immediately.

The phenomena of ligature and levitation are too well known to need much description. In the former, the mystic loses the sensory contact with the environment, and even the rational activities are so rigidly channeled that he is compelled in a way to dwell on the objects of his contemplation to such a degree that he can hardly avoid it. He is thus unwilling to and almost incapable of performing the simpler kinds of mental prayer to which he had formerly devoted himself. He confesses that he is, as it were, living in a new world, letting himself be possessed and directed by the events produced in him by God.

In levitation the persons feel that they are in a gravitationless world and it is reported that observers have seen them rise from the ground. Other bodily changes would place this state somewhat on a par with the deep coma spoken of by physiologists. Breathing slows and almost ceases; body temperature drops; the physical state resembles death to an onlooker. Yet with this collapse of the bodily organism there is a superabundant psychic life, showing itself in great progress in virtue after the trance.

During the trance there are experienced visions and revelations, distinct in character—as the Saints realized—from images had by that kind of contemplative who is especially subject to illusions. Spiritual directors are always instructed to warn their subjects that they must not "seek such experiences, that it is better not to have them." Yet St. John of the Cross lays down certain rules according to which the director will help the religious person detect "evil, snares, and illusions" in the visions. The general opinion is that whenever the experiences lead to virtuous living rather than to its opposite, to improvement in goodness rather than to deterioration, they are likely to be genuine. Because the ideas of the mystic are communicated to the mind without sensory images, or any given data of sense, they may on that account be described in rather vague, exaggerated and unrealistic terms. Analogies and symbols will be used which make the picture seem quite impossible to the outside observer. Nevertheless, the experiences must be taken as real when honest and trustworthy persons report them and they are all the less illusory because they are more supernatural. The mystic is generally able to tell for sure whether or not he feels this immediate contact with God, and one trusts the description of the experience. So why doubt the fact of what is experienced! A sample from St. Theresa will be illustrative:

> "But," you will ask me, "if the mind cannot afterwards remember the sublime favors Our Lord bestows in this mansion, what profit do they bring it?" O my daughters! their value cannot be over-rated, for though the recipient is incapable of describing them, they are deeply imprinted in the center of the soul and are never forgotten. "How can they be remembered, if nothing is seen, and the powers of the soul do not comprehend them?" I, too, do not understand this, but I know that certain truths of the greatness of God remain so impressed on the spirit by this favor, that, did not faith teach it Who He is and that it is bound to believe He is God, it would henceforth worship Him as such, as Jacob did when he saw the ladder. St. Theresa, *Interior Castle*, Mansion VI, Chap. IV, Par. 6—quoted by Howley, *Psychology and Mystical Experience*, p. 267.

The reader who is interested in studying this matter at greater length should, by all means, consult the works of A. Poulain, S.J., particulary *The Graces of Interior Prayer*, Part IV. This whole section comprising 99 pages deals with the question of visions and revelations and how to judge them. One or another excerpt should be of particular interest to the psychologist. It is an attempt to interpret the remarks made by the mystic much in the same way that one might try to interpret similar remarks made by his friends. For example, "When X came in church and knelt next to me, I was distracted; not merely distracted—for I could just feel the person." Says St. Theresa, speaking of herself:

> "She sees nothing either outwardly or inwardly ... but without seeing anything, she understands what it is, and where it is, more clearly than if she saw it, only nothing in particular presents itself to her. She is like a person who feels that another is close beside her; but because she is in the dark she sees him not ... without a word, inward or outward, the soul clearly perceives who it is, where he is and occasionally what he means. Why or how she perceives it, she knoweth not; so it is." Relation VII, 26, to Father Rodrigo Alvarez, Life, p. 454.

Pere Poulain, speaking of the manner in which a director should handle certain "seers of visions," might compare favorably with a doctor trying to delve into the hallucinations of his patients. One short quotation will point up what is meant:

> When a seer wishes to be believed on his bare word, we can generally get rid of him by saying: "You assure me that God speaks by your mouth. I have no right to believe you unless you prove it. What sign do you bring?" In his ingenuousness he has not expected this question, and retires abashed. Poulain, *Op. cit.*, p. 399.

One of the wisest counsels and directions which Poulain gives deserves to be publicized and it is given here in its entirety. He is speaking of the rules for the spiritual director and on the manner in which he should regulate his actions, not by revelations but by sound reasons; how he should deal gently with those who believe themselves to have revelations. Quoting St. Theresa, he says:

> At times, indeed, very often this (voice) may be nothing but a fancy, especially with persons of a lively imagination or who are afflicted with melancholy to any marked extent. I think no attention should be paid to such people when they say they see, hear, or learn anything supernaturally. Do not disturb their minds by telling them it comes from the devil, but listen to them as if they were sick persons. Let the Prioress or confessor to whom they tell their story, bid them think no more of it, for such matters do not conduce to the service of God; the devil has deceived many Christians thus, although perhaps it is not so in their case; therefore, they need not trouble themselves about it. St. Theresa, *Interior Castle*, Mansion VI, Chap. III, Par. 2, 3.—quoted in Poulain, *Op. cit.*, p. 399.

THE HIGHEST LEVEL: TRANSFORMING UNION

The climax of all mystical experience is called the "transforming union" or the "spiritual marriage"; it has caused no end of grief to doctors and spiritual directors alike. It is nevertheless possible that a genuine mystic could experience it. Only a few lines will be needed to describe it, and with that the whole matter may be turned over to the spiritual director, in the hope that his psychological training, along with his supernatural virtues, will enable him to guide the soul experiencing this transforming union:

> This is a trance of the senses and faculties of the soul, for everything else combines, as I told you, to make the agony more intense. The understanding realizes acutely what cause there is for grief in separation from God, and His Majesty now augments this sorrow by a vivid manifestation of Himself, thus increasing her anguish to such a degree that the sufferer gives vent to loud cries, which she cannot stifle, however patient and accustomed to pain she may be, because this torture is not corporal, but attacks the innermost recesses of the soul. St. Theresa, *Interior Castle*, Mansion VI, Chap. X, Par. 3.

Actually St. Theresa is here speaking more of the third purgation which precedes in many cases the highest state of union with God or the spiritual marriage. One finds words inadequate to depict what is meant by this union; let it be said briefly that it involves a total annihilation of the self and a new creation of the human person now totally immersed in the Divine; he lives, not now by himself but God lives in him. And this new life is experienced first hand, as it were.

By way of summary, the mystical experiences described above will be reviewed. The prayer of simplicity melts into the prayer of quiet, and quiet deepens toward union, union flames to ecstasy, and ecstasy passes into transforming union. These are rather subjective distinctions, it is true, and the experiences vary from person to person. They are all in the order of faith and thus transcend our feeble intelligence to grasp them in their entirety.

The negative idea of God, incapable of full description by those not endowed with it, has such stupendous dynamism when impressed on the will that the soul is totally transformed. Yet the beginnings of such a concept are possible for anyone using natural reason. It may well be that the element of the faith of the everyday Catholic which links his idea of God with that of the mystic, or with the ecstatic orison of the great Saint, is the unknown psychic element bridging one's imagined idea of God with the imageless intangible idea of the mystic. Then there could be traced a gradual progress of spiritual experiences starting from conversion, passing through several degrees of charity and altruism, and culminating in the felt union of being immersed in the Deity. A general caution can and should be sounded with regard to this matter. The mystics themselves advise that one ought not seek to attain mystical experience by his own efforts. These experiences could be harmful, especially if one is not adequately prepared for them.

Note: The author is deeply indebted to numerous insights received from classes in psychology of religion held at Loyola University during the years 1955 through 1962. Especially helpful have been the efforts and advice of Rev. James J. Doyle, S.J., professor of ascetical theology, West Baden College, West Baden Springs, Indiana. The author requested Fr. Doyle to add a short sketch of his own views on mysticism, since he has had years of experience in teaching this subject to theology students. This he very kindly agreed to do and the result will be found in the following pages.

FATHER JAMES DOYLE ON MYSTICISM AND PSYCHOLOGY

At the very start some methodological considerations are not out of place. We begin by posing three questions, and giving brief answers to them. First, does mystical experience in any way transcend the sphere and method of the psychologist? Second, if so, does it in any way still furnish matter for the psychologist? Third, if not, is the psychologist the sole purveyor of truth concerning it? It would, perhaps, be better not to begin or even try to begin with a definition of mystical experience. It might be wiser simply to state that there are a large number of experiences which everyone connects with religious mysticism, as well as a large number of analogous experiences whose religious significance is disputed. This is sufficient to mark out our field.

Of much more importance is the question of the limits of psychological method, if question two is answered affirmatively. Psychology cannot transgress these limits without denying its own methodology. Psychology is limited to the study of conscious states and acts which can be discovered and systematized by behavioristic and introspectionist methods. If there is an assumption of the omni-competence of these procedures, so that mystical experience will be held to be identical in kind and continuous with other human experience, psychologists may claim that the third question must be answered in the affirmative. That there is a profound continuity of the mystical states with the fundamental modes and general forms of human psychology, there can be no doubt. If the psychologist will be content with this profound continuity without wishing to make it into an identity, then all will be well. If he will assume and carry out an attitude of neutrality, then there can be agreement between him and the theologian. We ought to note that this attitude may be difficult to maintain, unless the psychologist is also at the same time a philosopher and a theologian.

We turn again to the second question: even if mystical experience does transcend the sphere of the psychologist, does it still furnish subject matter for him? As was indicated, we can give an answer to this, but an abstract one: even if the experiences of the mystic are supernatural and follow other laws, there is still a profound continuity between them and our natural mental structure. There is room for the psychologist. But how can we apply this principle in practice? Some points may be considered perfectly clear and agreed upon: the age, sex, nationality, historical circumstances of his existence—all influence the mystic. These can be traced and investigated by the psychologist. Further, in regard to those phenomena which are called para-mystical (sensible visions, levitation, haloes, odors, stigmata, prolonged fasts or vigils, etc.) theologians are the first to consult experts in psychology and medicine. But is this all? Is the psychologist content with this? Does he not want to investigate the essential mystical experience itself? If so, then the precautions mentioned before with regard to method must be observed. In other words, let us admit that he may treat of mystical experience itself, and try to discover its continuity with and similarity to ordinary experience.

If we proceed to the investigation, we must make ourselves very clear on the ordinary elements or the ordinary structure of our properly human experience. Structure here is to be distinguished from content, and refers to the invariable features of human knowledge-experience, namely understanding and judgment. It would be difficult to exaggerate the importance of this point. Properly human knowledge occurs in the judgment and only in the judgment. Any way of describing or explaining any human knowledge (except the beatific vision) which neglects or denies this is not likely to give a correct account of mystical experience.

A second point, of no less importance, is that our so-called general concepts, those especially of metaphysics and, with due regard for the necessary distinctions, of both Natural and Sacred Theology, are not had by any process of abstraction, and certainly not by any process of abstraction from phantasms. True, the mind must grasp some reality in the phantasm, but when it comes to elaborating the concepts of being, truth, goodness and so forth, the attention must be paid to their genesis from what we should term rational consciousness. Rather they are grasped by grasping the structure of the mind; they are heuristic rather than conditioned concepts. (Cf. Lonergan, *Insight.* pp. 359-363; 369, 371, 683-684), that is "they are definitions at second remove." Our intellects, being potential, can define being "only at a second remove as whatever is to be known by intelligent grasp and reasonable affirmation." (*Ibid.*, p. 371)

The enormous consequences of this appear at once. If being is so conceived, and if our concepts of God are to be sought also in some process, not of abstraction, but of an attempt to grasp what an *unconditioned* act of understanding would be, then we must interpret with extreme care some of the statements which the mystics make about "knowledge without concepts, immediate knowledge, etc." This, it seems, follows from the modest part allowed to the psychologist in handling not merely the concomitants of mystical experience, but the experience itself.

There is no doubt that the characteristic of mystical experience, that which distinguishes it from ordinary religious experience, is the felt presence of God, the realization that "God is here," that He is within me, etc. But one ought to add that these experiences are all had "in the faith," or better, "in Faith." If we recall that faith is a matter of judgment, that the concepts it uses are already supplied prior to the grace of faith, then we have moved a long way toward grasping the new element that emerges in mystical experience. It is an element relative to judgment rather than to concept. It is a modification of the judgment of faith. The ordinary Catholic says: "This is true because God has revealed it, etc." It is the act of grasping and contemplating the truth that characterizes faith. Now the mystic continues this, but his faith is an "illuminated faith," as St. John of the Cross tells us. The added grace of mystical experience or realization is surely not confined simply to the truth that "God is here," but any truth of our Faith can be the object of mystical experience. The element of realization, of immediateness comes rather from the fact that the conditions for the judgment are now more and more on the side of the subject. This does not, emphatically, make the act purely subjectivistic, but it is the internal experience of the subject, and not external experience that begins to play a role here. Moreover, it is a question of attention to elements in internal experience which were not attended to before that promotes this experience to the point where the mind in judging takes account of them. It is a case of a judgment by way of inclination, or by way of connaturality (with one's good subjective dispositions) that the reflex act of understanding grasps as evidence for the judgment and the modalities of the judgment. The mind uses its own reactions, inclinations, its felt love, joy, reverence, etc., as a basis for the judgment. Since the judgment is, as St. Thomas teaches, a mental word, distinct from the first mental word or concept, the mind making this judgment can rest in it, and enjoy it.

Another way of putting the same matter is to state that in mystical experience the mind attends to the supernaturality of its acts. By infused faith, hope and love the mind is supernaturalized, put into immediate contact with God. St. Thomas likes to speak of the mind as adhering to God immediately (*mens Deo adheret*). But in ordinary religious experience the supernaturality of these acts, though present, and in a true sense conscious, is not and cannot be attended to. Their supernatural passivity goes unnoticed. But with mystical graces, there comes the attention to their very supernaturality, to the fact that they do unite us to God, though still in the darkness of faith. Again, the mind is now aware of and attending to its union with God. For the union is actual in and through the supernaturality of these acts.

Recall now what we said earlier about the statements of the mystics concerning non-conceptual knowledge, and how we indicated that our concepts of metaphysical truths do not arise by an abstraction from phantasm, but by grasping the structure of the mind in reference to *any* phantasmal presentation. Here we get the notions of the true, the intelligible and the good. Now, when the supernaturalized mind attends to its new structure, its relation to God who is the supreme intelligible, supreme truth and goodness, it proceeds in exactly the same way to get a concept of Him and all that pertains to Him. It seems like an empty concept, like the concept of the intelligible, the true which is achieved by natural reason. For this reason the mystic is led to speak of non-conceptual knowledge.

If the theory proposed for explaining mystical experience is admitted to be a psychological one, as we think it must be, and if it is to be an adequate one, then it ought to serve to explain all the characteristics commonly attributed to mystical experience. Let us see if this is the case.

We have claimed that the characteristic of non-conceptual knowledge is explained. Along with this goes the explanation of what mystics experience when they pass from what is called the prayer of simplicity (which is non-infused prayer) to the first stage of mystical prayer, namely the prayer of quiet. They say that they seem to be passing from light and day to darkness and night; that their thought becomes less clear, less distinct, etc. Now, this is just what one would expect if the mystic is being led to attend to the structure of the mind and its acts rather than to their content, especially their content as connected with special and particular phantasmal presentations. Is this not what happens when metaphysical notions are arrived at? The mind is turning away from distinct phantasmal contents to consider the structure of the mind itself as it is realized in the grasp of such content. The content seems so clear, so distinct, so *real*, and the ideas of the intelligible, the true, and the good, so unreal, that when the structure is considered apart from any definite content, the experience is like passing from light to darkness.

Next there is the characteristic of certitude. The mystic cannot doubt that God is present during the course of the experience. Later involuntary doubts, even great doubts may arise. Clearly, the explanation is in the passivity experienced when the mystical grace is actually bestowed. This passivity is simply another way of designating the characteristic, so often and so much insisted on by St. Theresa and other writers, of supernaturality. The experience, they say, is one that the mind knows it cannot produce by its own powers; special power must be added which is called the grace of contemplation. These writers

224 / religious psychology

insist further that God grants this grace to whom He wills, when He wills and as He wills. Little wonder then that once this special grace is withdrawn and the mystic finds himself with his ordinary powers of prayer, by which he cannot produce this experience, he begins to doubt the actual experience.

So far we have considered the common characteristics of mystical experience and tried to show how our explanation fits the facts. It will not be out of order here to warn ourselves of the ever-present danger of the "psychologist's fallacy." It threatens both the one who presents the explanation and the one who reads it. The explanation is a theory and is merely intended to explain, not to give the reader the mystic experience itself, any more than the equations of thermodynamics are meant to give the mathematician the feeling of the drowsy breezes of summer, or the cool winds of autumn.

Are there stages of growth in mystical experience? The answer is in the affirmative, as seen above, and this answer is based on the writings of the mystics themselves. Writers have found various numbers of degrees: the division most commonly accepted and solidly based is that given by St. Theresa in her book, *The Interior Castle.* Seven stages of prayer are enumerated and described. The first three stages are levels of non-mystical prayer: discursive prayer, affective prayer, and simplified affective prayer or prayer of simplicity. The next four levels are mystical prayer: prayer of quiet, of full union, of ecstasy, and finally, the spiritual marriage. Our concern is limited to the last four. Of course, other writers give other names to these stages and, as was said above, find many more divisions than these. But these four stages can be distinguished fairly clearly and with some systematic exactness. Since we will later study ecstasy and show that it is not clearly a different stage, let us say that there are three principal degrees or levels: they are recollection and quiet, full union, and transforming union or spiritual marriage. In the first degree it is the will in which the passivity is experienced. It is held, fixed and the other powers of the soul can suffer distractions, and in fact effort is needed to keep them fixed. At this stage, even the intellect is subject to distractions, for the fixity of the will does not influence it very much; or at least, influences it with varying degrees of intensity.

In the second principal stage, called above the degree of full union, God lays hold of all the powers of the soul, and renders them fully passive, so that the soul no longer suffers any distractions and need make no effort to preserve union. Note then that in ecstasy there is a twofold element; the one negative and the other positive. The negative element is the impossibility of using the senses or the power of motion, and this is often manifested in phenomena which can be matched in abnormal psychology, such as the states which accompany hysteria and other deviant mental processes. The positive element is the union of the intellect and will with God. The external phenomena of ecstasy have captured the attention of psychologists and have led some of them to rather startling conclusions.

It is said that in mystical experience we have a "swoon," that the mystic is a victim of mono-ideism, that it is a more or less self-induced pathological state. Now here is where we must recall the methodological considerations set down at the beginning of this section. Does one claim that the external phenomena are the essence of what the mystics thought their experience to be? If so, then those startling conclusions are justified. But what do the mystics themselves tell us? That along with these phenomena they experienced a very great union with God. To excise this clear simple report, based on consciousness itself, from the accounts of the mystics is surely to commit a methodological blunder; it is to claim, implicitly at least, that no such union as the mystics describe is at all possible, or to judge the experience from its external characteristics only. It should be emphasized, we believe, that there have been mystics who have gone on to the highest degree of union, the transforming union, and have never experienced ecstasy. Further, ecstasy is not the only degree of mystical prayer and experience. To treat it as such and to reduce it to an identity with some abnormal pathological states is to transgress the limits of method.

The final stage of mystical prayer is called the transforming union. Volumes could be devoted to this beautiful and inspiring phenomenon, but we must be content with just a few of the famous Maxims of St. John of the Cross. *"One desire only* does God allow, and suffer in His presence, within the soul,—the desire of keeping the law perfectly, and carrying the Cross of Christ.... The goods of God, which are beyond measure, can be contained *only* in an *empty* and *solitary* heart ... it is by an act that the will is united with God, and rests in Him; that act is *love....*"

10 empirical studies on relevant topics

1. ATTITUDES TOWARD RELIGION AND SCIENCE

A study on attitudes toward religion and science was done by Miss Petros-Johnson and had as its purpose a sampling of common reactions to questions concerning religious motivations. College students were the subjects of these questionnaires. This hopeful investigator is to be praised for the attempt, at least, to gather empirical data on a question that is most difficult and elusive, namely, the inner reasons for church attendance, for prayer and conversions, for virtuous living generally. The flaws in the study far outweigh the good points, but credit will be given the author for making a serious attempt to fathom some of the depths of thought which give rise to the apparent conflicts between religion and science, in the minds of young educated persons.

The questionnaire used was short, with only ten questions dealing with the respondents' idea of psychology, religion and science. Only six of the questions proved meaningful for this study of the psychology of religion. These six are listed, together with some hints for improving the scale.

One of the questions used was: What is the place in our society of converters, such as Billy Graham? Fifty percent of the respondents thought that works such as his had a value in our society, in so far as they helped to bring men to realize God's mercy and love.

The next question: Have you seen any long-term results of

conversion? This received an overwhelming "yes," but the yeas were always qualified with some such expression as: If conversion does last, it has to be built upon some deeper convictions than those aroused by the emotional appeals of the converter. The investigator might easily improve his tool by supplying multiple-choice answers for the respondent. The alternative choices should be derived from preliminary interviews with the potential respondents.

The next question was: What percentage of church-goers would you estimate go as a result of parental influence rather than of conviction? Answers range from 75% to 90%. This high figure will be especially meaningful when taken in conjunction with the findings of other investigators in the same area.

The fourth question had to do with the meaning and importance of the ideas "scientific psychology of religion" in our modern times. All the respondents thought that this "science" had value today, and some of the reasons which were most frequently given are the following: Science will do much to purify religion of its emotionalism; there will be, as a result of science, a better analysis of just why men go to church.

A multiple-choice answer would be strongly suggested here also; otherwise it is next to impossible to analyze the responses accurately. In addition, it must be remembered that the respondents will judge to be objectively important that which they themselves engage in. Hence full data regarding the church-going activities and other related behavior should be had from all the respondents, if at all possible, in view of the personal character of the questions asked.

Part one of the last question: Are space-age developments causing people to return to the security of their churches? A common answer to this was, "Suffering and threats of suffering remind men of God, and make them go to God in prayer." Part two of this question read: Why are the churches so well attended at Christmas and Easter? Common responses here were: "A sense of guilt," or "Tradition, and the desire to engage in symbolic behavior with all its pageantry often motivate church attendance at these times."

On the whole, the answers were meager, probably due in

large part to the kind of questions used in the list. Even with the best possible list it will be found that it is not an altogether easy matter to motivate subjects to answer honestly and truthfully, as soon as they learn that they are to be questioned on such delicate matters as these.

2. RELIGIOUS EXPERIENCES OF JUNIOR HIGH SCHOOL GIRLS: A STUDY BASED ON SEVENTY-FIVE QUESTIONS

A study was made by Mary Lou Doherty which had for its purpose an analysis of the religious experiences of young girls. The questionnaire method was used and the respondents were kept anonymous. Such personal questions were asked as: What is your experience of the love of God most like? The love of mother for a child; that of the mother for the father; that of one child for another, etc.? Each question gave five choices for the respondent. The answers were subsequently counted, and the end result is really an analysis, made by the girls themselves, with the aid of leading questions, of their own religious experiences. Some of the main findings will be sketched here.

By actual count, Miss Doherty found that 38% of the girls compared the love of God with love for a parent, but 60% found it unlike any human relationship. Those same girls who found the love of God unlike any human relationship still were able to say that these same relationships occasioned in them a reaction of loving God, mostly when the girls had been aware of the goodness of someone toward themselves.

The investigator was also able to tally responses in regard to elements which might be called intellectual in their love for God. Forty-four percent said that they at least occasionally loved God from motives which were primarily intellectual rather than emotional. Twenty-eight percent said that they loved God by a strong effort of their wills, and only 8% loved God by a purely intellectual decision that God ought to be loved. Only 4% ever seriously questioned, over a long period of time, the existence of God, and 4% questioned the divinity of Christ. Another finding, indicative of some of the difficulties adolescents

have, is the folowing: In describing their most common reactions
to the love of God, 24% were unable to feel as they should
about God, 24% feared what God could do to them, and 18%
had a confused, uncertain, or guilty reaction. This low percentage
reacting out of fear is quite different from the one published by
Leonard Gross in his stimulating but inaccurate and misleading
book called *God and Freud.*

Some personal and emotional reactions found in this study
are of special interest and value for a psychology of religion.
For instance, 62% of the girls feel that God has a personal
interest in them; 22% feel their love of God more than that for
their mother, 18% more than that for their father, and 28%
more than that for their best friend. Again 54% are in some
way physically-emotionally moved by their experience of God,
with half of these feeling a very warm emotional experience,
the others feeling a sense of physical aliveness.

Finally, in describing God's attitudes toward them, 62%
of the girls always feel that God has a personal love for them,
20% frequently feel this, and 12% occasionally do. Fifty percent
always feel that they are helped by God's love when they feel
depressed, 26% frequently feel so, and 18% occasionally do.

The student who carried out the research felt that the girls
she questioned gave out spontaneous and perhaps unreliable
responses. One could grant that the answers might have been
very spontaneous, but it is not altogether obvious that they are
on this account unreliable. The investigator says that the fact
that the biggest majority of the girls have never questioned the
existence of Christ shows that they have not yet been faced with
very strong opposition to their religious pattern . . . or that they
have not yet questioned their motivations. To this, it may be
answered that nevertheless these answers do show, when taken
at their face value, that doubts are not so common in adolescents
as one might expect, and that religion gives comfort to these
girls in their everyday lives. Religion also helps them in their
doubts and difficulties. On the whole, these 50 girls had a good
personal relationship with their teacher who gave them the
questionnaires, or else they would not have taken the trouble
to answer the long list of questions. For this reason readers will

probably trust the findings even more than they would trust those of a priest or nun making such a study. In these latter cases the girls might well have yielded much more to the temptation to give the "expected" answer wherever possible.

3. CHANGES IN RELIGIOUS ATTITUDES FOLLOWING CLIENT-CENTERED THERAPY

The third study was done by Rev. A. Ramierez, O.F.M., and was undertaken for the precise purpose of discovering whether or not there would be a change in religious feelings and attitudes following upon therapy. The reason for choosing the client who had undergone this type of therapy was that it is often heard that the permissiveness of the method would be likely to engender irreligious or even immoral attitudes in the subject. The only way in which an investigator could learn whether or not the client did change or develop hostility toward religion during a dozen or more sessions, was to study the recorded sessions, the actual pronouncements of the client during the treatment process. Father Ramierez decided to do just this with a couple of cases which had terminated somewhat successfully, in the mind of the therapist, at least.

Father Ramierez studied intensively the first session, the middle one, and the last one, with some difficulty in deciding which statements would be interpreted as reflecting a religious or an ethical attitude. He partially solved this problem by applying a standard definition to the concept of religion, which was: a system of beliefs and moral precepts which the client held and which regulated him in his relationship with the Deity. This would, then, include ceremonial acts as well as moral judgments. Father Ramierez then prepared a set of categories of response which would reflect the client's state of mind with regard to the religious-moral attitudes of his life. These categories were: (1) Believing versus unbelieving. Examples were: "God is a forgiving Father," "The idea of God and heaven is silly"; (2) Morally good versus morally evil. Examples were: "I've given up drinking, it's not good for me," "I want full freedom in finding succesful sexual experiences"; (3) Worshipping versus atheistic attitudes. Examples were: "I get true peace of mind out of worshipping God," and "I see no use spending time and money in churches." As a check, neutral responses were also counted. This category included all other statements not subsumed under the above six categories and yet which had some sort of religious connotation.

A typical case was used as a beginning. It was that of H. Brian, published by Rogers in its entirety. The units counted in the various categories were always single sentences, that is complete propositions. "Hum—" and "Yes" responses were taken as units only when they clearly endorsed attitudes reflected by the therapist.

As stated, the first, the last, and the middle counseling sessions were the ones analyzed. These represented the series which lasted three months, and the length of each weekly treatment period was approximately 50 minutes. In the first interview there were 85% neutral responses and 15% unbelieving or atheistic and immoral responses. In the middle sessions, these percentages change to 87.6% and 12.4% respectively, with a fraction of one percent only in the "unbelieving and morally good" category. In the final session the following proportions are seen: 84.6% neutral responses, 8% irreligious and morally evil responses, 7.4% believing and morally good responses.

Although these figures merely indicate trends, it appears that the kind of responses designated as "neutral" tend to remain constant throughout the series. The only notable changes are from the category of atheistic-immoral to that of believing-moral responses. The accuracy of the count was verified by a second rater who approved all of the first rater's categorizations. The study is being pursued with many more cases, and promises to give conclusive evidence that "permissive" therapy has not been shown to make a person more immoral and more irreligious than he was before the treatment.

The author of the study concludes: "Non-directive techniques and attitudes cannot have reinforced any anti-moral and anti-religious attitudes on the part of the clients studied."

4. A STUDY OF RELIGIOUS MATURITY IN ADOLESCENTS

Mr. Thomas Schaefer, in an attempt to secure deeper insights into the religious beliefs and feelings of adolescents, interviewed an 18-year-old boy and an 18-year-old girl at considerable length. He was interested principally in seeking out differences between the boy and the girl, but he also wished to try his hand at evaluating the religious maturity of these persons. He noted that very little had been done along these lines with Catholics, but a good deal with non-Catholics. Hence he selected for his study two young Catholics, and decided to apply to them some norms of religious maturity found in W. Clark's *Psychology of Religion*, Macmillan, 1958.

The method used for collecting the data was the directed-interview method. He based his study on 58 very personal questions, of such a nature that the inner desires and aspirations of the subjects would be uncovered to some degree at least. He later evaluated the answers to these questions in terms of Clark's criteria of religious maturity. These criteria are the following: Religion must be primary, fresh, growing, self-critical, free from magic, integrating, humble, socially effective, and meaningfully dynamic.

The same procedure was followed for the boy as for the girl. The investigator then concluded that the religion of the boy is of about average maturity, and so is that of the girl. For both he makes the comment: Their religion is neither so great as to class them in the area of saintliness, nor is it so meager as to class them in the area of the lax.

Several students and the teacher decided to push the investigation a little further. They selected certain key questions and assigned to each of them a maximum score of 20, so that the highest score a person could get for religious maturity would be 100 and the lowest, zero. The questions were: (1) Do you believe in God? (2) Are you frankly more concerned with and anxious about the affairs of your life than the inevitability of your death? (3) How often do you attend church? (4) Which motive is stronger, loving God for Himself, or loving Him mostly because if you don't you will get thrown into hell? (5) To what extent, if any, do you enjoy praying? Do you perform prayers as a dull chore, or out of a sense of duty, or in imitation of another person?

There was no difficulty in getting a score for the persons singly, on their religious maturity. The maturity score for the 18-year-old boy turned out to be 57, and that for the 18-year-old girl, 65.

Thus the shortened form of the same test gave the boy and the girl an average rating in maturity, with the girl somewhat above the boy, as would be expected from common opinion in these matters. Then it was decided to use the shortened form of the test, namely, the five questions, on a sample of the citizenry taken more or less at random. The tester took this as his criteria of selection: anybody he would meet on the elevated train going from 6500 North to 800 North. Thirty persons were interviewed in this fashion, and their distribution by religion turned out to be 4 agnostics, 1 atheist, 3 "gentlemen of the road," 3 graduate students who would not declare their religion, and 19 casual workers who also did not declare any religious affiliation. The average score for these 30 persons, using the above-mentioned scale, was 37. The atheist and the agnostics scored lowest, as would be expected from the system of scoring used.

The questionnaire, as well as the method of scoring, leaves much to be desired. Yet even with such crude instruments, the private religious feelings and experiences of individuals who are willing to speak can be somewhat roughly described. As for Clark's eight criteria of a mature religion, it seems that they are too complex and "indescribable" to enable an investigator to score them accurately. The five questions selected by the researcher do however tend to throw some light on the matter of whether or not a person's religion is fresh and active, integrating and elevating, socially effective to the extent of his being willing to discuss it with an interviewer who is a total stranger to him.

5. A STUDY OF THE ATTITUDES OF ADOLESCENT GIRLS TOWARD PRIESTS

This study was carried out first in Brussels, at the International

Center for Studies in Religious Education, and the results were published in *Lumen Vitae*.[1] The authors of the study were four nuns, who prepared the questionnaire and secured the data, and prepared the article as well. Here only those parts of the research which seem pertinent to the psychology of religion will be given, together with a comparison between the responses given by Belgian girls and by American girls.

The number of subjects tested in Brussels was 300. They were what would be classed here as high-school students, and rather homogeneous from an educational and from a social standpoint. Their ages ranged from 14 to .20, with 80% of them between 15 and 18. Their socio-economic level would be called middle class and upper middle class.

The questions were of such a nature that the "expected" answers could not easily be found. Moreover, in some of the questions the subjects could easily and naturally project their own feelings and preferences upon the problems presented in the test. The form of the test was partly yes-no, with space for a qualification, partly multiple-choice, and partly comment on small case histories.

The same set of questions was presented to a group of high-school girls in Chicago. The women who collected the data were members of the Loyola University Alumnae Sodality. Whereas in the Belgian study, only the most and least desirable choices were recorded by the testee, the Loyola study required the students to rank all the alternatives, sometimes ten or more, in the order of preference. This enabled the investigator to perform more operations upon the data than were possible in the Belgian sample. The subjects in Chicago were 150 girls within the same age range as those of the Belgian sample. The economic level of the American girls was also middle and upper class. A sample of American boys is also being prepared, in order to compare the religious attitudes of boys with those of girls, in so far as their reaction to various aspects of Catholic priesthood is concerned.

In the analysis which follows, the remarks made by the four

1 Lumen Vitae, XII, 1957, No. 2, pp. 342-352.

nuns with respect to the Brussels sample will not be noted, but percentages will be computed here, so as to make a comparison between the Belgian and the American samples. The question will be stated and, immediately afterward, the kind of responses given by the American and the Belgian samples respectively. Question One reads: "To which role is that of the priest nearest?" (Six different professions were listed for choice.) The preferred similar role for the Belgians was that of the doctor (69% choosing this), and so was it for the Americans (54% choosing it). The second most desirable role was for Belgians that of professor (12%) and for Americans, professor (14%). The profession to which the priesthood was least similar was that of director for Belgians, and soldier-tied with lawyer—for Americans. Here we see that the pattern of thinking of Catholic girls in widely different parts of the world, though stereotyped to a degree, differs from place to place.

When asked to state positive similarities between the priesthood and other roles, they agreed very well; when asked for dissimilarities there is less agreement, as would be expected from the principle that the number of possible differences is unlimited. Neither of the above percentage differences is significant at the .05 level of confidence, when tested by chi square corrected for continuity by Yates formula. (Hereafter differences significant at or beyond the .05 level will be marked with an asterisk.)

The second question was worded: "Why is it that only men are called to the priesthood?" Then seven answers were suggested; the first number in parenthesis will indicate the Belgian percentage, and the second, the American. "Because Christ, the first priest, was a man." (32) (43); "Because certain features in a woman's character would be unsuitable in a priest." (25) (12); "Because Christ, the first victim, was a man." (11) (13). In this comparison it seems that there is a tendency for Brussels girls to stress the unsuitableness of the woman's character for the priesthood. Americans, on the other hand, stress the character of Christ, whose place the priest is taking.

The third question read: "Have you ever wondered why Catholic priests in our country cannot marry? Underline the reason:" "In order that they may be freer for their apostolate." (35) (42); "So that they may belong more completely to God." (36) (36); "So that they may more resemble Christ." (17) (7). Here again it is seen that the institution of celibacy is understood in practically an identical fashion by the girls in Brussels and by the girls in Chicago. The nuns in Belgium state that: An examination shows that the motive of belonging to God tends to increase with age. And in Belgium, as well as in Chicago, the replies show that little value is attached to the psychological reasons, namely, "So that they may speak more authoritatively about the sixth and ninth commandments," and "So that people will have confidence more readily in the absolute secrecy of the confessional." In both places also the motive of imitation of Christ who was not married did not seem to be a very powerful one. Finally, in both places the comments written in by the students did not add much to the choice already given. They only exemplify one or another of the reasons suggested in the questionnaire.

Question Four read: "If you had to give one single counsel to a priest appointed to be chaplain to a group of young girls, which would be your primary choice?" The answer most frequently chosen by Belgians was: "Do not be afraid to tell them home truths." (44); this was second in frequency for Americans (21),* and here for the first time there is a significant difference. The reason for the difference lies, in all probability, in the meaning which the girls in the two places attach to the term "home truths." But it seems noteworthy that there is here too a change with age, among the Americans at least. The older they get, the less they think the priest should tell girls "home truths." So the second choice for Belgians was: "Don't talk too much about vocations." (16), which was the first for Americans (33). The Belgian third choice was almost tied with their second, and it was: "Do not judge their conduct too severely." (14), which for Americans was also (14).

Question Five was: "What qualities would you most prefer in a priest?" The traits will be listed in rank order for Belgians first, and then for Americans. They are: understanding, sincerity, will power, hope in God ... politeness. And then: understanding, sincerity, humility, hope in God . . . zeal. It is noticed that, where-as there are not any differences in the top two traits, there are in the third trait and in the last. In this question we have a case in which the girls differ least, whether we consider the scatter of scores within either nation, or whether we consider the two nations together. The priest is not considered to be much in need of "intelligence" when this trait is compared to the others in the list. Traits next to the bottom in both groups are "abnega-tion regarding comfort," and "respect for people."

The nuns in Belgium consider that Question Five is a real case in which the girls projected their own desires upon the character of the priest. They say that understanding, sincerity, and will power have always been highly valued in adolescent girls, and that this might be the reason why the girls selected these traits for their priests. If that is true for Belgium, then the same argument would hold for the Americans, since they selected the same two traits as most desired in their priests. It will only become evident after further research with larger groups, whether or not this choice of traits is a matter of "adolescent projection."

Question Six read: "To which reason do you principally attribute the fact of ceasing to practice religion?" The answers: "Because religious instruction was insufficient." (48) (29)*; and, "Because of the Church's moral demands about marriage." (13) (34)*; and, "Because of the influence of the husband upon the wife." (21) (22). In this case there is a complete reversal of the answers which occupy first and second places, and both reach significance. Apparently the Belgian girls value their instruction very much as a means of keeping the faith, whereas Americans believe that the restraints placed upon marriage by the Catholic Church are a frequent cause of loss of faith. How-ever, the frequency with which Americans selected their "top-rating" cause is still below the frequency of the Belgian selection, namely, 34%, as compared to 48%. Further questioning of these adolescents would be necessary in order to receive the full import of their answers to this important question. Another noteworthy feature of the responses to this question is the fact that both groups, American and Belgian, attribute the same small amount of responsibility to the priests' behavior as a cause of loss of faith, that is, exclusive of his activities in giving instructions. The percentages of the three low-rating choices are given: "Because a priest has offended them." (8) (3); "Because some priests are engaged in politics." (1) (0); "Because of some priests' misbehavior." (5) (3).

The nuns who wrote the Belgian report think that the tendency for even 20% of their girls to blame the loss of faith upon "insufficient instruction" may perhaps show a form of "aggressive criticism" usual at this age. The argument they give for this interpretation is that the girls selected this reason with increasing frequency the older they became. Without some interviews it would be impossible to state the real reasons for blaming the loss of faith upon poor instruction.

Question Seven reads: "If you marry would you like your son to be a priest? Why?" The answers are: "Yes" (74) (78); and "No" (16) (13). And as one would expect, those girls who have more relatives already in the religious life or in the priesthood, do actually wish their sons to be priests with greater frequency—significantly greater. And this is true for Belgium as well as for America. In each nation, some very egocentric or non-altruistic motives are stated as the reasons for wishing their sons to be priests. Examples are: "It is an honor for the family"; "More blessings are received from one's priest"; "Know that someone is praying for me"; "I shall be more certain of gaining salvation." A few non-selfish reasons were given also, such as: "The priest would help to redeem my own life which is too self-centered."

Question Eight is a short anecdote describing the fact that an adolescent girl who comes home from a boarding school to spend the summer with her family always finds a priest, a friend of the family, coming to her home for visits. She always finds some pretext for slipping away as soon as the priest arrives. The questions are: "Do you understand her behavior?" "How do you explain it?" The "yes" responses for Belgians were (94), whereas for Americans they were (57),* and here again there is a significant difference. The "no" responses were (5) and (35) respectively. In trying to analyze the reasons given, this difference for the two groups in "yes" responses should be remembered, as well as in the "no" responses. The most frequently given reason for Belgians was: "Affective relationship with the priest" (21); next came: "Shyness" (17); then, "Something on her conscience" (16). The answer, "Something on her conscience" occurred more often among the older girls, whereas shyness was more often cited by the younger girls. It is difficult to make exact comparisons because of the shades of meaning given to such terms as "shyness" and "affection," but there does not seem to be any obvious national difference in the frequencies for the various explanations, apart from the fact that Americans seem to be less able to "understand" why the girl should slip away whenever the priest arrives.

Question Nine deals with the question of whether or not a girl would be indifferent to receiving absolution from a priest in a state of mortal sin. The percentages of "yes" and "no" are almost identical for the two countries, namely (45) "yes," and (35) "no." Among the reasons given by Belgians for not being indifferent to receiving such absolution was found the following, with rather astounding frequency: "The absolution would be invalid." Thus, about one-fifth of the girls simply do not know their doctrine. It is most interesting that, in the other added reasons, about the same percentage was found in America as in Belgium holding this reason.

The last question dealt with a story in which a girl is found in an embarrassing position, and confides to her girl friend. This girl friend advises her to go to a certain priest who solves difficult problems. The question was: "Do you entirely agree in this?" "Yes" (72) (70); "Categorically disagree?" "Yes" (14) (4); "Distinguish certain types or situations?" "Yes" (10) (25). Here again in both localities we find age differences in the answers. The replies in which a distinction is drawn between situations where the priest is a good counselor, and others in which parents, or a friend, would give better advice, are given mostly by girls over 17 years of age.

(Note: In listing the percentages, no account was taken of persons who did not respond and hence the total percentage is always less than 100.)

General comments could be made about the answers in this

very interesting questionnaire. It would seem that adolescent girls do not evaluate their priests in the cold and rational manner of neutral adults, i.e., adults who are not parents. They seem to respond in most instances more emotionally than logically. In this it is just possible that they reflect the emotional or sentimental kind of reaction which characterizes their parents. On the other hand it is conceivable that the reaction is one of immaturity and insecurity, and obviously these two traits are present in adolescents to a rather notable degree. Both parents and adolescents could be better instructed in the real "sacramental" role of the priest. They could also be told that most priests are now being trained to engage in "pastoral" counseling with their parishioners. Most priests now as of yesterday are actually fairly well-trained in handling problems normally expected to occur day by day during the natural process of growing up and maturing.

(These empirical studies have been included in the hope that the reader may wish to repeat some or all of them with other groups.)

11 tools and methods of psychology of religion

INTRODUCTION

AFTER reporting on these few empirical studies it is proper for us now to explain how far it is possible to use scientific method in the psychology of religion. Whenever mention is made of method one likes to think that he is modern and scientific, or at least reliable in his approach to a given subject. Scientific canons particularly stress the need for repetition, the requirement that repeated observations are needed in order to confirm a certain hypothesis. This is as it should be; otherwise the first observation may have been an accident. Science also requires a possibility of prediction that, under like circumstances, like phenomena will occur. Much of the benefit to be derived from scientific investigations lies in the ability to foreknow and forecast the turn of events. However, pure science would not stop at the prediction stage, but would push on to the further goal of defining the natures of the things studied. The highest of all sciences in the natural order, then, is metaphysics, which defines beings by reason of essential attributes and their inter-relationships.

Religious psychologists rightly shy away from the concept of scientific method portrayed here. They do so partly because religious phenomena rarely permit of precise repetition; that is, no set of circumstances can be repeated with that amount of exactness and control needed for a scientific experiment. Again, even though it might happen accidentally that we would encounter repetition of certain religious events, nevertheless prediction of the outcome of these events is the exception rather than the rule. One reason for this lies in the inability on the part of the observer of religious phenomena to report all the relevant data and to observe the situation fully or even in such a manner that significant variables may be isolated for further study. For example, an experienced pastor might be able to predict with a high degree of accuracy the increase of worshippers to be expected at Mass on Easter Sunday. However, at least in individual cases, it does not follow that he understands their motives or can foresee the course of their future religious life. These limitations in method place very real restrictions upon the conclusions which can be drawn from scientific studies in this field.

Nonetheless, the psychology of religion will be approached, but not of course by the experimental means of causing an event to occur by placing all the necessary conditions. Rather the investigation will follow the method of accurate empirical observation of factual data pertaining to religious phenomena. There should be no fear lest attempts to delve into religious experience with scientific tools will make a mockery of religion. Religion itself has no need to be bolstered up or verified by the tools of science. On the contrary, positive science, taken to mean the search for the latent causes of observable phenomena, has a real need for religion. Without the data furnished by religionists, whole areas of scientific investigation would be shut off, such as yoga, magic and mysticism.

The methods which psychology of religion uses in gathering its data and formulating its principles will be sketched briefly. Since methods are means or instruments, their character will be determined largely by the purpose for which they are used. For example, one such purpose will be the clarification of the relationship between human beings and their striving for happiness. Hence, the need for clarifying this relationship makes it urgent to use every means available for studying this relationship. If an interview with a person will help, then that is an acceptable method. If speculation about the nature of man (that is, deductive inference from principles of philosophy or of revealed theology) will help, that too should be used. And scarcely anyone would dare to claim that deductive inference is not a fruitful method of obtaining new knowledge, provided the facts or data about which one speculates are *bona fide* facts. For instance, if the experience of conversion and of ecstasy are really given in the lives of certain people, then they too belong to the subject matter of the psychology of religion. But if none of these phenomena exists, or if they are incapable of being reliably reported by anyone in whose life they occur, then no amount of speculation or inference will ever make them intelligible or meaningful.

Thus the methods used will be to some extent those used in any kind of psychological study, because the psychology of religion deals with men, with real, live, breathing human beings. Their needs and strivings, hopes and ambitions, goals and satisfactions interest the psychologist especially. In so far as these very aspects of human living express or imply a relation to the deity, they belong to the psychology of religion; and the analysis of these phenomena will be based upon three simple kinds of techniques, all of which involve to some extent the use of measures, numbers or quantities.

The first technique to be described is that of handling empirical data by means of character-trait estimation. The second is that of finding mathematical tools of testing for significant differences for clusters of traits and rank correlations. The third is a speculative view of religion from which valuable conclusions can be drawn concerning the nature and characteristics of the religious person. In the first and second techniques empirical data can and will be used. In the third, the combined speculative-deductive elements will predominate.

A. *Methods of Handling Empirical Data*

ATTITUDE STUDIES

The most important single topic of interest to social psychologists generally is the process of attitude formation, consolidation, and change. An attitude can be described as a predisposition to act in a certain fixed manner in response to a whole series of widely differing stimulations. Thus if Person X has a hostile attitude toward Group Y, almost any actions of any specified person in Group Y will evoke predictable behavior in Person X. Also, if Group X is notably communistic, and Group Y is anti-communistic, then most, if not all, of the behavior of persons in Group X is interpreted by the persons in Group Y as if it were an expression of some opposition or even hostility. This tendency to follow patterns of predictable behavior is readily observable in war time. In fact, propaganda agencies specialize and vie with each other in their efforts at inculcating hostile attitudes among the members of the groups which are opposed to each other.

There are any number of clearly isolable emotionally-loaded religious attitudes to be found in various groups. A Mohammedan is predisposed to act differently toward the sacred cow than is a Hindu. His readiness to act, or his "set," is called an "attitude." If the object in question is of a religous nature then the attitude is designated religious. Herr and Kobler have perfected a two-factor religious attitude scale. Permission to use this scale may be had by writing to the author.

Attitudes may be ranked on a continuous scale from positive to negative with neutrality in the middle; or they may be scaled in terms of high to low inclinations—high to low positives—with no real neutrality point. Which scaling model is used depends largely upon the taste of the investigator, but also to some extent upon the nature of the case. For example, were one to scale the attitudes of Americans toward democracy, he would probably have a more discriminating scale if he made the continuum extend from neutrality to high positive. This is, of course, on the well-founded assumption that few Americans are really very hostile toward their government.

But should the investigator wish to scale the attitudes of Americans toward atomic warfare, he might profitably choose a continuum from high positive to high negative, with a neutral point in the center of the scale. Generally speaking, when fineness of discrimination between persons tested is desired, an all positive or an all-negative continuum is preferred. This is a consequence of the fact that, as far as some classes of objects are concerned, there may actually be no person or only a very few persons in existence who would declare themselves strictly neutral toward them.

The optimum kind of attitude scale in existence today, as admitted by most contemporary psychologists, is that of Thurstone-Chave. It selects items for the scale on the basis of judgments by experts merely as to the meaning, i.e., the degree of favorableness or its opposite inherent in a given expression of an attitude. This scaling process must take place prior to the testing process and is very tedious and time-consuming. When the scale is finished, it is reliable, as can be shown by comparisons made between scores of favorableness and instances of favorable behavior. The main objection to the scale arises from the fact that the judges are presumed to read into the items they are judging the identical meaning which the testees themselves are going to see in them. There does not seem to be any solution to this difficulty except perhaps to have the judges chosen from the same socio-economic level as those who are tested by the scale. When this precaution is taken, fairly consistent patterns of favorable, neutral and unfavorable attitudes emerge from the use of the scale.

Throughout all the efforts of social psychologists to measure attitudes runs the latent assumption that attitudes do lead to behavior. To test this assumption, some have tried another device to measure the attitude, namely the "what would you do if—?" technique. This consists in a set of hypothetical behavior samples to which the testee responds by indicating his own behavior under specified circumstances. Many studies are in progress at the present moment using this method, under the direction of the author, to study religious concepts of children. An anecdote is narrated involving some form of behavior on the part of a fictitious person. The testee is then asked to make a choice of several alternatives; for instance, to agree or to disagree with the fictitious person. This way of approaching the study of attitude by stressing the real likelihood of behavior of a given kind has been found fairly useful. Its unreliability stems from the fact that the subject can deceive the experimenter if he wants to, and pretend to agree when he really does not. Also, as in public-opinion polling, there is another source of possible error in predicting behavior: the person may not know what he will do—he may not even know his own attitudes; and, moreover, if he does know, he may not wish to communicate the knowledge.

An easy way out of the dilemma might be to study behavior alone and infer the attitudes from the behavior. The obvious flaw in this procedure is simply this: The person does not always act consistently. In other words, he does not always behave according to the pattern of his inner attitudes.

Nevertheless, much valuable information about religious motivation has arisen from the apparently helter-skelter mass of studies which go under the name of measures of attitude. For instance, it is indisputable that the earliest attitudes toward the Church, namely those formed in the home, are the strongest, most enduring and most influential in directing adult behavior.

Before leaving the topic of attitude-scaling it should be noted in passing that Webb,[2] Kobler, Rimoldi and others (working on the N.I.M.H. Project at Loyola) have devised an interesting technique of attitude scaling, combining strong points of the Thurstone and Likert techniques. The finished scale has given a very valid and reliable measure of the attitudes and attitude changes of adult human beings toward the profession of psychiatry. One novel feature in this National Institute of Mental Health supported project technique is the fact that items for the scale were derived through the interview method. Another is the fact that scale-values were obtained by an equal-interval normalizing process, that is, by the multiple-category method of scaling.

PERSONALITY AND CHARACTER STUDIES

Psychologists have come a long way in perfecting methods whereby personality variables can be measured. There are paper-and-pencil inventories, case-history methods, and projective

2 Webb, Neil J., and Kobler, F. J., Clinical-experimental Techniques for Assessing the Attitudes of Religious toward Psychiatry, *Journal of Social Psychology*, Vol. 55, 1961, pp. 245-251.

techniques; but all leave much to be desired in the way of validity, that is, the ability of the test actually to measure the same trait which it is supposed to measure. They are also low in reliability that is the ability to give any dependable score for a trait upon repeated measuring of such a trait. In other words, such tests give less hope of successful prediction than do attitude studies and much less than do ability and aptitude tests. However, for whatever value the tests possess, religious workers should be acquainted with some of them.

From pre-scientific days observers of human behavior have noticed trends; somehow men behave according to a pattern. Complex experimental designers in psychology may one day arrive at the secret of the complexity, touch the core of the human personality and be able to designate personality types. The Kretschmer school, for example, has attempted to classify all persons into two main types. They are the tall, slim introverted type and the short, stocky extraverted type. The two types are not so easily distinguished as Kretschmer supposes. There is good evidence for the fact that most people share attributes of both types; that is, they are both extraverted and introverted, of average height and weight. As yet we have to be content with a lesser goal. There are as yet no fully acceptable measures of simple personality traits, taking the term *trait* to mean that in a person which is consistently manifested, despite variations, within a considerable range of circumstances. Probably no one ever will be fully successful here because of the fact that each trait exists in a totality of the person and this over-all totality gives a peculiar meaning to each and every trait. Even the most validly measured trait, namely intellectual ability, has been known to operate differently in the presence of radical changes in personality, or even when there has been an interference with the motivational systems within the individual.

Nevertheless, everyone who deals much with people or mixes with his friends does somehow predict their behavior. This ability to predict is a very desirable quality and one eagerly sought for by sociologists and clinical psychologists; they speak of an ability to "understand people." It may be safely said, and without redundancy, that if people act "true to form"—and they sometimes do just this—then trained observers can predict their behavior. Such predictable behavior is said to arise because of a quality, a trait or habit system of the person reacting. Such a quality must have some sort of permanence, since it shows itself repeatedly over an extended period of time. It must have some generality because it goes into action when widely different situations are present. In this way a trait resembles an attitude. Both show up under widely differing situations. The attitude is, however, "value-laden," that is, it connotes either acting for or against some object. Traits have no such connotation; they are used merely to catalogue and describe behavior. Only a criterion of goodness, or efficiency, or health, which is external to the sphere of activity of the trait, can be utilized in order to evaluate the trait.

The earliest personality trait to be measured was sociability. But this trait concept has been found too generalized to be of much service in prediction. Another popularly measured trait has been that of emotionality. Again, it has become exceedingly doubtful that such a generalized unitary trait really exists. The same must be said for suggestibility. All these supposed traits seem rather to be a function of highly specific aspects of particular situations. This means, for example, that Person A is likely to be very emotional, suggestible and even sociable with regard to Persons A1, A2, and A3 (his own clique), but quite the opposite with respect to Persons B1, B2, and B3.

Now, what of the time-honored traits of honesty, truthfulness, unselfishness and cooperativeness? Some authors speak as if these also were non-existent, as if there were even no valid scientific grounds for asserting that such action-tendencies exist in any generalized fashion in anyone. Hartshorne and May were pioneeers in research in this area. They claim to have proved that no generalized trait, of honesty, for example, exists. Rather, honest behavior is a function of specific situational determinants. From the evidence which they present their conclusions seem unjustified. Their test for honesty, for instance, has a heavy loading of intelligence. The more intelligent the children, the more they are able to avoid being detected in dishonest behavior. As for the trait of sociability, some experts say that this trait must be present in many persons, but that we do not yet have any adequate measure for it.

Regardless of what one holds about the existence of unitary traits, it remains a fact that some people are better than others in predicting the behavior of their friends. Evidently certain habit systems are at work which give the behavior of these friends a kind of uniformity, and this is what makes the prediction possible.

One reason why prediction so often fails, when tried with respect to human behavior, is the fact that human beings, though habit-directed, are fortunately not habit-bound in all respects. Every teacher knows, after the first few tests in class, which students are most likely to cheat during an examination. This does not mean that we know that these persons are dishonest in all circumstances. It is none the less true that he knows the habit system of cheating will probably operate under these restricted circumstances.

The same may be said—and is implied—by educators, particularly religious educators, when they employ procedures in their character education classes to prepare the youth for facing life. The exercises of behavior, the trials in which human adjustment skills play a part during school days, all predispose our youth toward acceptable social and individual behavior. Yet these situations do not predetermine them. Just because prediction is possible, there are no adequate grounds for holding that behavior is or will be absolutely determined.

With these brief comments on the trait-type question finished, the question of some inter-personal or group-determined traits can now be sketched.

A particularly fruitful approach to the whole question of character education and evaluation of its effectiveness is to be found in Ernst Ligon's "Dimensions of Character," Macmillan. N. Y. 1956. Here may also be found references to the most useful tests of religious personality.

SOCIOMETRY AND INTER-PERSONAL RELATIONS

In religious circles the role of authority is stressed. In other parts of this work reasons were given to account for this fact. Let it be pointed out here that when it comes to the question of estimating the quality of leadership in special social situations the statements in the above paragraphs about the difficulty of measuring and rating character traits do not hold true. There are some check-lists available, techniques of rating and the like, which will enable the religious teacher to select from a class the most successful leader. Of course this does not imply the use of simple balloting or voting. Rather, the success in effectively selecting leaders seems most often to be traceable for the most part to the judicious pooling of ratings made by the acquaintances of the potential leader. His acquaintances, his peers, each rate him upon a certain small, but well-chosen, battery of traits.

In the Sociometry studies of Moreno, Dreikurs and others, it has been repeatedly shown that the "simple counts" of behavior samples (that is, counts of certain kinds of interaction among members of a group) make prediction of leadership possible. The technique is similar to one in which two or three observers, such as teachers of the same class, watch the children at play day to day, or in social gatherings, and keep a continuous record on a chart, containing the names of all group members, of all instances of person-to-person responses. The more any one individual tends to be sought out by his peers (or avoided by the same) the more likely is he to be accepted as a leader (or rejected). Thus from group behavior samples, prediction is possible to other behavior samples within the same group. This possibility highlights the idea that socially conditioned behavior does follow fairly well-defined pattern so long as the same group structure is maintained.

It was largely as a result of studies like the above on the fields of force existing within social groups that practicing psychologists have come to recognize the importance of interpersonal relations among human beings. These relations are strongest and most resistant to change when formed in early childhood. Unless they are of such kind that the child gets his needed amount of gratification at these early levels, he may suffer an enormous amount of difficulty later on in adjusting to his superiors and peers. Thus the grain of truth is emphasized which we see so much exaggerated by psychologists, namely the need to safeguard the early childhood development of every child. The same need is very well brought out in the doctrine of churches generally, and the Catholic Church in particular: make the early days happy and secure, guard the child and protect him, but do not coddle or neglect him.

B. *Mathematical Tools For Getting The Most Out of Data*

INTRODUCTION

This treatise would not be complete unless something were stated about the newer tools of measurement and assessment. It used to be thought that only measurable data could be handled by the computing machines of science. Now our thinking on these subjects must be revised somewhat. Data can be handled scientifically even though they are not quantified in the strict sense. That is, there is a way in which numbers and number counts can be used without implying the existence of a measuring scale with its own zero point and equal scale units.

Discovery of this fact is one of the most startling advances in modern psychology, and an attempt will now be made to show how serviceable these newer methods will be in studying phenomena pertaining to the influence of religion on human attitudes and behavior. There will be given in sub-section 1, the technique of finding how significant are the differences between distinct groups; in sub-section 2, a glance at the field of self-evaluation studies for comparing ideal with real selves, and lastly, in sub-section 3, a quick survey of factor analysis and correlational studies.

1. HOW SIGNIFICANT ARE THE DIFFERENCES?

It often happens that a count of events results in a certain number of individuals in one group possessing the quality in question, and a different number of individuals in another group, or in the same group under different circumstances, possessing the quality of which there is question. The crucial question for science is whether or not the differences are as great as one could expect from mere chance variations among people or within the same person under different circumstances.

From the use of a statistical technique called x^2 (chi square) applied to the frequencies of detecting the quality in question, one can tell with a certain degree of certainty whether or not the observed difference in frequency is due to chance. An example in point might be the following: Girls experience religious conversion before age 20, in the groups under consideration, about 25% of the time (25 out of every hundred had the experience and 75 did not). Boys, on the other hand, in a group similar to that of girls in every respect except sex, had the experience only 15% of the time. Now it can be calculated by the use of the X^2 formula (or by a similar formula for the significance of proportions) whether or not a difference of 10% is significant at the degree of certainty desired. In other words, one can say with a certain degree of assurance whether a variation as large as 10% one way or the other could be due to chance.

It is really impossible to overestimate the value for scientific research which is inherent in these statistical appoaches to the question of real versus chance differences. An estimate of how great a difference can be attributable to chance, and how much difference will be over and above this chance amount, will dictate how much risk is involved in predicting this same difference under similar circumstances some other time. An example of such a prediction might be making predictions about religious conversion in another entirely distinct group of boys and girls.[3]

Any of the other tests designed to ascertain whether an observed difference is due to chance rather than to deliberately introduced factors relies heavily upon this same kind of reasoning. Mean scores for any group or medians may actually be different because of the errors of sampling. These errors, however,

3 Underwood, Benton J., Duncan, Carl P., Taylor, Janet A., Cotton, John W. *Elementary Statistics*. Appleton Century Crofts N. Y. 1954.

characteristically turn up as often in a positive as in a negative direction. If one wants to be sure, to a certain degree, that a difference in means between two groups is greater than the calculated allowance for the error of that difference, he calculates the Critical Ratio. This is defined as the ratio of a difference, to its standard error. It is equivalent to applying a t test to the differences, in order to predict the likelihood of obtaining such differences in the future.

Again, it is important to emphasize that there is enormous value for religious psychology attaching to the fact that these mathematical formulas may be used in predicting the flow of events both desirable and undesirable.

Note here the important caution: Just knowing what will occur by no means tells us why it should occur, especially in the area of personality study and in that of religious psychology. The answer to the delicate question of why predicted personality changes occur in predicted directions more than could be expected merely by chance, or merely by reason of changes which occur due to age or cultural trends, must await further analysis of the phenomena of concomitant variations. In the meantime, one is not justified in arguing that all attempts at predicting human behavior will be failures because of man's free will. After all, God knows what man is going to do, yet this knowledge by no means destroys human freedom. Are the scientists, then, claiming a kind of divine fore-knowledge of the outcome of human behavior? On the contrary, some of them are trying to know more and more about the kind of circumstances and environmental influences, e.g., education, which will be likely to bring about desirable behavior patterns. It would not be disrespectful to God to state that He Himself would give His stamp of approval to this kind of scientific endeavor: It is largely due to the materialistic elements in science that Catholics sometimes oppose a scientific study of religion. They will have less and less ground for opposing a scientific and experimental mathematical study of personality determinants the more they reflect upon the fact that man's strivings for happiness are given him by God and must be realized in human relationship before man is able to go back to God.

A sane psychology of religion, then, fosters and favors thorough scientific investigation into the causes and accompaniments of personality changes by whatever legitimate means these may be pursued.

2. THE CLUSTERS OF DIFFERENCES

A vital question in the area of personality study is: How well do attributes fit the person to whom they are ascribed? This is another way of asking how dependable is the test that is used on any particular person.

One of the most fruitful ways of assessing personality variables is the one recently discovered by Stephenson and Cattell called the "Q Sort." This technique is a method whereby a person rates himself on certain qualities; he does so merely by checking which of a large sample of trait descriptions he thinks apply to himself. Then, after a period of time has elapsed, he can repeat the process; and one has or can have a kind of measure of change in himself, at least as rated by himself between two different occasions.

Another valuable modification of the "Q Sort" is used by Rogers and his school. It consists in having a person rate himself first, i.e., sort out the qualities given him as they apply to himself, as he really is. Then at a later time he is given the task to re-sort or re-check the items, but according to the kind of person he would like to be, namely his ideal self. Discrepancies between these two selves often give useful hints as to the causes of maladjustment within the person.

The same sortings can, of course, be made by an external observer, rating a group of persons on what he thinks they really are like. Then measures of agreement or disagreement, between self and self-as-rated-by-other, can be obtained. In all these studies the mathematics become very laborious. Researchers are learning to diminish the amount of labor involved in the computations, but much time is still found necessary if one wishes to plan and carry out a meaningful experiment.

A college instructor used the "Q Sort" technique recently, in order to find out whether or not the students in his class tended to rate their teacher according to idealized traits they attributed to themselves.

We quote from Lambin's doctoral dissertation:

> If a judge of personality is called upon to rate another person, he first views this other person's behavior, and other attributes ... attains a high degree of accuracy, unless he is asked to describe the other's needs, motives, and unobserved behavior, (for these) ... he turns within himself for the answer. He describes the other in terms of his own patterns of values, attitudes, and emotions associated with this behavior.[4]

The interpretation of such experimental results is not unambiguous, yet evidence seems to be accumulating from many angles pointing toward the fact that most people do think of themselves in at least two ways: first, as they really are; and secondly, as they would like to be. And the view they take of some others around them seems to be profoundly influenced by the view they take of themselves.

One could turn the process around. Viewed from the obverse side, this projection of ourselves into others becomes an indication of the fact that people need others very much in order to evaluate themselves. What one thinks of others depends on what he thinks of himself, and what he thinks of himself depends upon what he thinks others think of him.

From the religious point of view, considerations such as this bring out the fact of the brotherhood of man, and even of the fatherhood of God. Awareness of these relationships can and must emerge from the two-fold fact that we depend upon our fellow-man in many ways for mental health and happiness in this life. It also emerges from the consideration of the fact that our idealized self, when allowed to perfect itself to its utmost, turns back to God Who is the Author of the real self and the ultimate goal of all our striving.

4 H. A. Lambin, unpublished doctoral dissertation, Loyola University, 1960.

It would be challenging at this point to design an experiment which would propose to learn how much one tends to evaluate his real and ideal self in terms of the known personal attributes of our changeless Friend, the Man God Jesus Christ.

3. RELATIONS BETWEEN TRAITS: CLUSTERS OF TRAITS

Since each individual person functions as a unit, it would be expected that all measures of ability and achievement would have some correlation between them. It is expected that if Person A is talented, next to the highest in his class, for example, in mathematics, he would also be near the top of his class in science, because it is a known fact that the two subjects have much in common with each other. This is the same as saying that there exists an ability in the person which serves him both for mathematics and for science. Similar reasoning might be applied to a comparison between a given person's leadership score, for example, and his sociability score. In other words, what we are saying here is that the methodology most fruitful for gaining information about a person is that which seeks the degree of inter-correlation between his scores in the various dimensions of his personality.

If the person is endowed with a high degree of consistency, his qualities will be maximally interrelated. It could hardly be true of any man that there is zero relationship between his various functions. Yet when a low or zero correlation (one not significantly different from zero) is found, we may be tempted to think of a very chaotic or randomly organized individual. It would be logical, however, to think that perhaps our measures or scores are faulty. There is one powerful argument to show that traits or clusters of traits within a person are never totally unrelated: the fact that they all have the same origin or reference point, namely the person himself. It must be remembered that, in order to run a correlational study, the investigator must be sure he knows which scores come from which people, so that he then correlates two or more tests from the same person. This, of course, complicates the process of keeping records, especially when the persons being tested wish to remain anonymous. Since the experiment starts, in each case, with each of several persons getting scored on each of several variables—as when we make a personality profile, or chart indicating relative importance of traits in a person—there is at least this basic relationship of common origin that must be ascribed to all the traits. That is, Person X is the same one who ranks second in mathematics, fifth in science and tenth in language, etc.

This latter consideration brings us to a few practical notes with regard to the use we make of correlations or measured interdependencies.

It is not necessary to possess real quantified scores in order to find a correlation. In fact some theorists in psychology think our test scores are rarely of such a nature that they permit the use of parametric, i.e., quantity, statistics upon them. Spearman's Rank Difference correlational method is capable of being used with the greatest variety of different measures. To use this, all we need to know is the fact that persons differ from one another in a certain order. We need not know their real scores at all, nor how much they differ from one another. Thus, Dad is older than Mom; Mom older than Jerry, the son; and Jerry older than Mary, the daughter; and so on for all other gradations. A second-growth forest may have short and tall trees about 20 to 60 feet high, and an undergrowth of trees two to ten feet high. All the trees together may be ranked according to size, and the age probably would correlate positively with the size. But certain measures might be more closely related within the group of young trees whereas others would be interrelated within the group of older trees. These clustering of traits give the basis for factor analysis. Correlations and clusters of correlations may be analyzed to give us detailed information about the degree of parallelism which exists between various qualities in several individuals or in several groups. The clusters so analyzed become especially significant in predicting behavior of a group.

As far as prediction for an individual in a group is concerned, it is rare that this is possible. The failure to make such prediction arises partly because of a weak connection between the variables measured. In either case, more and more evidence is needed to justify an estimate of what the future will bring.

This type of personality assessment, through analysis of correlated activities in a person, is especially valuable for the psychology of religion. It has enabled investigators like Gordon Allport to predict that frequent churchgoers and those who participate very actively in their religion will score high on an attitude scale measuring favorableness to the church, will have fewer serious crimes committed among them, and will engage in more humanitarian projects than their less religiously active brethren. The possibilities here seem literally endless, and each year a new technique or two is added to the psychological armamentarium. Correlational personality study has also made it possible for the workers in the Schenectady Character Research Project[5] to plan the teaching of character traits to children, and to arrive at predictions such as the following: Learning something in one context gives no assurance that it will automatically become a generalized skill. It will usually not be generalized, but will remain specific to a few situations. But one way to be sure of an increased probability of generalization is to create learning situations in several roles in the learner's life experience.

Another positive finding of the Character Research Project is that there will be a greater likelihood of transferring materials learned in childhood to the later years of life if the parents learn the same thing at the time the children learn it. The parents' sharing in the learning experience enables the child to see how the thing does apply to adult life. It would be a challenging experiment to test this hypothesis, that coordinated learning of parent and child makes for better retention in the life of the child.

Numerous other testable hypotheses can emerge in the study of religious influences upon personality. Outstanding examples would be the influence of religious counseling upon bereaved persons, or that of religious devotional exercises upon emotional life generally.

5 Ligon, Ernst. The Dimensions of Character, N. Y.; Macmillan, 1956.

C. The Inferential Method

THE TECHNIQUE OF CONCEPT ANALYSIS

When an investigator adds a bit of speculation to his otherwise factual approach to any problem he often meets with opposition. This is because other investigators may have points of view and basic assumptions different from his. Thus, materialists assume that religion cannot be a value and that pleasure is the only goal of human striving. Others hold, however, that whatever of value attaches to religious practice must be for the higher spiritual good of man and may not necessarily be a pleasurable good. The difference between these points of view lies in the fact that spiritual goods serve to unite man to his Creator, whereas pleasurable, sensory or utilitarian goods rather unite him to himself or to his egotistically sought goals. Conversely evil, the privation of good in a being which ought to have it, may also be either spiritual or material. The non-materialists speculate rightly in this manner: Whatever furthers the highest and ultimate good of man eventually removes him from merely material goods simply because these latter are not the ultimate goods or goals for human striving.

By a simple analysis of concepts we see that a religious psychologist need not condemn pleasure as evil. Nor may he posit as the supreme and ultimate goal of man, possession of and union with God, as man's *only* end. True, it is the only adequate or satisfactory goal. But many, many intermediate and partially gratifying goals will have to be reached by man, as intermediate steps or stages, before he reaches God, his ultimate end. All through life man strives for intermediate goals, and when he reaches full and mature use of all his spiritual and psychic powers, he still uses them as means for attaining his ultimate end. When he reaches out toward God in thoughtful prayers or in acts of worship and homage, his spiritual and material powers cooperate with each other, in order that he may grow and perfect himself in the service of God for which he was created. Considerations such as these are necessary in a psychology of religion, for they help us immeasurably toward an understanding of the deeper meaning of man's relation to his Creator.

RELIGION, ANALYZED CONCEPTUALLY, HIGHLIGHTS THE GOD-MAN RELATIONSHIP

1) The relationship between God and man is recognized as having produced men dominated by motives of service to mankind. This phenomenon—for it is as much a reality as any fact of history—cannot be speculated out of existence by the claims of behaviorists who say that one cannot know what mentally motivates men; they can no more prove by scientific method that conditioned reflexes produce humanitarians than can the psychoanalysts, who say that it is the basic instincts and drives which produce the humanitarian.

2) Behavior mechanisms, analyzed conceptually, turn out to be dynamisms; the energy which is supplied for these compound chain-reacting processes gets its source not only from sunlight and cosmic rays but from the divine spark of truth, from the flame of the love of righteousness, both of which energizers are constantly being renewed through the resources of religion and religious motivation. Men of religious zeal and conviction are notoriously goal-directed and hard-driven.

3) Religion gives the grounds for inspiring in men the hope that all will find happiness and better days ahead. This expectancy is not bolstered up merely by reason of technological advances; it is continually growing in dynamic power in the hearts of religious men, mostly by reason of contacts with transcendental reality, i.e., by immersing themselves in the Divine Being.

4) Religion, finally, brings men close together with one another when they all trust fully in the notion that all creation is good and all men are friends and even brothers to one another. The concept of the fatherhood of God and the brotherhood of man can scarcely be reached by purely empirical methods. Only men's meditation and self-stimulation through spiritual com-

munion with divine truth can and surely will be effective pro-
ducers of true brothers.

RELIGION CONSIDERED SPECULATIVELY AS WELL AS PRACTICALLY FOSTERS A PARTICULAR KIND OF ENNOBLING GOD-MAN RELATIONSHIP

1) Religion makes men peculiarly sensitive to the needs of
other men. Acute sensitivity will create clusters of attitudes,
and even of character traits in line with the virtues of charity
and social solidarity. Depressed and goalless people become
lively and goal-striving when they reach out to God for help.

2) The special kind of relationship also becomes evident in
the fact that religion urges man to give every other person his
rights to equal chances for obtaining happiness and success.
In other words, flowing from the doctrine of brotherhood of
man, and devotion to the service of humanity, are the notions
of the fundamental equality of all men and the freedoms. When
writers proclaim that religion makes men slaves to law and precepts, they overlook the fact that it has always been religion's
dominant ambition to produce in all men a real love of liberty.
From true human liberty alone comes the notion that each man
needs the opportunity to serve God and to make the best use
of his capacities.

3) Religion makes man try to enlarge the scope of his thinking,
to expand his humanitarian sentiments so as to love all men,
no matter to which nation or race they may belong. It therefore
makes for better social living, lessening of social conflicts and
wars, heightening of a hope that man can eventually come to
act differently from animals, where might is equivalent to right.

4) In the last analysis of our methodology, we see how religion leads man to value such a thing as sacrifice. This value
does not remain in the abstract order. It motivates men to exercise themselves in deeds of heroism at times, once the conviction
of value is present.

Without religion one would look in vain over history's pages
for genuine instances of vicarious sacrifice, of one man's being
willing actually to suffer for his fellow man. With religion we

know not what impetus may move men onward, what energy may drive them. Yet onward they move, in group after group of devoted humanitarians, desiring the hard lot of poverty, obedience, and suffering that their fellow man may be enriched.

To summarize briefly: Attitudes, personality traits, and social endowments have been described which allow of treatment under the psychology of religion. All the scores and measures arrived at under controlled conditions admit of statistical handling, whose chief purpose is to enable the investigator to predict. Many true and significant predictions are also made possible by reason of a conceptual analysis of man and his relation to God. This last type of analysis uses methods as old as the history of human thought. All the great religions of the world, in the past up to the present, have prospered and benefited humanity as a result of their speculative approach to religion, at least as much as science has by measurement and prediction.

selected bibliography

General Reference. MEISSNER, W. W. (S.J.), Annotated Bibliog. in Religion and Psychology, N. Y. Acad. R & M H 1961.

Allport, G. W., The Individual and His Religion. New York: Macmillan, 1950.

Ames, E. S., The Psychology of Religious Experience. Boston: Houghton Mifflin, 1910.

Clark, W. H., The Psychology of Religion. New York: Macmillan, 1958.

Coe, G. A., The Psychology of Religion. Chicago: Univ. Chicago Press, 1916.

Conklin, E. S., The Psychology of Religious Adjustment. New York: Macmillan, 1929.

De Sanctis, S., Religious Conversion (tr. H. Augur). New York: Harcourt, Brace, 1927.

Doniger, S., (Ed.) Religion and Human Behavior. New York: Association Press, 1954.

Edward, Kenneth, Religious Experience. Edinburgh, Clark, 1926.

Fromm, Erich, Psychoanalysis and Religion. New Haven, Conn.: Yale Univ. Press, 1950.

Girgensohn, Karl, Der Seelische Aufbau des Religioesen Erlebens. Leipzig, 1921. (This and the next two were typical of the "non-emotional" school.)

Grensted, L. W., Psychology of Religion. New York: Oxford Univ. Press, 1952.

Gruen, W., Die Froemmigheit der Gegenwart. Muenster: Aschendorffsche Verlagsbuchhandlung, 1956.

Hickman, F. S., Introduction to the Psychology of Religion. New York: Abington, 1926.

Hiltner, S., Self-understanding through Psychology and Religion. New York: Scribner, 1951.

James, William, Varieties of Religious Experience. London: Longmans, 1902.

Johnson, P. E., Psychology of Religion. New York: Abingdon-Cokesbury Press, 1945.

Josey, C. C., The Psychology of Religion. New York: Macmillan, 1927.

Jung, C. G., Modern Man in Search of a Soul. New York: Harcourt, Brace, 1933.

Keenan, A., O.F.M., Neuroses and Sacraments. New York: Sheed and Ward 1950.

Leuba, J. H., A Psychological Study of Religion. New York: Macmillan, 1912.

Lindworsky, Joseph, (S.J.) The Psychology of Asceticism. London: Edwards, 1936.

―――Psychologie der Aszese. Winke fuer eine Psychologischrichtige Aszese. Freiburg: Herder, 1935.

Maréchal, Joseph, S.J., Studies in the Psychology of the Mystics. London: Burns, Oates & Washbourne, 1927.

Menninger, Karl, The Religion of a Psychiatrist. Univ. Chicago Round Table, 1951.

Outler, A. C., Psychotherapy and the Christian Message. New York: Harper, 1954.

Pratt, J. B., The Psychology of Religious Belief. New York: Macmillan, 1907.

―――The Religious Consciousness. New York: Macmillan, 1920.

_____Eternal Values in Religion. New York: Macmillan, 1950.

Roberts, D. E., Psychotherapy and a Christian View of Man. New York: Scribner, 1950.

Schaer, Hans, Religion and the Cure of Souls in Jung's Psychology. New York: Pantheon, 1950.

Selbie, W. B., The Psychology of Religion. Oxford: Clarendon Press, 1924.

_____Christianity and the New Psychology. London: Centenary, 1939.

Starbuck, E. D., The Psychology of Religion. New York: Scribner, 1903.

Stern, Karl, The Third Revolution; a study of psychiatry and religion. New York: Harcourt, Brace, 1954.

Strickland, F. L., Psychology of Religious Experience. New York: Cokesbury, 1924.

Thouless, R. H., An Introduction to the Psychology of Religion. Cambridge: Cambridge Univ. Press. 1923, 1936.

Underhill, Evelyn, The Essentials of Mysticism. New York: Dutton, 1920.

Willwoll, A., (S.J.), Psychologie de l'ascese. Dictionnaire de Spiritualité, I. Paris: Beauchesne, 1937, Col. 1001-1010.

index

Duncan, Carl P., 308 note
Dynamics in infancy, 49 ff.
Dynamism of hope and love, 90 ff.

Early childhood, 52 ff.
Ecstasies, 204
Education, 63
Effects of faith, 85
Egan, John J., 12
Egan, Joseph M., 12
Egan, Mary Kay, 12
Ego reaction, 43
Ego strength, 51, 95, 124 ff., 162, 164, 166, 169, 178, 199
"Elementary Statistics," 254 note
Emotional elements, 43, 229 ff.
Emotional learning, 49 ff., 85
Empirical method, 243
Eranos Group, 44
Escape, death as, 36
"Escape" theory, 30
Evidence, 80
Example in altruism, 93 ff.
Existentialists, 122 note
"Experience of Worth," 44

Faculty theory, 121
Faith, 79 ff.
Family devotions, 56
Farrell, Walter L. 12, 13
Fasting, 162
Fatherhood of God, 48, 62, 87
Feldman, Raymond, 11
Felix, Robert R., 11
Flagellation, 83

Foley, Malachy P., 12
Foundations, 25, 31
Fractionating of experience, 42
Frazer, J. G., 30
Free will and prediction, 255
Freud, Sigmund, 21, 29, 30, 35, 230
Frivolity, 68
Frustration, 50
Fulfillment, 32, 114
"Future of an Illusion, The," 30

Ghandi, Mahatma, 97, 173
Generalizing, 111
Girgensohn, 42 ff.
Girls' concerns, 70
Giving, 59, 92
Goal guidance, 51
Goals, infant, 50
Goals, intermediate, 261
"God and Freud," 230
God's attributes by negation, 210
God's love, 136
"Golden Bough, The," 30
Grace, 39 ff.
"Graces of Interior Prayer, The," 206
Gross, Leonard, 230
Group activities, 56
Group awareness, 59
Group dynamics, 126
Group example, 60
Group identification, 94
Group need, 33
Group prediction, 259

ALBA HOUSE is staffed by the Pauline Fathers and Brothers. All the operations going into the making of this book were carried out by the Fathers and Brothers as part of their publishing apostolate. The Society of St. Paul was founded to work exclusively in communications. By this is meant that it was instituted to spread the teachings of Christ via the press, radio, motion pictures and television.

PAULINES reach thousands daily — by each book, pamphlet, production — multiplying the good message and carrying it into all manner of places. It is their job in the Church to staff editorial offices, publishing plants, film studios, etc., and to develop those fields of communications still comparatively un-touched for Christ.

PAULINES, aside from living a balanced religious life, perform their apostolic work according to their talents and training as: editors, designers, directors, proofreaders, writers, artists, photographers, pressmen, typesetters, binders, compositors, photoengravers, as well as in many other editorial and technical fields. The **Vatican Council's** decree on the media of social communications has been a great source of renewed energy for them.

INTERNATIONAL as the air-waves, the Pauline Fathers and Brothers are located in twenty-three countries, with headquarters in Rome. In the United States they are in New York City, Boston, Buffalo, Detroit, and Youngstown.

A BROCHURE on the Society and its aims can be obtained for yourself, or any young man whom you feel might qualify to become a Pauline Priest or Brother, by simply sending a card to: The Pauline Fathers and Brothers, Vocation Office, 2187 Victory Blvd., Staten Island, N. Y.